SILVERPOINT AND METALPOINT DRAWING

Silverpoint, and metalpoint more generally, is the practice of marking with soft metal on a specially prepared drawing surface. Experiencing a resurgence in recent years, contemporary metalpoint art is realist and abstract, traditional and conceptual.

Silverpoint and Metalpoint Drawing is the essential manual of metalpoint technique, written by Susan Schwalb and Tom Mazzullo, contemporary masters of the medium. This book is the first treatise on the subject for artists and art teachers, with chapters on early history; materials, including grounds, supports, metals, and tools; techniques for working in metalpoint and artwork in mixed media; and care of metalpoint artworks. Not only is it beautifully illustrated, this book also demonstrates how to photograph and exhibit metalpoint art. Featuring a gallery of drawings by contemporary artists, along with their tips and insights, *Silverpoint and Metalpoint Drawing* is a perfect introduction for students of the medium and an inspiration for those already more familiar with it.

Susan Schwalb is one of the foremost figures in the current silverpoint revival. She was born in New York City in 1944 and studied at Carnegie Mellon University. She has had over 50 solo exhibitions in galleries and museums worldwide, and her work is represented in most major public collections, including the Museum of Modern Art, the Metropolitan Museum of Art, the Kupferstichkabinett, Berlin, the Ashmolean Museum, Oxford, the Yale University Art Gallery, and the British Museum, London. Schwalb was one of only three living artists included in the historical metalpoint exhibition *Drawing in Silver and Gold: Leonardo to Jasper Johns* at the National Gallery of Art, Washington, DC. She lives in New York City.

Tom Mazzullo was born in Williamsport, Pennsylvania in 1968 and attended Tyler School of Art, where he was awarded a BFA in Printmaking in 1990. He earned an MFA from Syracuse University in 1993 and has taught drawing at Hamilton College in Clinton, New York, the University of Denver, and the Art Students League of Denver, and he has lectured and demonstrated silverpoint all over the country. He has exhibited his silverpoint drawings in museums and galleries nationwide, has work in several notable collections, and is a member of Spark Gallery, Denver. He lives in Westminster, Colorado.

SILVERPOINT AND METALPOINT DRAWING

A Complete Guide to the Medium

Susan Schwalb and Tom Mazzullo

Routledge
Taylor & Francis Group
NEW YORK AND LONDON

First published 2019
by Routledge
52 Vanderbilt Avenue, New York, NY 10017

and by Routledge
2 Park Square, Milton Park, Abingdon, Oxon, OX14 4RN

Routledge is an imprint of the Taylor & Francis Group, an informa business

Library of Congress Cataloging-in-Publication Data
A catalog record for this title has been requested

ISBN: 978-0-8153-6588-4 (hbk)
ISBN: 978-0-8153-6590-7 (pbk)
ISBN: 978-1-351-26036-7 (ebk)

Typeset in Bembo
by Apex CoVantage, LLC

CONTENTS

FIGURES

FOREWORD

During the course of a warm winter afternoon lunch in 1982 in West Palm Beach, Florida, I casually informed the late New York art dealer Vance Jordan that I was thinking of organizing an exhibition devoted to American artistic investigation of the medium of silverpoint. This idea was spurred on by my knowledge of outstanding work in the medium by a handful of American artists, among them Thomas Dewing, Joseph Stella, Leo Dee, and Harvey Dinnerstein. Vance responded with unbridled enthusiasm, and so the investigation began.

With the encouragement and support of Richard Madigan, Director of the Norton Gallery of Art (now the Norton Museum of Art), where I served as curator of collections, and the enthusiastic assistance of several staff members, research ensued, and typewritten letters were sent to over a hundred American museum registrars, asking them to identify both European and American silverpoint drawings in their collection in preparation for a potential exhibition on the subject. This process was especially useful and rich in identifying the names of late nineteenth- and twentieth-century American artists who had worked or were currently working in silverpoint. With this information in hand, I was on my way to putting together *The Fine Line: Drawing with Silver in America*, which opened at the Norton in the spring of 1985 and travelled to three institutions in the United States.

These are heady days for the metalpoint medium, and I am in rapture. The present volume serves as a marvelously comprehensive one-step guide to learning the history and technical ins and outs of metalpoint. The publication follows in the wake of the National Gallery of Art's 2015 exhibition *Drawing in Silver and Gold: Leonardo to Jaspar Johns* and its accompanying publication (for which I contributed an essay on American and European metalpoint drawing created from the late nineteenth century to today, updating and adding to my essay for the catalog of the Norton exhibition) and Thea Burns's important 2012 study, *The Luminous Trace: Drawing and Writing in Metalpoint*. In addition to the welcome proliferation in recent years of exhibitions around the country of contemporary efforts, a special highlight has been the recent retrospective at the Arkansas Arts Center (for which I authored the catalog essay), which celebrates Susan Schwalb's career-long exploration of metalpoint in multitudinously inventive ways.

A few memories draw me back in time. The amazing encouragement and support for the Norton exhibition and publication from the great art historian Agnes Mongan, who contributed an essay on the practice of silverpoint by the Old Masters and spread the word about both the show and catalog to her wide network of colleagues in the field of drawing. Also, the lukewarm response by her old friend, the American writer, art connoisseur, impresario, philanthropist, and cultural figure Lincoln Kirstein (whose circle included a group of artists who worked in the medium, including Pavel Tchelitchew, Paul Cadmus, and Jared French), who dissed the effort as silly and no more worthy of an exhibition than plumbago. One further flashback: on the afternoon of the opening of the Norton exhibition, the deputy director of the National Endowment for the Arts was visiting with Richard Madigan. Following the visit, Dick gave her a preview of the show, whose works elegantly and distinctively glistened in the dimly lit galleries. She came over to me while I was busily directing final details on the installation and profusely apologized for the NEA's turning down the museum's request for funding.

Since the mid-1980s, I have tried to keep aware of discoveries and breakthroughs in the metalpoint medium. It is rare to discover American artists of the past to add to the roster of its practice (though just recently I learned of Dewing Woodward's silverpoints, created around 1915 in Shady, New York, outside Woodstock). Meanwhile I was informed in 2004 by the artist Jeannine Cook that the catalog for *The Fine Line* had inspired widespread interest among contemporary artists in metalpoint drawing in America. In retrospect, I understand why – I had aimed to solicit enthusiasm for the then-even-less-known medium and the fascinating ways it had been employed. I was also making a semi-unconscious call for artists to try their hand and embrace metalpoint's unique and special qualities. I do the same today – go on, try your hand. You will be surprised and delighted.

Bruce Weber
Saugerties, New York
18 May 2018

PREFACE

Why Metalpoint Now?

In 1974 one could only find a handful of contemporary artists who had heard of metalpoint, much less used the technique. Within a few years more and more artists from around the country began to work in this medium. They were located in areas where there had been a significant teacher who specialized in metalpoint. Among those early leaders, one would have to count Paula Gerard, who taught artists during her years at the Art Institute of Chicago (1962–1975) and the Layton School of Art (1945–1962); James S. Watrous, who taught John Wilde and numerous others at the University of Wisconsin (1930–1976); Roger Anliker at Carnegie Mellon University (1948–1963) and later at Tyler School of Art (1963–1988); and Charles Schmidt, also at Tyler (1967–2008). In 1957 Watrous published *The Craft of Old-Master Drawings*, an important book with some technical information, but until today it was the only book with a chapter on metalpoint technique. Many artists were inspired to try metalpoint after seeing amazing Renaissance drawings in museums such as The Morgan Library and the Metropolitan Museum of Art in New York.

In 1985 the landmark exhibition *The Fine Line: Drawing with Silver in America*, curated by Bruce Weber, opened at the Norton Museum of Art in West Palm Beach, Florida. Drawings by 40 American artists of the nineteenth and twentieth centuries were gathered together, and the show toured to three other venues (Pensacola Museum of Art, Florida; Arkansas Art Center, Little Rock; and Museum of Fine Arts, Springfield, Massachusetts). The works were primarily figurative, but there were also a study for an abstract sculpture by John Storrs along with several abstract drawings by Michiko Itatani and Susan Schwalb. This exhibition (and its illuminating catalogue) seems to have been the catalyst for an expanding interest in what was once a little-known art medium. Numerous museum and university gallery shows followed along with solo and group exhibitions in commercial galleries.[1] As the internet has grown, sites like Facebook, with several metalpoint groups of over 700 members, continue to introduce artists to the medium and, as they share techniques and ideas, the circle continues to widen.

As more artists begin to draw in metalpoint they have given workshops in their studios, libraries or community centers, in universities and schools like the Art Students League, and in museums during exhibitions. In 2015 the first historical exhibition, *Drawing in Silver and Gold: Leonardo to Jasper Johns*, was held at the National Gallery of Art, Washington, DC, and at the British Museum, London, leading to simultaneous shows in galleries in New York City, Little Rock, and London.[2] More and more artists were inspired to try the technique, and today there is a full range of abstract and figurative artists exploring the medium.

Margaret Mathews-Berenson, in a recent essay, has suggested another view on why silverpoint has reemerged:

> At a time when art is being redefined by new and rapidly changing digital tools and technology that often deny the man-made mark, silverpoint offers artists a connection with a potent creative tradition. The fine delicate lines inevitably reveal the artist's hand: an affirmation of human presence. . . . A drawing medium made for quiet meditation, silverpoint remains a venerable instrument of intimate communication for artists today and provides welcome distraction from the dizzying pace of our technocentric world for artists and viewers alike.[3]

But no matter what the reason, there is an impressive revival of metalpoint drawing in the United States and the United Kingdom as it slowly reappears around the world.

Notes

1 Since *The Fine Line* there have been several other major museum shows of contemporary silverpoint drawing: *Silverpoint Etcetera: Contemporary American Metalpoint Drawings*, curated by Charles Schmidt, which toured to several museums beginning in 1992; *The Luster of Silver: Contemporary Metalpoint Drawings*, curated by Holly Koons McCullough at the Telfair Museum of Art, Savannah, Georgia, in 2006; and *The Luster of Silver: Contemporary Metalpoint Drawings*, curated by the artists Koo Schadler and Jeannine Cook at the Evansville Museum of Arts, History and Science, Evansville, Indiana, in 2009. Cook and Schadler used the original Telfair show as the source for the Evansville show. In addition, there have been numerous solo and group shows of metalpoint drawings in commercial galleries, plus two recent shows in non-profit venues: *Reinventing Silverpoint: An Ancient Technique for the 21st Century* at the Kentler International Drawing Space, Brooklyn, New York, in 2009, curated by Margaret Mathews-Berenson and Susan Schwalb; and *Luminous Line: Contemporary Drawing in Metalpoint*, curated by Margaret Mathews-Berenson at Scripps College, Claremont, California, in 2010. In 2013, Sherry Camhy curated a show at the National Arts Club, New York, entitled *The Silverpoint Exhibition*. In 2018, *Silver Lining: Contemporary Works in Silverpoint*, co-curated by Kristen Miller Zohn and Hannah Israel, was shown at the Lauren Rogers Museum of Art, Lauren, Mississippi, and the Illges Gallery at Columbus State University, Columbus, Georgia.

2 *Metalpoint Now* at Garvey | Simon Gallery, New York; *Drawing with Metalpoint* at Patrick Heide Contemporary Art, London; *National Silverpoint Invitational 2015: Drawing in Silverpoint*, coordinated by artists AJ Smith and Marjorie Williams-Smith at Hearne Fine Art, Little Rock, Arkansas and Greg Thompson Fine Art, North Little Rock, Arkansas; *Tarnished*, a two-person show with Susan Schwalb and Erica Winstone at Arthouse 1, London; and *Lustrous Lines: Contemporary Metalpoint Drawing* at the Morris Graves Museum of Art, Eureka, California.

3 Mathews-Berenson, Margaret. *Reinventing Silverpoint: An Ancient Technique for the 21st Century* (Brooklyn, NY: Kentler International Drawing Space, 2009).

ACKNOWLEDGMENTS

We would like to thank all the artists who generously contributed their work for this book, as well as the dealers and museums who provided images, including Michael Rosenfeld Gallery, New York; Didier Aaron, New York; Marlborough Gallery, New York; Davidson Contemporary, New York; Arkansas Art Center, Little Rock, Arkansas; Portland Museum of Art, Portland, Maine; and The Hunt Library at Carnegie Mellon University, Pittsburgh, Pennsylvania; as well as the estates of Nancy Lawton, Leo Dee, John Wilde, and Roger Anliker for agreeing to participate. We would also like to thank Brook Prestowitz of the Williamstown Art Conservation Center and Talia Steinman of the Metropolitan Museum of Art for their assistance. To Carol Prusa, Thea Burns, and Bruce Weber, a special thank you for their contributions, as well as to numerous metalpoint artists who have offered insights and examples. Last but not least Susan would like to thank her loving and supportive husband, Martin Boykan, who took on the job of in-house editor for the project, and her assistant, Elle DioGuardi, whose assistance has been invaluable, and Tom would like to thank his wife, Maggie, for all her patient love and support.

Susan Schwalb and Tom Mazzullo
July 2018

CONTRIBUTORS

Thea Burns received a BA in Fine Arts from McGill University, an MAC in Art Conservation from Queen's University, Kingston, ON, a certificate in Paper Conservation from the Fogg Art Museum, Harvard University, and a PhD, from the Courtauld Institute, University of London. She taught paper conservation at Queen's University (1987–2001) and was Senior Paper Conservator of Collections, Weissman Preservation Center, Harvard University Library (2002–2008). She is the author of *The Invention of Pastel Painting* (2007), *The Luminous Trace: Drawing and Writing in Metalpoint* (2012), *L'Art du Pastel* (2014), with Philippe Saunier, and *Compositiones Variae: A Late 8th-Century Craftsman's Technical Treatise Reconsidered* (2017).

Carol Prusa, born and raised on the south side of Chicago, received her BS from the University of Illinois and her MFA in painting from Drake University. Known for her contemporary and large-scale use of silverpoint combined with fiber optics, she has been awarded fellowships from the South Florida Cultural Consortium, the State of Florida and the Howard Foundation. Her work is in the collections of the Museum of Arts and Design, New York, and the Telfair Museum of Art, among others. Gallery representation includes Brintz–Palm Beach, Jenkins-Johnson–NYC/San Francisco, Bluerider–Taipei, Kostuik–Vancouver, and Le Salon Vert–Geneva.

INTRODUCTION

What is Silverpoint and Metalpoint?

Overview and History

Simply stated, metalpoint drawing means making art using soft metal tools to mark on specially prepared surfaces. Although the term is often used interchangeably with silverpoint, many different metals can be used; the subtle differences in the lusters of metals and the fact that metals can tarnish, combined with the unusual quality of a drawing surface prepared with a coating, are the key components that attract artists to this medium. As metals tarnish, they lighten, darken, or take on hues that make works in metalpoint distinct from those in any other medium. The prepared surfaces metalpoint artists use range from common paint and homemade grounds applied onto papers and boards to commercially-available treated papers. Contemporary metalpoint artists experiment with grounds, metals, supports and concepts, infusing a traditional drawing medium with fresh ideas.

Metalpoint has been around since antiquity, much longer than the modern pencil, which it resembles in a superficial way. Along with ink and chalk, metalpoint was one of the three main methods of producing sketches on paper before the modern era. It was in the late Middle Ages that metalpoint done in silver or lead on surfaces coated in natural materials grew in favor as a choice for drawing. Cennino Cennini, in *Il Libro dell'Arte*, written around 1400, describes how a ground made from nine coats of pulverized, burned bones combined with animal-skin glue, white lead, and saliva or oils makes a suitable surface for marking with a silver stylus[1].

Silverpoint in the Renaissance reached its zenith with such artists as Jean Fouquet (Figure 0.1), Filippino Lippi, Leonardo da Vinci, and Albrecht Dürer. In the sixteenth century artists began to abandon metalpoint as styles changed and easier-to-use materials became more available. There were some artists who continued with the technique well into the seventeenth century – Rembrandt, for example, made a few silverpoint drawings – but metalpoint virtually disappeared during the eighteenth century. It was not until the end of the nineteenth century that metalpoint was revived and then adapted for modern use by artists in England. It was at this time that commercially-made tools and clay-coated papers first became available. Once rediscovered, silverpoint became more common and was brought to the United States, where it continues to

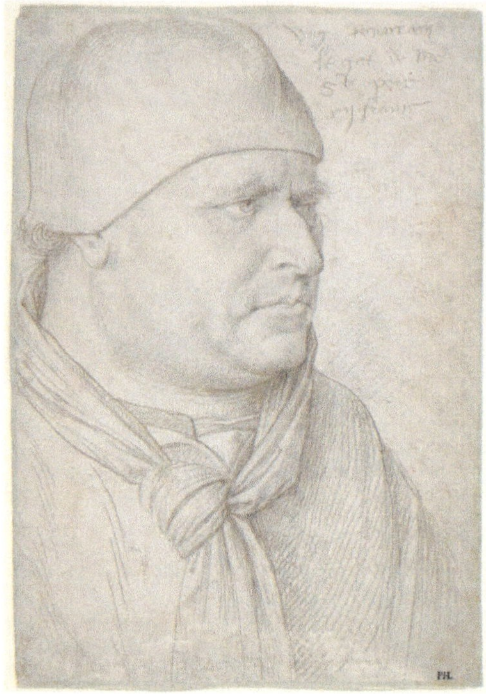

FIGURE 0.1 Jean Fouquet (French, Tours ca. 1425–ca. 1478 Tours); *Portrait of an Ecclesiastic*; ca. 1461, metalpoint, black chalk on white prepared paper; 7 13/16 × 5 5/16 in. (19.8 × 13.5 cm); Metropolitan Museum of Art, New York. Purchase, Rogers Fund and Gift of Mrs. Benjamin Knower, Bequest of Ogden Mills, and Bequest of Collis P. Huntington, by exchange, 1949

grow in popularity due to dozens of contemporary artists who have devoted their lives to producing metalpoint drawings and teaching others how to use the medium.

Distinguishing Characteristics

Metalpoint has distinguishing characteristics, some to be exploited, others to be adapted to or overcome. First is that all metalpoint is done on special surfaces – papers, boards or panels coated with some preparation, be it paint, a clay-coating, or a homemade ground tinted with pigment or made of unusual materials like bone ash or marble dust. The ground imparts particular characteristics to the mark: rough grounds make an uneven mark, tinted grounds reduce contrast, many-layered grounds take a darker mark. Clay-coated papers are very smooth and somewhat shiny, and new plastic-like papers work with metalpoint and come in a variety of colors. Anything that can be painted can be used as a metalpoint support; a prepared surface can be a major clue that one is looking at a metalpoint drawing.

Another characteristic is the metal mark itself; rather than looking like shiny metal, metalpoint works are often pale and gray on white grounds, especially when compared to work in graphite or charcoal (Figure 0.2). The color of metals is subtle, but distinct; exploiting the cast of metals is one of the main contemporary approaches to this medium. A metal tool can be sharpened to a

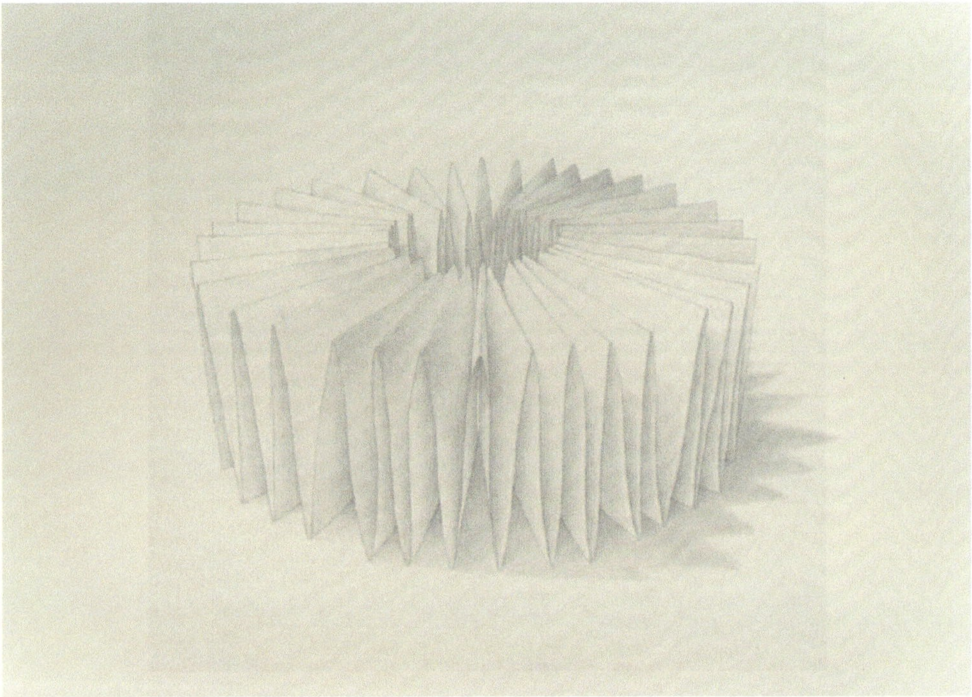

FIGURE 0.2 Tom Mazzullo, *Ruff*, 2017, silverpoint on prepared paper, 12 × 15 inches (30.48 × 12.7 cm), private collection

very fine point, thinner than a pencil point and capable of producing a more consistent fine line. Extra pressure on a metalpoint tool will not produce a darker mark; more pressure often damages the fragile ground. Changing the shape of the point will produce a variety of marks, and using different metals will create some tonal variation. Some artists experiment with adding materials into the ground preparation to give a wider value range to their drawings. Additionally, drawings in metal will react with the atmosphere and other art materials in a process called *tarnishing*. Silver marks will start out gray, but can turn warm brown, gaining a patina similar to sepia-toned ink; copper can fade and turn yellow or greenish, and other metals will react (or remain inert) in their own particular way.

Metalpoint drawing has some qualities that may turn people away from the medium. The process involved in preparing paper and making tools is not commonly taught in schools; metalpoint drawing materials are not easily found on the shelves of art supply stores; and there is some research and experimentation involved in preparing even the simplest of materials for metalpoint. There are also technical and stylistic obstacles. A drawing in metalpoint is difficult to correct by erasing. Drawing on top of paint has a different feel from drawing on paper, and marking with metal feels very different from marking with graphite, ink, or chalk. Also, finished metalpoint drawings require special handling; they are fragile works and have their own considerations with regard to photography, storage, and exhibition. There is a certain need for an experimental outlook when working with metalpoint, and while some artists welcome the chance to tinker, other artists will rebel against anything that adds roadblocks to their creative process.

FIGURE 0.3 Susan Schwalb, *Currents I*, 2017, 30 × 30 × 2 inches (76.2 × 76.2 × 5.1 cm) silverpoint, aluminum wire brush on navy blue gesso on panel, courtesy of the artist

There are many reasons why drawing in metalpoint is an endeavor worth investigating, not just for its historical importance or for its mysterious disappearances and rediscoveries, but also because of its expressive qualities and its unique place in the pantheon of drawing techniques. Being an artist who works in metalpoint is a special thing. The technique itself needs some explanation to many outsiders and also to experts, so that dialogues between artist and viewer can be very rewarding. The chance to break new ground in metalpoint drawing is still wide open, with new adherents every day developing their own spin on materials, techniques, or creative possibilities within the confines of the medium (Figure 0.3). Learning all aspects of metalpoint can be a lifetime's work, but it is the best way for an artist to arrive at his or her creative voice.

Note

1 Broecke, Laura. *Cennino Cennini's 'Il Libro dell'Arte': A New English Translation and Commentary with Italian Transcription* (London: Archetype, 2015), 28.

1

THE HISTORY OF METALPOINT AS A DRAWING TECHNIQUE

Thea Burns

Introduction

There are various styles of writing about artworks. To be useful, a history must be selective; therefore, this chapter will investigate the practice of metalpoint drawing at specific moments in its history, focusing on detailed analyses of selected works, rather than imposing on the technique a progressive narrative of development and evolution.

Despite seeming distinct from subject matter, meaning in a work of art is intimately bound up with its physical form. Historical metalpoint drawings, studied in this chapter, are approached through careful visual examination of their material composition and physical features. To deepen understanding, the information revealed will be juxtaposed with appropriate cultural, social, and other evidence that suggests why artifacts look as they do. At the same time, it is important to recognize that meaning is constructed by and for audiences not just at the point of origin but at each historical moment of the life of the object.

The Origins of Drawing in Metalpoint

The scholar Joseph Meder (1857–1934), in his seminal book on the history of Western drawing practice, *The Mastery of Drawing*, assumed that the origins of early modern stylus drawing lay in the metalpoint drawings of classical antiquity.[1] Because it is difficult, in the absence of scientific analysis, to correctly identify the metal source of a particular line, the generic term *metalpoint* is preferred. In fact, no artefactual evidence of metalpoint drawings – basically, line drawings on a parchment or paper support – has survived from antiquity. Meder hypothesized that drawings existed in classical times, and he conflated them with ancient writing supports, about which more evidence survives. He sought the roots of metalpoint drawing in classical writing systems that incised texts into the surfaces of wax tablets with metal styli. No artefactual evidence survives to support his assumption.

Medieval Metalpoint

During the Middle Ages, images served monastic, clerical, courtly, and, later, secular urban society. Medieval drawing practice – in which images are composed of lines – has been characterized as either a way to present conventional subjects for practical purposes or to prove evidence of the artist's creative mind through spontaneous sketches and nature studies.[2]

In this period direct physical and literary evidence for metalpoint drawing is limited, and its uses were relatively humble. Blind stylus (or drypoint) rulings, made to guide the hand-inscribed texts of manuscripts and documents, incised a furrow on the recto and raised a ridge on the verso of the parchment membrane, providing the armature of the page. Evidence of leadpoint has survived from as early as 700 CE, in rulings, underdrawings, and marginalia of illuminated manuscripts.[3] Lead was soft enough to leave a visible and, importantly, erasable pale grey line on parchment and, later, on unprepared paper surfaces. Leadpoint permitted the draughtsman/scribe to experiment, encouraging flexibility and complexity in the design process.[4] Pen and ink or pigments applied over the underdrawings sometimes left visible the metalpoint lines.[5]

In the few analyses undertaken of metalpoints, leadpoint was identified in rulings and designs of the *Lindisfarne Gospels* and several other late eighth- to early ninth-century English and Irish manuscripts.[6] In southern Italian Greek manuscripts of the eleventh and twelfth centuries, lead (sometime with siliceous impurities) and iron (as a component of *plombagine*, a carbon-based form of graphite rich in iron impurities) were identified in the stylus lines as well as an ink containing iron, potassium, and sulphur. The ruling and preparatory drawings of the *Erfurt Giant Hebrew Bible* (1343) are a lead-tin alloy.[7]

Texts were incised by metal styli into wax tablets, leaving visible marks. The practice of composing on wax tablets and the features of their structure – layers of wax applied to tablets made of various materials (wood, ivory, bone) – were inherited by the Middle Ages from the Romans.[8] Wax tablets were temporary supports; until the thirteenth century, information recorded there was copied onto parchment for posterity, and the wax surfaces were erased and reused. Their use for sketching has been debated, but no images on medieval wax tablets survive.

To interpret the results of the technical or scientific analysis of medieval writing and drawing, a knowledge of historical materials is essential. Reference may be made to medieval artists' technical manuals, often called *recipe books* because their format is similar to modern cook books. Craft recipes that appear to transmit practical information in a neutral, transparent way are, in fact, fraught with uncertainties of which readers may be unaware.[9]

Artisanal recipes probably originated in classical antiquity and were reproduced throughout the Middle Ages in numerous and varied compilations. Scholars express a variety of opinions about their function as practical, literary, or straightforward documentary sources for the study of medieval art.[10] The amount of information about metalpoint drawing preserved in medieval texts is very limited.

More practical recipes for working in metalpoint are found from the late fourteenth century on. Jean le Begue's 1431 version of Alcherius's *De Coloribus Diversis Modis Tractator*[11] describes a way of preparing

> parchment, or paper, primed panels, and linen, so that you may be able to draw on them in black with a pencil or stile of gold, silver, bronze or brass, as is done on panels of boxwood whitened or covered with bone, or stag's-horn burnt and whitened in the fire.[12]

Italian Renaissance Metalpoint Drawings

Metalpoint on prepared paper is known as a drawing genre particular to Italian Quattrocento artists; it was the most widely used drawing technique in fifteenth-century Florence and the standard apprenticeship practice. To the late Quattrocento, the materials and techniques remained largely unchanged from those described by Cennini in the late Trecento.[13] A ground of finely pulverized bone mixed with mineral color, white lead, and glue was brushed thinly or thickly onto the paper support. Often, only one side of the paper was prepared by the artist or assistant, or paper was purchased ready-made from a stationer.[14] Cennini recommended a metal-tipped stylus with a lead point for the sketch or underdrawing and a silver point for strengthening the contours and details of the definitive design.[15] Grounds were often brightly colored.[16] Artists worked from the mid-tone of the ground through a range of darks, using metalpoint and, often, additional media, heightening with white body color to suggest the fall of light and sculptural solidity.[17]

The *Head of a Man with a Short Beard* by the Umbrian painter Pietro Vanucci, called Perugino (ca. 1450–1523), demonstrates how metalpoint drawings served to prepare a painting (Figure 1.1).

Figure 1.1 is a study for the head of an apostle on the extreme right of a painting of the Ascension, now in Lyon, made to clarify details of modelling, probably after the composition had been established, but perhaps before the cartoon (a large, often full-scale, finished preparatory drawing for a painting) was executed; it explores only those parts of the composition that were to be visible in the finished painting.[18]

In the later fifteenth century, the Florentine artist Filippino Lippi (1456–1504) produced an exceptional number of metalpoint figure studies (Figure 1.2).[19] He often combined marks made with two different metals in one drawing; they were heightened with white body color on a prepared paper. One point was lead alloyed 2:1 with tin; this corresponds with Cennini's recipe

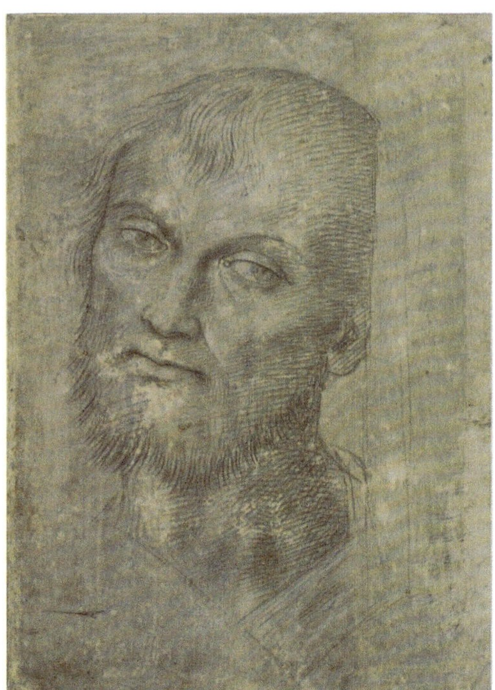

FIGURE 1.1 Pietro Perugino, *Head of a Man with a Short Beard*, ca. 1496–1500, metalpoint (probably silverpoint) heightened with white on cream-colored prepared paper, outlines indented, 7 1/8 × 5 inches (18.2 × 12.5 cm), London, British Museum, 1895, 0915.597

and the composition of other Quattrocento leadpoints. Pure leadpoint was soft; when alloyed it became a more satisfactory drawing tool. Pure silver was also too pliable for drawing, but a minimal amount of added copper and zinc was also a well-established composition. Lippi used the two metallic points in distinct stages of the elaboration of his drawings, taking into account their individual expressive potential. Lead, because of its eraseability, was selected for the preliminary light sketch; silverpoint, applied next, reinforced the hatched shading, confirmed the outlines, defined facial details, and softened the hair. Sometimes lead was more appropriate for describing soft shading on the skin while the silverpoint accentuated boundaries and shadows with defined contour and hatched lines.[20]

The Umbrian painter Raphael (1483–1520) used drawings to train his eye and hand and to execute his projects.[21] He was exceptional in his mastery of metalpoint, valuing it for the precision, fluidity, delicate clarity, and freedom it afforded; unlike pen and ink, the drawing tool did not need to be recharged while working.[22] Raphael was exceptional in his adherence to silverpoint throughout his career; it reinforced his inclination toward "pure, carefully calculated forms and controlled, orderly practices" (Figure 1.3).[23] Unprecedented were his underdrawings in colorless metalpoint lines (blind incisions) made into the paper to establish the compositional layout in preparation for a fuller study in pen and ink.[24] Raphael also made rapid sketches in prepared paper notebooks, for which silverpoint was particularly convenient.[25]

By the early sixteenth century figure drawing in natural black and red chalks, with their richer tonal possibilities, increased and, at Raphael's death in 1520, metalpoint was no longer used by

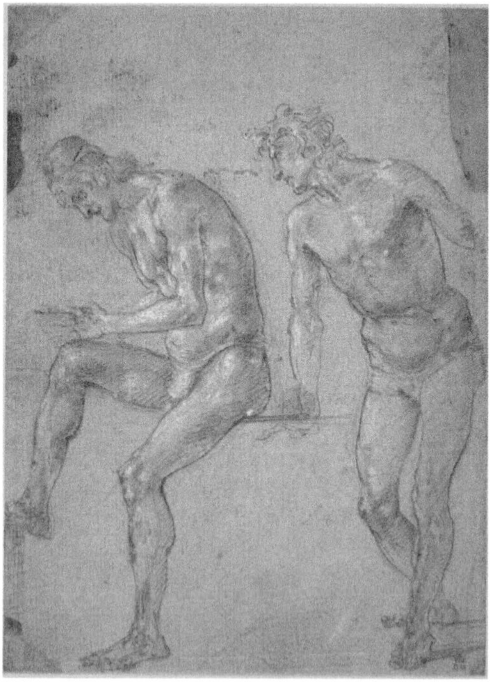

FIGURE 1.2 Filippino Lippi, *Two Nude Men, One Sitting with a Book to Left . . .*, 1485–88, silverpoint (left figure) and leadpoint (right figure), heightened with white (partly discolored), over blind stylus, on grey prepared paper, 10 1/4 × 7 5/16 inches (26.0 × 18.6 cm), London, British Museum, 1858, 724.4

FIGURE 1.3 Raphael, *Studies for the Christ Child in the 'Madonna di Loreto'*, 1507–1510, silverpoint on pink prepared paper, 6 1/2 × 4 5/8 inches (16.7 × 11.8 cm), London, British Museum, Pp.1–72.

Italians.[26] With its restrictive discipline, it was superseded by more flexible tools that did not require prepared paper and were easier to erase. The art historian Kenneth Clark went so far as to suggest that metalpoint was "sharp, brittle and precise . . . which men of the high Renaissance disliked."[27]

The curator Hugo Chapman suggested that in Italy metalpoint usage had always been limited because it was largely a studio-bound activity. Northern European artists realized its potential, appreciating its portability and durability, which allowed them to draw wherever and whenever they chose. It spread more widely in the North than it had ever had in Italy, which ensured its continuation, especially in Holland, until the mid-seventeenth century.[28]

Nevertheless, metalpoint drawing continued to carry cultural meaning for Italian humanist elites. The *Portrait of Alessandro de' Medici* depicted the noble "drawing in the rather outmoded . . . medium of metalpoint."[29] Painted by the Florentine Pontormo (1494–1556) about 1534–1535, the image may allude to the ancient and Quattrocento understanding of *disegno* as the basis of the arts and to its origin as described by classical writers and Renaissance artists.[30]

Metalpoint in Late Medieval and Early Modern Northern Europe

Even in Northern Europe the use of the metalpoint stylus for drawing was limited and intermittent from the mid-fourteenth to the late eighteenth century. In fact, relatively few drawings in any technique have survived, and drawings conceived by the artist as independent aesthetic products may always have been rare, partly because paintings were mostly planned and executed on the panel. Once the paint layer was applied, the underdrawing disappeared from view.[31]

It is unclear whether Jan van Eyck's (c.1390/95–1441) image of *St Barbara*, now in Antwerp, elaborately drawn with a "gossamer-fine brush"[32] and, possibly, a metal stylus on panel and dated 1437, is the underdrawing for an unfinished painting or was intended by the artist as an independent drawing.[33] The translation of an artist's thinking into a linear idiom and the appreciation of drawing as a display of artistic originality were concepts only developed later.[34]

Late Gothic drawings were made as workshop resources or learning exercises, often copying model drawings – partial or deliberately altered copies of single figures or parts of compositions. Some drawings may have been pictorial inventions to be added to the studio's image stock or preliminary sketches to give clients an idea of how a completed work would look. Survivals from this early period are also rare because workshop drawings were used repeatedly and wore out.[35] They were not meant for collectors nor did they have value on the open market beyond the network of workshops.[36] Albrecht Dürer's later addition of a monogram and date to his drawings connected them to a moment of creation by an artist-creator and marked the drawing as a collectible of value to non-artists.[37]

The preparatory purpose of Jan van Eyck's exceptionally detailed metalpoint drawing of an old man, now in Dresden, is clear, since the painting made after it, now in Vienna, survives.[38] Handwritten color notes at the left-hand side of the drawing correspond closely to the painted panel, showing that the artist based the painting on the drawing.[39] Recently, scientific analysis revealed that, exceptionally for the period, it appears van Eyck used several different metal styli to execute his drawing: a silver stylus containing a small amount of copper, a second silver stylus with about 24 percent copper, and a goldpoint with about 20 percent silver.[40] Different styli produced different marks exploited by the artist to achieve subtle painterly modelling.[41]

What remains suggests that metalpoint, during the fifteenth century, was used by artists to study portrait heads and make copies; this practice changed late in the fifteenth century, and metalpoint was sometimes used for portrait sketches drawn freely from life.[42] Surviving drawings feature simple materials – metalpoint on a paper usually coated with white, greenish-white, or ivory ground, rather than brightly colored surfaces, to provide the required tooth. The reduced color range may be appreciated as the best accommodation for the clear objective manner of northern drawings. Technical analysis undertaken at the British Museum confirmed that bone-white ground and silver styli used were almost exclusively.[43]

Metalpoint drawings, featuring stock pictorial images for workshop reference, also survive on small wood- or ivory-leaf tablets; they are sometimes gathered together into multi-leaf codices or bound volumes.[44] The *Morgan Library Boxwood Sketchbook* consists of six boxwood leaves with nine drawings and an associated drawing framed separately, dated about 1400; perhaps they were models for illuminators.[45] Some panels were washed with a thin, translucent white coating, possibly gesso, on which the drawings were executed in silverpoint or leadpoint; the grey color, typical of both, that results from the drawings' protection within a bound structure might indicate either metal, but the incision of the line into the surface of the wood is typical of the harder metal, silver. The conservator Kristi Dahm cautions us about the difficulty of identifying the particular metal used by visual inspection alone.[46]

Two German artists chose metalpoint, favoring it for portraiture because of the subtlety and delicacy with which it captured facial expressions. Hans Holbein the Elder (ca. 1465–1524) produced elaborate Gothic altarpieces in a large, successful Augsburg workshop. Holbein specialized in face and figure studies from life; these were drawn on small sheets that he kept in his workshop in the form of sketchbooks of prepared paper. Only two survive.[47] Holbein often applied a grey preparation and combined silverpoint with other drawing materials: chalks, including red chalk, leadpoint, and/or ink.[48]

The second German artist to favor metalpoint for drawing was Albrecht Dürer (1471–1528) of Nuremberg. His graphic practice made use of all available tools and materials. His work was admired for the fineness and delicacy of his drawn and painted lines. Drawings that have been scientifically analyzed reveal that Dürer drew with a silverpoint on a bone-white ground; lead white is sometimes present.[49]

By the sixteenth century northern interest in the metalpoint technique waned. Holbein's son, Hans Holbein the Younger (1497/8–1543), used it in his earliest portraits on prepared paper. The conservator Victoria Button analyzed the stratigraphy of his early drawings and found that he used metalpoint to draw contours, shade and model faces, and darken strokes (by repeated applications).[50] He also used the metal stylus to trace over his drawings and transfer, by means of blind incisions, the composition to a panel prior to painting. However, Button found little evidence of metalpoint in his later drawings on pink prepared paper.[51]

Early in his career the Haarlem printmaker Hendrick Goltzius (1558–1617) made small portrait drawings in metalpoint on prepared surfaces, some intended as preparatory studies for engravings and others as independent works of art. Many of the small supports are drawn on both sides, suggesting that they originated in pocket-sized drawing books, later cut up.[52] With the exception of his pupils, no other artists in the northern Netherlands in the 1570s and 1580s worked in metalpoint; it was an old-fashioned choice, one which may have been in use in the Goltzius family workshop and/or was perhaps influenced by his admiration of sketches in silverpoint by Dürer, recognized as the most important German artist even during his lifetime.[53] In more highly finished works, Goltzius combined silverpoint with other drawing materials.[54]

The curator Marjorie Wieseman marveled at the fine delineation Goltzius achieved. "Even under magnification the impossibly fine hatching of the face can hardly be distinguished, while the hair and costume are drawn with rather freer, highly differentiated strokes that suggest the varied textures of fabric and fur."[55] Elsewhere the artist may have "rubbed over the [metalpoint] lines with a stump, creating a velvety effect and extremely subtle gradations of grey."[56] Goltzius's works gradually gained in size, his drawing became freer, and he increasingly favored the more fluid properties of softer leadpoint.[57]

The supports of his drawings are often described as tablets of card or parchment, coated on both sides with a layer of gesso and then polished; an annotation on the verso of a metalpoint portrait dated 1580 records that the "thick" tablet is coated with "White of an Egg and ground."[58] However, instrumental analysis by French scientists of two drawings by Goltzius revealed that they are supported on wood slips covered with a layer of bone white; a yellow surface layer, over the bone-white ground, is lead-tin yellow.[59] The silverpoint drawings were executed on the yellow layer, once dry. Technical analysis at the British Museum of four Goltzius metalpoints detected a yellow surface layer of lead-tin yellow over a smooth burnished, white, chalk-based ground applied to vellum.[60]

The Eighteenth Century and the Waning of Metalpoint

Drawings into the eighteenth century still functioned as tools, resources for the artist's workshop, and, rarely, as independent works of art. However, by then, drawings were acquiring increasing status as collectibles and became useful in an emerging science of art or history of artists;

connoisseurs prized initial thoughts and sketches that captured the spontaneity of the artist's hand "because their allegedly less calculated and labored nature made them more immediate and thus authentic."[61] The first ideas of artists were now valued as proof of their fertility and intense genius.[62] This new reception of drawings crystallized in France in the circle around the wealthy banker and collector Pierre Crozat (1665–1740).[63]

In such an environment, it is difficult to see a role for metalpoint. In fact, few examples have been identified to date and, without undertaking scientific analysis, it can be difficult to distinguish metalpoint marks from graphite. According to the curator Stacey Sell, metalpoint was used by only a few minor portraitists; she has suggested that its stability, in contrast to the more friable graphite, permitted artists to overpaint their underdrawings with watercolors and avoid muddied colors.[64] David Boudon (1748–1816), an established European miniaturist in silverpoint and watercolor before his emigration to America in 1794/5, used this technique.[65] Anton Graff (1736–1813), also of Swiss origin and active in Germany, combined metalpoint and graphite in small portraits.[66]

Metalpoint has also been identified in mixed media drawings of the late eighteenth century. The art historian Sonia Couturier described two drawings by the French neoclassical architect Thomas de Thomon (1754–1813) – *A View of Ancient Rome, with Figures at a Well beneath a Statue of an Amazon*[67] and *Tullis Driving Her Chariot Over the Body of Her Father*[68] (both 1798) – as executed in graphite, metalpoint, and traces of brown wash; in addition, the latter also contains drypoint incisions and is executed on paper prepared for metalpoint.[69]

The Nineteenth and Early Twentieth Centuries

Metalpoint has left relatively few traces in nineteenth-century drawing practice.[70] Fine line drawings were normally executed in synthetic graphite pencils, increasingly available in a broad range of hardnesses. Nevertheless, a taste for linear delicacy, firmness, and precision sometimes recommended metalpoint as an additional technical option. English artists in particular benefitted from opportunities to study large numbers of Old Master and contemporary drawings made increasingly accessible through exhibitions in museums and galleries, along with photographic reproductions.[71] Cennino Cennini's *Il Libro dell'Arte*, published in English translation in 1844, provided English artists with basic instructions for working in metalpoint.[72]

The case of Frederic, Lord Leighton (1830–1896), a prolific English draughtsman highly regarded for his delicate drawings, is instructive; metalpoint might have been a natural choice for him, but there continues to be confusion in the literature about whether he worked in graphite or metalpoint.[73] The painter Edward Burne-Jones (1833–1898), obsessed with drawing and knowledgeable about Old Master (especially Florentine) drawings, rarely used metalpoint; a rare example, from 1877, is in the Ashmolean Museum, Oxford.[74] Usually he drew with hard graphite, sharpened to a point, which allowed him "to emulate the crisp contours associated with Florentine drawings."[75]

The art historian Susan Owens has suggested that artists engaged creatively with earlier drawings and made works emulating the appearance of metalpoint without necessarily adopting the technique itself.[76] Partly, she attributed this to the dearth of commercially available metalpoint materials before Winsor & Newton's introduction of labor-saving kits about 1892.[77] The 1896 wholesale catalogue advertises silverpoint supplies, including "silver-point drawing paper" in two sizes, sketchbooks with metallic pencil, and "Sterling Silver Points."[78]

In late nineteenth-century England, a "silverpoint revival" occurred; it featured a wider, more sustained use of the tool.[79] A taste for small-sized drawings and a reorientation of art education toward academic principles and the classical tradition renewed veneration for Italian Renaissance drawing and emphasized technical skill. This privileged the role of line in the representation of three-dimensional forms and encouraged a reliance on fine linear marks.

Alphonse Legros (1837–1911), a French painter and etcher and Slade Professor from 1876 to 1892, studied Old Master techniques; he was an enthusiast of metalpoint, as were his students William Strang (1859–1921) and Charles Prosper Sainton (1861–1914).[80] They appreciated the rigor with which he taught drawing "with the point alone" (using a pale grey Italian natural chalk and graphite in addition to silverpoint), emphasizing pure line and contour.[81] Legros did not record why he chose metalpoint;[82] it would have met his requirement for muted rather than tonally contrasted images, for working with line and shading through hatching. Furthermore, as an etcher he would have been comfortable working with needle-like tools. Analysis has confirmed Legros's use of goldpoint, a metal which resists oxidation, retaining its pale grey lines.[83] At times Legros used a commercially prepared baryta paper; its ultra-smooth surface permitted a more refined line and further restricted the tonal range.[84]

American interest in metalpoint dates from the mid-1890s, motivated by renewed enthusiasm for Renaissance art, knowledge of the British metalpoint revival, and growing interest in fine draftsmanship sparked by academic training abroad.[85] The American tonalist painter and draftsman Thomas Wilmer Dewing (1851–1938) studied at the Académie Julien in Paris. There he was introduced to the Old Masters along with their traditional materials and techniques and learned to favor clear composition and a careful definition of form.[86] His earliest metalpoints from the 1890s portrayed his female sitters in strict profile poses that were probably inspired by Renaissance compositions, but, at the same time, he was doubtless aware of metalpoint's appeal to devotees of the English Aesthetic Movement, including Legros's students.[87] Dewing's metalpoint drawings were the perfect complement to his paintings – in both genres he portrayed refined women of the Anglo-American elite as dematerialized aesthetic objects in an ambiguous pictorial space, capturing an abstract beauty with soft tonalities and smooth surfaces that radiated a luminous sheen. Drawn in faint, tiny, straight parallel lines,[88] his heads barely emerge from the chromatic mist that dominates the pictorial surface (Figure 1.4).

The origins of metalpoint drawing in America in fact go back to the interest in historical techniques of Charles Eliot Norton (1827–1908), appointed first professor of fine arts at Harvard University in 1875. Influenced by his close friend John Ruskin, the English polymath, Norton adopted for the new Harvard curriculum the educational methods and instructional materials developed by Ruskin for Oxford University.[89] Lacking suitable textbooks, Norton and his assistants gathered together illustrative materials, both good reproductions and original works, including metalpoint drawings. Norton was convinced of the significance of the artist's outlines as evidence of his "first idea" and believed that this creative stage was captured in the outline drawing.[90] Ruskin's conviction that manual practice accompanying art lectures would aid students in "understand[ing] the nature and difficulty of executive skill" led Norton to supplement his own lectures with studio art classes.[91]

Fine art teaching at Harvard continued to be informed by Ruskinian tenets into the twentieth century. Students were encouraged to look at original works of art and to reproduce them using historical materials and methods. Edward Forbes, director of Harvard's Fogg Museum from 1909 to 1944, believed that historical artists' recipes would repay study and experimentation;

FIGURE 1.4 Thomas Wilmer Dewing, *Head of a Girl*, c. 1909, silverpoint on prepared wove paper, sheet: 13 5/8 × 11 3/4 inches (34.61 × 29.85 cm), *Corcoran Collection (Bequest of James Parmelee)*, 2015.19.498

disputed points would be clarified, ensuring better care of old pictures and more durable execution of new ones. Forbes introduced his student and, later, assistant, Daniel Varney Thompson, Jr. (1902–1980), to metalpoint drawing. Thompson experimented with the technique and wrote about his efforts in his correspondences; they were reflected in his later translation of Cennino Cennini's *Il Libro dell'Arte*.[92]

Artists – traditionalists and modernists – drew in metalpoint in early twentieth-century America. Some American midwestern artists chose metalpoint as a direct result of the influence of James Watrous (1908–1999), a Public Works Administration artist who gained his PhD from the University of Wisconsin, Madison, in 1939 and subsequently taught art history and studio art there. His passion for late medieval and Renaissance art led him to develop a hands-on course in historical techniques. His students Silvia Fein (b. 1919) and John Wilde (1919–2006) and other midwestern artists were fascinated by the technical and expressive capabilities of historical materials and passionate about making art with them.

Preliminary drawings played an important part in the working method of the American regionalist painter Marsden Hartley (1877–1943), who had received a traditional academic education at the Cleveland School of Art. Bruce Weber has suggested that Hartley became interested in silverpoint through his friendship with the sculptor John Storrs (1885–1956) in the late 1920s.

In silverpoint drawings from 1926 on, Storrs worked out the relationship between edges and surfaces, "the glide of the silver needle over the prepared paper," he explained, "is easier than even the softest pencil, and that very smoothness invites a subtler, more flexible line. The resulting drawing is evanescent. . . ."[93]

Before he embarked on a painting, Hartley, a prolific draftsman, sought to capture the essence of his subject mentally and visually, subsequently painting in the studio from sketches made at the site.[94] Many drawings survive, some executed in metalpoint, usually identified as silverpoint, on paper sometimes described as "prepared" or "white coated" but often not well characterized. He drew still lifes and delicate silverpoint landscapes around Aix-en-Provence from May to November 1927; in these "parallel-line drawings" – characterized by outlines and single-hatched, diagonally oriented strokes, he sought to eliminate everything extraneous to the formal truths of his motifs and capture the essence of a place, emulating Cezanne.[95] Drawings from Hartley's Bavarian sojourn, in the fall and winter of 1933–1934, may have been made in a metalpoint sketchbook.[96]

Between 1931 and 1944, Otto Dix (1891–1969), a German social realist painter, printmaker, and virtuoso draftsman, made over 200 silverpoint drawings – portraits, nudes, landscapes, and preparatory studies for paintings.[97] He mastered a disciplined academic draftsmanship as a student in Dresden and later taught at the Dresden Academy of Art (1927–1933), a center for the study of artists' techniques and material science. Although he greatly admired the northern Renaissance Old Masters, especially Hans Baldung Grien, he was less interested in reconstructing historical techniques as an end in itself than in exploiting metalpoint for his own purposes: "One uses techniques according to one's needs at the moment."[98] He lost his teaching position after 1933, when the Nazis came to power, and retreated into the countryside, where he drew controlled, precise, but politically inoffensive landscapes, children, his family, and others, often in silverpoint on white prepared paper.

A Russian-born surrealist painter, stage designer, and draughtsman, Pavel Tchelitchew (1898–1957) moved to Western Europe in 1920 and lived in New York City from 1934 to 1949. Described by the art historian Robert Rosenblum as "a cosmopolitan butterfly," he was, nevertheless, an artist of considerable individuality.[99] It was after a trip to Italy in 1935 that he apparently took up metalpoint to execute portraits and figure studies.[100] His metalpoint drawings, identified as silverpoints, were made mainly in 1937 and 1938.[101] Tchelitchew admired the technique's "crystalline perfection" and noted its "extreme demands of absolute skill."[102] His elegant, hard, thin line was incised into commercially prepared paper to create compelling images characterized by clarity, delicacy of contour, and precise linear modelling.[103]

Conclusion

This chapter has introduced the materials and techniques that have defined metalpoint drawing practice at historical moments. Following a brief methodological introduction, it considered whether the origins of metalpoint drawing are to be found in classical antiquity. No archaeological or literary evidence survives from the ancient world to support this assumption; ancient styli that have been recovered were likely used for writing on clay and wax surfaces. Material and literary evidence for the use of the metalpoint for writing and drawing during the Middle Ages and through the Trecento were reviewed next. The chapter suggested that throughout this long period the stylus served varied but limited and relatively humble functions.

It was in Florence during the Quattrocento that numerous artists enthusiastically and quite suddenly embraced the metalpoint for drawing. Why? Artists were not continuing a strong drawing tradition. Other tools and materials – charcoal and variously colored chalks, pen and ink, and, increasingly, watercolor – were readily available, flexible, and easier to use. Possibly artists exploited the linear incisions made by the stylus in the ground preparation because such marks, preserved in ancient metal and ceramic artifacts, reflected how they imagined ancient drawing might have appeared, had it survived.[104]

Metalpoint continued in limited use through the early modern period and into modern times. In the present, this technique, generally perceived as exclusively linear with a narrow tonal range, has experienced a renaissance. Particularly in America, artists have created metalpoint drawings of "exceptional beauty and remarkable craftsmanship."[105] The process attracts contemporary artists who enjoy its refinement, its precision, and the quiet, meditative discipline of careful mark-making. Those attracted by the challenge and beauty of metalpoint will appreciate the information distilled in the chapters that follow, drawn together by Susan Schwalb and Tom Mazzullo, consummate contemporary masters of this exacting yet richly expressive technique.

Notes

1 Meder, Joseph and Winslow Ames. *The Mastery of Drawing*. 2 vols. (New York: Abaris Books, 1978). First published as *Die Handzeichnung: Ihre Technik und Entwicklung* in Vienna in 1919, it was translated into English by Winslow Ames and published in 1978.

2 Burns, Thea. *The Luminous Trace: Drawing and Writing in Metalpoint* (London: Archetype, 2012), 44, 211: n. 7.

3 Brown, Michelle P. *The Lindisfarne Gospels: Society, Spirituality and the Scribe* (London: British Library, 2003), 204–205, 216–217, 219.

4 Ibid., 283.

5 *Barlaam and Josaphat*, Los Angeles, J. Paul Getty Museum, 83.MR.179, a fifteenth-century German illuminated manuscript, features tempera colours, coloured washes, and ink over leadpoint underdrawing on paper. www.getty.edu/art/collection/objects/1441/follower-of-hans-schilling-from-the-workshop-of-diebold-lauber-rudolf-von-ems-et-al-barlaam-und-josaphat-alsatian-1469/. Accessed 25 June 2018

6 Brown, *The Lindisfarne Gospels*, 204, 216. Burns, *The Luminous Trace*, 64.

7 Burns, *The Luminous Trace*, 64–65, with further references.

8 Ibid., 54–61 and figs. 29–34.

9 Ibid., 68–69 summarizes the concerns.

10 The issues are complex. For a summary, with references to basic bibliographical sources, see Burns, *The Luminous Trace*, 68–73; for a detailed study of the earliest surviving medieval recipe collection, Lucca, Biblioteca Capitolare Feliniana, Cod. 490, folios 217r–231r, see Burns, Thea. *Compositiones Variae: A Late Eighth-Century Craftsman's Treatise Reconsidered* (London: Archetype, 2017).

11 A Treatise Upon Colours of Various Kinds.

12 Merrifield, Mary P. *Original Treatises: Dating from the XIIth to XVIIIth Centuries on the Arts of Painting in Oil, Miniature, Mosaic, and on Glass; of Gilding, Dyeing, and the Preparation of Colours and Artificial Gems*, vol. 1 (London: J. Murray, 1849), 274–278.

13 Broecke, Laura. *Cennino Cennini's "Il Libro dell'Arte": A New English Translation and Commentary with Italian Transcription* (London: Archetype, 2015), 26–33.

14 Bambach, Carmen. "Technique and Workshop Practice in Filippino's Drawings." In *The Drawings of Filippino Lippi and His Circle*, George R. Goldner, Carmen Bambach, and Filippino Lippi, 21–28 (New York: Metropolitan Museum of Art, 1997), 24.

15 Melli, Lorenza. "I disegni a due punte metalliche di Filippino Lippi: una scelta funzionale." *Mitteilungen des Kunsthistorischen Instituts in Florenz* 52, no. 2/3 (2008): 88–108, 102.

16 Broecke, *Cennino Cennini's "Il Libro dell'Arte"*, 35–43, with additional references.

17 Aceto, Angelam. "Raphael's Materials and Techniques." In *Raphael, the Drawings*, edited by Catherine Whistler and Ben Thomas (Oxford: Ashmolean Museum, 2017), 22–27, 27.

18 Dreyer, Peter. "A Forgotten Drawing by Perugino." *The Burlington Magazine* 139, no. 1132 (1997): 465–469, 467. Aceto, "Raphael's Materials and Technique," 24.

19 Melli, "I disegni a due punte metalliche." Bambach, "Technique and Workshop," 21

20 Melli, "I disegni a due punte metalliche," 95, gives a more extensive and nuanced description of Filippino's metalpoints.

21 Ames-Lewis, Francis. *The Draftsman Raphael* (New Haven, CT: Yale University Press, 1986), 12.

22 Aceto, "Raphael's Materials and Techniques," 25–26.

23 Ames-Lewis, *The Draftsman Raphael*, 13–14.

24 Ibid., 20.

25 Ibid., 17.

26 Bambach, "Technique and Workshop," 25–26. Aceto, "Raphael's Materials and Techniques," 26.

27 Clark, Kenneth and Carlo Pedretti. *The Drawings of Leonardo Da Vinci in the Collection of Her Majesty the Queen at Windsor Castle*. 2nd revised ed., vol. 1, 3 vols. (London: Phaidon, 1968), 27.

28 Chapman, Hugo. "Introduction." In *Northern European Metalpoint Drawings: Technical Examination and Analysis*, edited by Joanna Russell, Judith Rayner and Jenny Bescoby, 1–3. (London: Archetype, 2017), 1–2.

29 Simons, Patricia. "Disegno and desire in Pontormo's Alessandro de' Medici." *Renaissance Studies* 22, no. 5 (2008): 650–688, 655.

30 Burns, *The Luminous Trace*, 113, fig. 51, with further references.

31 Messling, Guido. "The Art of Drawing Before van Eyck." In *The Road to Van Eyck*, Stephan Kemperdick and Friso Lammertse, 66–68 (Rotterdam, the Netherlands: Museum Boijmans Van Beuningen, 2012), 66.

32 Jan van Eyck (ca.1390/95–1441), *St Barbara* (1437), drawing, possibly metalpoint, on wood panel prepared on both sides with a white ground, 41.2 x 27.5 cm, Antwerp, Koninklijk Museum voor Schone Kunsten, inv. No. 410. Lammertse, Friso. "Jan Van Eyck, St Barbara (1437)." In *The Road to Van Eyck*, edited by Stephan Kemperdick and Friso Lammertse, 300 (Rotterdam, the Netherlands: Museum Boijmans Van Beuningen, 2012). Illustrated in Burns, *The Luminous Trace*, 121, fig. 53, and at http://vlaamseprimitieven.vlaamsekunstcollectie.be/en/collection/saint-barbara. Accessed 25 June 2018.

33 Ainsworth, Maryan W. "Review: Early Netherlandish Drawings from Jan van Eyck to Hieronymus Bosch, ex.cat, Fritz Koreny, E. Pokorny and G. Zeman, eds." *Master Drawings* 41, no. 3 (2003): 305–316, 307, opts for its being the underdrawing of an unfinished panel painting.

34 Koreny, Fritz. "Introduction: Early Netherlandish Drawings Issue." *Master Drawings* 41, no. 3 (2003): 201–203, 201.

35 Ainsworth, "Review: Early Netherlandish Drawings," 305.

36 Wood, Christopher S. *Forgery, Replica, Fiction: Temporalities of German Renaissance Art* (Chicago, IL: University of Chicago Press, 2008), 346. Buck, Stephanie. "An Approach to Looking at Eyckian Drawings." In *Investigating Jan Van Eyck*, edited by Susan Foister, Sue Jones, Delphine Cool, and Jan Van Eyck, 185–195 (Turnhout: Brepols, Belgium: 2000), 160: n. 24, records written sources that document the economic significance to and theft of early drawings by artists.

37 Wood, *Forgery, Replica, Fiction*, 49–50. Koerner, Joseph Leo. *The Moment of Self-Portraiture in German Renaissance Art* (Chicago: University of Chicago Press, 1996), xviii, 46, 203–223.

38 Jan van Eyck (ca.1390/95–1441), *Portrait of an Elderly Man* (ca. 1435), silverpoint on prepared paper, 21.4 x 18.1 cm, Dresden, Staatliche Kunstsammlungen, Kupferstich-Kabinett, C775. Messling, "The Art of Drawing Before van Eyck.", 66. Illustrated in Burns, *The Luminous Trace*, 129, fig. 57.

39 Buck, Stephanie. "An Approach to Looking at Eyckian Drawings."

40 Ambers, Janet, Catherine Higgitt, and David Saunders. *Italian Renaissance Drawings: Technical Examination and Analysis* (London: Archetype Publications, in Association with the British Museum, 2010), 13–14.

41 Reiche, Ina, Martin Radtke, Achim Berger, Wolf Görner, Thomas Ketelsen, Silke Merchel, Josef Riederer, Heinrich Riesemeier, and Michael Roth. "Spatially Resolved Synchrotron-Induced X-ray Fluorescence Analyses of Metalpoint Drawings and Their Mysterious Inscriptions." *Spectrochimica Acta Part B: Atomic Spectroscopy* 59, no. 10/11 (2004): 1657–1662, 1662.

42 Bartrum, Giulia and An Van Camp. "Masters of Metalpoint in Northern Europe." In *Northern European Metalpoint Drawings: Technical Examination and Analysis*, Joanna Russell, Judith Rayner, and Jenny Bescoby, 5–12 (London: Archetype Publications, in association with the British Museum, 2017).
43 Chapman, "Introduction," 3. Russell, Joanna, Judith Rayner, and Jenny Bescoby. "Technical Examination and Analysis." In *Northern European Metalpoint Drawings: Technical Examination and Analysis*, Joanna Russell, Judith Rayner, and Jenny Bescoby, 21–52 (London: Archetype Publications, in association with the British Museum, 2017), 49.
44 Burns, *The Luminous Trace*, 120–128.
45 *Morgan Library Boxwood Sketchbook*. New York: Pierpont Morgan Library M 346 & 346A, illustrated in part at www.themorgan.org/manuscript/158212. Accessed 25 June 2018.
46 Dahm, Kristi. "The Stylus Revealed: A Metalpoint Identification Study of Fifteenth- and Sixteenth-Century Italian Drawings in The Metropolitan Museum of Art." *The Paper Conservator* 28 (2004): 75–86, 75.
47 Bartram and Van Camp, "Masters of Metalpoint in Northern Europe," 7.
48 Russell, Rayner, and Bescoby, "Technical Examination and Analysis," 30. Burns, *The Luminous Trace*, 128.
49 Burns, *The Luminous Trace*, 134–136.
50 Button, Victoria. *The Portrait Drawings of Hans Holbein the Younger: Function and Use Explored Through Materials and Techniques*. Ph.D. Thesis (London: Royal College of Art, Victoria and Albert Museum, 2013), 117–119.
51 Ibid., 120.
52 Bartram and Van Camp, "Masters of Metalpoint in Northern Europe," 10.
53 Schapelhouman, Marjin. "Many Fine Likenesses: Portrait Engravings and Drawings 1578–1590." In *Hendrick Goltzius (1558–1617): Tekeningen, Prenten en Schilderijen*, edited by Huigen Leeflang, Ger Luijten, Jaap Engelsman, and Lawrence W. Nichols, 56–79 (Zwolle, the Netherlands: Waanders, 2003), 61–62. Burns, *The Luminous Trace*, 140–141.
54 Russell et al.., "Technical Examination and Analysis," 45.
55 Wieseman, Marjorie E. "Between Paint and Print: Plumbago Portraits in Britain and the Netherlands." In *Perfect Likeness: European and American Portrait Miniatures from the Cincinnati Art Museum*, Julie Aronson and Marjorie E. Wieseman, 33–47 (New Haven, CT: Yale University Press, 2006), 36.
56 Schapelhouman, "Many Fine Likenesses," 73–75.
57 Ibid., 62.
58 Ibid., 63.
59 Duval, Alain, Helen Guicharnaud, and Jean-Claude Dran. "Particle-induced X-Ray Emission: A Valuable Tool for the Analysis of Metalpoint Drawings." *Nuclear Instruments and Methods in Physics Research B* 226 (2004): 60–74.
60 Russell et al.., "Technical Examination and Analysis," 43–49.
61 Turel, Noa. "Genius Disrobed: The Early Netherlandish Underdrawing Craze and the End of the Connoisseurship Era." *Journal of Art Historiography*, no. 16 (2017): 1–16, 6.
62 Michel, Christian. "Le goût pour le dessin en France aux XVIIe et XVIIIe siecles: de l'utilisation à l'étude désintéressée." *Revue de l'art* 143, no. 1 (2004): 27–34.
63 Crow, Thomas. *Painters and Public Life in Eighteenth-Century Paris* (New Haven, CT: Yale University Press, 2000), 39–44.
64 Sell, Stacey. "The Silverpoint Revival in Nineteenth-Century Britain." In *Drawing in Silver and Gold: Leonardo to Jasper Johns*, Stacey Sell and Hugo Chapman, 189–223 (Washington, D.C.: National Gallery of Art, 2015), 189.
65 Richards, Nancy E. "A Most Perfect Resemblance at Moderate Prices: The Miniatures of David Boudon." *Winterthur Portfolio* 9 (1974): 77–101.
66 Burns, *The Luminous Trace*, 143.
67 London, Jean-Luc Baroni Ltd., 20.7 x 27.5 cm.
68 Ottawa, National Gallery of Canada, acc. no. 41858.
69 Couturier, Sonia. "Une fantaisie historique ou la fabrication du néoclassicisme: *Tullie conduisant son char sur le corps de son père* par Jean-François Thomas, dit Thomas de Thomon." *National Gallery of Canada Review* 6 (2008): 36–51.
70 Sell, "The Silverpoint Revival," 189–190, presents several continental works in metalpoint, possibly inspired by Renaissance examples.

71 Owens, Susan. "'A Dose of Paradise': Some Effects of Renaissance Drawings on Victorian Artists." In *Burning Bright: Essays in Honour of David Bindman*, Diana Dethloff, edited by T. V. Murdoch, Kim Sloan, Caroline Elam, and David Bindman, 180–189 (London: UCL Press, 2015), 180–181.
72 Burns, Thea. "Cennino Cennini's Il Libro dell'Arte: A Historiographical Review." *Studies in Conservation* 56 (2011): 1–13, 5.
73 Burns, *The Luminous Trace*, 150–3 and figs. 67, 68.
74 Wildman, Stephen and John Christian, with essays by Alan Crawford, and Laurence Des Cars. *Edward Burne-Jones, Victorian Artist-Dreamer* (New York: Metropolitan Museum of Art, 1998), 148–150.
75 Owens, "'A Dose of Paradise,'" 184.
76 Ibid., 182, 184.
77 Ibid., 182–184. Watrous, James. *The Craft of Old-Master Drawings* (Madison: University of Wisconsin Press, 1957), 8, 156: n. 10.
78 Winsor & Newton, Limited, Manufacturing Artists' Colourmen. *Wholesale Catalogue* (London: 1896), 51.
79 Owens, "'A Dose of Paradise,'" 182.
80 Burns, *The Luminous Trace*, 154–160.
81 Ibid., 154, 228, n. 31.
82 Sell, Stacey. "'The Interesting and Difficult Medium': The Silverpoint Revival in Nineteenth-Century Britain." *Master Drawings* 51, no. 1 (2013): 63–86, 74.
83 Sell, "The Silverpoint Revival in Nineteenth-Century Britain," 197, no. 43.
84 Ibid., 197, plate 83.
85 Weber, Bruce, and Agnes Mongan. *The Fine Line: Drawing with Silver in America* (West Palm Beach, FL: Norton Gallery and School of Art, 1985), 20.
86 Weinberg, H. Barbara. "Late Nineteenth-Century American Painting: Cosmopolitan Concerns and Critical Controversies." *Archives of American Art Journal* 23, no. 4 (1983): 19–26, 23–24.
87 Hobbs, Susan A., and Barbara Dayer Gallati. *The Art of Thomas Wilmer Dewing: Beauty Reconfigured* (New York: Brooklyn Museum, 1996), 13, 16, 210.
88 Ibid., 210.
89 Burns, *The Luminous Trace*, 161–163.
90 Gage, John. "Questions of Tone: Turner's Theme and Ruskin's Exposition." *Harvard University Art Museums Bulletin* 3, no. 1 (1994): 27–36, 32.
91 Dowling, Linda. *Charles Eliot Norton: The Art of Reform in Nineteenth-Century America* (Hanover, NH: University Press of New England, 2007), 136.
92 Cennini, Cennino and Daniel V. Thompson. *The Craftsman's Handbook* (New York: Dover Publications, 1954), 4–8. Burns, *The Luminous Trace*, 86, fig. 40, reproduces a metalpoint drawing on prepared paper by Thompson.
93 Weber, Bruce. "Modern and Contemporary Drawing in Metalpoint." In *Drawing in Silver and Gold: Leonardo to Jasper Johns*, Stacey Sell and Hugo Chapman, 224–239 (Washington, D.C.: National Gallery of Art, 2015), 228. Storrs's quote is cited more extensively on page 226; he gives the source on page 238, note 8.
94 Kornhauser, Elizabeth Mankin, and Ulrich Birkmaier. "Marsden Hartley's Materials and Working Methods." In *Marsden Hartley*, edited by Elizabeth Mankin Kornhauser, 265–277 (New Haven, CT: Wadsworth Athenaeum Museum of Art, 2002), 268.
95 Burns, *The Luminous Trace*, 169. Haskell, Barbara. *Marsden Hartley* (New York: Whitney Museum, 1980), 74–75, fig. 71.
96 Kornhauser and Birkmaier, "Marsden Hartley's Materials and Working Methods," 171–172.
97 Weber, "Modern and Contemporary Drawing in Metalpoint," 229.
98 Rewald, Sabine. "Dix at the Met." *Metropolitan Museum of Art Journal* 31 (1996): 219–224, 223. Miller, Bruce F. "Otto Dix and His Oil-Tempera Technique." *Bulletin of the Cleveland Museum of Art* 74, no. 8 (1987): 332–355, 332, 348. Beck, Rainier. "Dix et la tradition." In *Otto Dix et les maîtres anciens*, Rainer Beck and Otto Dix, 11–64 (Colmar, France: Musée d'Unterlinden, 1996).
99 Rosenblum, Robert. "Pavel Tchelitchew." *Artforum International* 37, no. 3 (1998): 107.
100 Soby, James Thrall. *Tchelitchew; Paintings, Drawings* (New York: Published for the Museum of Modern Art by Arno Press, 1972), 28. Dreishpoon, Douglas. "The Fine Line: Drawing with Silver." *Arts Magazine* 61, no. 1 (1985): 17.
101 Soby, *Tchelitchew: Paintings, Drawings*, 28, 93–95. Kirstein, Lincoln. *Pavel Tchelitchew Drawings* (New York: H. Bittner and Co., 1947), 11, 19, nos. 32, 33; 20, no. 36.

102 Kirstein, *Pavel Tchelitchew Drawings*, 8.
103 Weber, "Modern and Contemporary Drawing in Metalpoint," 230. Soby, *Tchelitchew: Paintings, Drawings*, 28
104 These ideas are developed more fully in Burns, *The Luminous Trace*.
105 Weber, "Modern and Contemporary Drawing in Metalpoint," 225.

Bibliography

Aceto, Angelam. "Raphael's Materials and Techniques." In *Raphael, the Drawings*, edited by Catherine Whistler & Ben Thomas, 22-27. Oxford: Ashmolean Museum, 2017.

Ainsworth, Maryan W. "Review: Early Netherlandish Drawings from Jan van Eyck to Hieronymus Bosch, ex.cat, Fritz Koreny, E. Pokorny & G. Zeman, eds." *Master Drawings*, 41, no. 3 (2003): 305-16.

Ambers, Janet, Catherine Higgitt, and David Saunders. *Italian Renaissance Drawings: Technical Examination and Analysis*. London: Archetype Publications, in Association with the British Museum, 2010.

Ames, Joseph, and Francis Ames-Lewis. *The Draftsman Raphael*. New Haven: Yale University Press, 1986.

Bambach, Carmen. "Technique and Workshop Practice in Filippino's Drawings." In *The Drawings of Filippino Lippi and His Circle*, George R. Goldner, Carmen Bambach, and Filippino Lippi, 21-28. New York: Metropolitan Museum of Art, 1997.

Bartrum, Giulia & An Van Camp. "Masters of Metalpoint in Northern Europe." In *Northern European Metalpoint Drawings: Technical Examination and Analysis,* Joanna Russell, Judith Rayner, and Jenny Bescoby, 5-12. London: Archetype Publications, in Association with The British Museum, 2017

Beck, Rainier. "Dix et la tradition." In *Otto Dix et les maîtres anciens,* Rainer Beck and Otto Dix, 11-64. Colmar: Musée d'Unterlinden, 1996.

Broecke, Laura. *Cennino Cennini's 'Il Libro dell'Arte': A New English Translation and Commentary with Italian Transcription*, London: Archetype, 2015.

Brown, Michelle P. *The Lindisfarne Gospels: Society, Spirituality and the Scribe*. London: British Library, 2003.

Buck, Stephanie. "An Approach to Looking at Eyckian Drawings." In *Investigating Jan Van Eyck*, Susan Foister, Sue Jones, Delphine Cool, and Jan Van Eyck, 185-195. Turnhout: Brepols, 2000.

Buck, Stephanie. "With Pen and Silverpoint." In *Rogier van der Weyden 1400-64: Master of Passions*, edited by Lorne Campbell and Jan van der Stock, 146-161. Zwolle: Waanders, 2009.

Burns, Thea. "Cennino Cennini's *Il Libro dell'Arte*: A Historiographical Review." *Studies in Conservation* 56 (2011): 1-13.

Burns, Thea. *The Luminous Trace: Drawing and Writing in Metalpoint*. London: Archetype, 2012.

Burns, Thea. *Compositiones Variae: A Late Eighth-Century Craftsman's Treatise Reconsidered*. London: Archetype, 2017.

Button, Victoria. *The Portrait Drawings of Hans Holbein the Younger: Function and Use Explored Through Materials and Techniques*. Ph.D. Thesis. London: Royal College of Art, Victoria and Albert Museum, 2013.

Cennini, Cennino, and Daniel V. Thompson. *The Craftsman's Handbook*. New York: Dover Publications, 1954.

Chapman, Hugo. "Introduction." In *Northern European Metalpoint Drawings: Technical Examination and Analysis*, edited by Joanna Russell, Judith Rayner and Jenny Bescoby, 1-3. London: Archetype, 2017.

Clark, Kenneth, and Carlo Pedretti. *The Drawings of Leonardo Da Vinci in the Collection of Her Majesty the Queen at Windsor Castle*. 2nd revised ed. 3 vols. London: Phaidon, 1968.

Couturier, Sonia. "Une fantaisie historique ou la fabrication du néoclassicisme: *Tullie conduisant son char sur le corps de son père* par Jean-François Thomas, dit Thomas de Thomon." *National Gallery of Canada Review* 6 (2008): 36-51.

Crow, Thomas. *Painters and Public Life in Eighteenth-Century Paris*. New Haven: Yale University Press, 2000.

Dahm, Kristi. "The Stylus Revealed: A Metalpoint Identification Study of Fifteenth- and Sixteenth-Century Italian Drawings in The Metropolitan Museum of Art." *The Paper Conservator* 28 (2004): 75-86.

Dreishpoon, Douglas. "The Fine Line: Drawing with Silver." *Arts Magazine* 61, no. 1 (1985): 17.

Dreyer, Peter. "A Forgotten Drawing by Perugino." *The Burlington Magazine* 139, no. 1132 (1997): 465-469.

Duval, Alain, Helen Guicharnaud and Jean-Claude Dran. "Particle-induced X-ray Emission: A Valuable Tool for the Analysis of Metalpoint drawings." *Nuclear Instruments and Methods in Physics Research B* 226 (2004): 60-74.

Gage, John. "Questions of Tone: Turner's Theme and Ruskin's Exposition." *Harvard University Art Museums Bulletin* 3, no. 1 (1994): 27-36.

Haskell, Barbara. *Marsden Hartley.* New York: Whitney Museum, 1980.

Hobbs, Susan A., and Barbara Dayer Gallati. *The Art of Thomas Wilmer Dewing: Beauty Reconfigured.* New York: Brooklyn Museum, 1996.

Kirstein, Lincoln. *Pavel Tchelitchew Drawings.* New York: H. Bittner and Co., 1947.

Koerner, Joseph Leo. *The Moment of Self-Portraiture in German Renaissance Art.* Chicago: University of Chicago Press, 1996.

Koreny, Fritz. "Introduction: Early Netherlandish Drawings Issue." *Master Drawings* 41, no. 3 (2003): 201-203.

Kornhauser, Elizabeth Mankin, and Ulrich Birkmaier. "Marsden Hartley's Materials and Working Methods." *Marsden Hartley*, edited by Elizabeth Mankin Kornhauser, 265-277 New Haven: Wadsworth Athenaeum Museum of Art, 2002.

Lammertse, Friso. "Jan Van Eyck, St Barbara (1437)." In *The Road to Van Eyck*, Stephan Kemperdick and Friso Lammertse, 300. Rotterdam: Museum Boijmans Van Beuningen, 2012.

Meder, Joseph, and Winslow Ames. *The Mastery of Drawing.* 2 vols. New York: Abaris Books, 1978.

Melli, Lorenza. "I disegni a due punte metalliche di Filippino Lippi: una scelta funzionale." *Mitteilungen des Kunsthistorischen Instituts in Florenz* 52, no. 2/3 (2008): 88-108.

Merrifield, Mary P. *Original Treatises: Dating from the XIIth to XVIIIth Centuries on the Arts of Painting, in Oil, Miniature, Mosaic, and on Glass; of Gilding, Dyeing, and the Preparation of Colours and Artificial Gems.* London: J. Murray, 1849.

Messling, Guido. "The Art of Drawing Before van Eyck." In *The Road to Van Eyck*, Stephan Kemperdick and Friso Lammertse, 66-68. Rotterdam: Museum Boijmans Van Beuningen, 2012.

Michel, Christian. "Le goût pour le dessin en France aux XVIIe et XVIIIe siecles: de l'utilisation à l'étude désintéressée." *Revue de l'art* 143, no. 1 (2004): 27-34.

Miller, Bruce F. "Otto Dix and His Oil-Tempera Technique." *Bulletin of the Cleveland Museum of Art* 74, no. 8 (1987): 332-355.

Owens, Susan. "'A Dose of Paradise': Some Effects of Renaissance Drawings on Victorian Artists," In *Burning Bright: Essays in Honour of David Bindman*, Diana Dethloff, edited by T.V. Murdoch, Kim Sloan, Caroline Elam, and David Bindman, 180-189. London: UCL Press, 2015.

Reiche, Ina, Martin Radtke, Achim Berger, et. al. "Spatially Resolved Synchrotron-Induced X-ray Fluorescence Analyses of Metalpoint Drawings and Their Mysterious Inscriptions." *Spectrochimia Acta Part B: Atomic Spectroscopy* 59, issues 10-11 (2004): 1657-62.

Rewald, Sabine. "Dix at the Met." *Metropolitan Museum of Art Journal* 31 (1996): 219-224.

Richards, Nancy E. "A Most Perfect Resemblance at Moderate Prices: The Miniatures of David Boudon." *Winterthur Portfolio* 9 (1974): 77-101.

Rosenblum Robert. "Pavel Tchelitchew." *Artforum International* 37 no. 3 (1998): 107.

Russell, Joanna, Judith Rayner, and Jenny Bescoby. "Technical Examination and Analysis." In *Northern European Metalpoint Drawings: Technical Examination and Analysis,* Joanna Russell, Judith Rayner, and Jenny Bescoby, 21-52. London: Archetype Publications, in Association with The British Museum, 2017.

Schapelhouman, Marjin. "Many Fine Likenesses: Portrait Engravings and Drawings 1578-1590." In *Hendrick Goltzius (1558-1617): Tekeningen, Prenten en Schilderijen*, edited by Huigen Leeflang, Ger Luijten, Jaap Engelsman, and Lawrence W. Nichols, 56-79. Zwolle: Waanders, 2003.

Sell, Stacey. "'The Interesting and Difficult Medium': The Silverpoint Revival in Nineteenth-Century Britain." *Master Drawings* 51, no. 1 (2013): 63-86.

Sell, Stacey. "The Silverpoint Revival in Nineteenth-Century Britain." In *Drawing in Silver and Gold: Leonardo to Jasper Johns*, Stacey Sell and Hugo Chapman, 189-223. Washington, D.C.: National Gallery of Art, 2015.

Soby, James Thrall. *Tchelitchew; Paintings, Drawings*. New York: Published for the Museum of Modern Art by Arno Press, 1972.

Turel, Noa. "Genius Disrobed: The Early Netherlandish Underdrawing Craze and the End of the Connoisseurship Era." *Journal of Art Historiography*, no.16 (2017): 1-16.

Watrous, James. *The Craft of Old-Master Drawings*. Madison: University of Wisconsin Press, 1957.

Weber, Bruce, and Agnes Mongan. *The Fine Line: Drawing with Silver in America*. West Palm Beach: Norton Gallery & School of Art, 1985.

Weber, Bruce. "Modern and Contemporary Drawing in Metalpoint." In *Drawing in Silver and Gold: Leonardo to Jasper Johns*, Stacey Sell and Hugo Chapman, 224-39. Washington, D.C.: National Gallery of Art, 2015.

Weinberg, H. Barbara. "Late Nineteenth-Century American Painting: Cosmopolitan Concerns and Critical Controversies." *Archives of American Art Journal* 23, no.4 (1983): 19-26.

Wieseman, Marjorie E. "Between Paint and Print: Plumbago Portraits in Britain and the Netherlands." In *Perfect Likeness: European and American Portrait Miniatures from the Cincinnati Art Museum*, Julie Aronson and Marjorie E. Wieseman, 33-47. New Haven: Yale University Press, 2006.

Wildman, Stephen, John Christian, Alan Crawford, and Laurence Des Cars. *Edward Burne-Jones, Victorian Artist-Dreamer*. New York: Metropolitan Museum of Art, 1998.

Winsor & Newton, Limited, Manufacturing Artists' Colourmen. *Wholesale Catalogue*, London: 1896.

Wood, Christopher S. *Forgery, Replica, Fiction: Temporalities of German Renaissance Art*. Chicago: University of Chicago Press, 2008.

2

TOOLS, METALS, AND TARNISHING

Introduction: Making Marks with Metal

Metalpoint, simply put, means drawing with soft metal tools. Almost any metal can be used, and while silver is the metal used most often, gold, copper, lead, and alloys such as brass and pewter will all work. Rarer metals, like magnesium, bismuth, aluminum, zinc, and platinum are also usable. The type of metal used has a great impact on the resulting drawing, as different metals reveal distinct lusters when used to make marks. Most metals are too hard to make a mark, so a *ground* is first applied to the drawing surface. Grounds and papers are covered in detail in Chapter 3, but, briefly, using a ground means that the plain paper, board, or other support is coated with a slightly abrasive substance that can grab particles of metal from the metalpoint tool. Each metal will impart a certain *cast* (coloration, reflective quality, etc.) when applied to the ground, and different grounds will take metals differently; some metals will draw darker or lighter or have a more recognizable color, depending on the makeup of the ground and how it is applied.

Many metals used for drawing tarnish by reacting with the ground, paper, atmosphere, or other art materials. Some will change color, and others will lighten or darken slightly. Silver, for example, starts out as a warm gray line on white surfaces, but will tarnish to a golden brown. Making a drawing that can tarnish is one of the signature charms of working in metalpoint, and there are even ways to hasten tarnishing through the use of special grounds, papers, or procedures.

Because tools used in metalpoint are not commonly found in art supply stores, artists make their own tools from common items like lengths of wire, jewelry, coins, wire brushes, shapes of metal, and bundles of metal wool (Figure 2.1). The most common metalpoint tool is the stylus, typically made from thin metal wire held by a pin vise or an ordinary mechanical pencil.

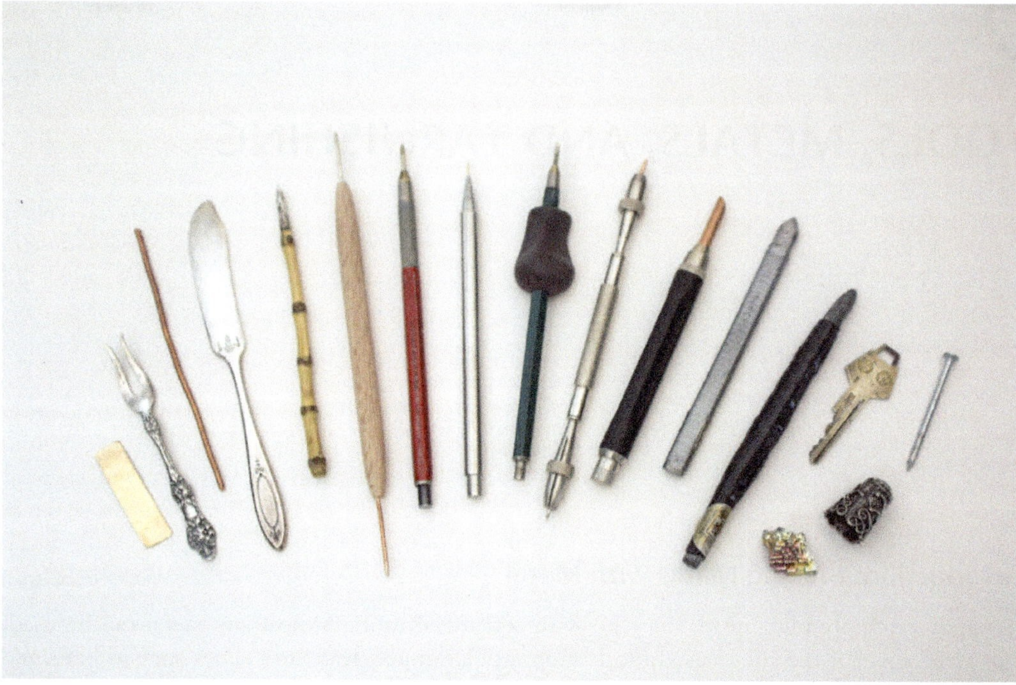

FIGURE 2.1 Metalpoint tools, including silverware, electrician's wire, mechanical lead holders with metal wire, a pin vise, a brass housekey, and other items

Types of Metals

Silver, Copper, and Gold

The metals most often used in metalpoint drawing today are silver, copper, and gold, due both to historical precedent and to their wide availability. Silverpoint is the most common type of metalpoint, because it draws darker than almost any other metal and because of the singular way it ages.

When used on light grounds, silver has a warm, medium-grey appearance, similar in value to a hard graphite pencil, with a reflective cast when viewed in raking light. On a black ground, silver reveals its white appearance. When silver reacts with sulfides in the air, it tarnishes to a warm, golden brown; even the thinnest and palest of silver lines in a drawing will change to a luminous sepia tone, but the effect is most noticeable in heavily worked areas. Silver often does not tarnish uniformly; some areas of a drawing may remain as fresh-looking as when they were drawn, while other areas may tarnish quickly and completely. Many factors affect tarnish; two drawings made in silver on the same type of paper at the same time and under the same conditions may tarnish differently. Changes in atmosphere can affect both the rapidity and degree of tarnish; dense, humid, polluted air will tarnish silver faster than clean, thin air. Working on low quality paper made from wood pulp can also increase the rate and degree of tarnish. In any event, a silverpoint drawing will not tarnish much beyond a golden brown; a drawing made of thin particles of silver will not blacken like a silver bowl. The quality of silver can affect tarnishing as well – sterling silver, which is an alloy of silver and 7.5 percent copper, will tarnish more than fine silver, which is 99.5 percent pure[1]. Silver is historically the most used metal for drawing after lead, and the degree to which it tarnishes as well as the luminous, warm color of the drawing make it the most interesting metal to work with. It is also one of the easiest metals to come by, since many art supply stores now offer silverpoint tools and silver wire, and jewelry findings, silver objects, and coins are all widely available and inexpensive sources of silver.

Copper, although appearing orange-red in its metal state, shows a warm, light gray luster and a barely noticeable red cast when used on a white ground; when worked on a black ground, copper looks more orange. Copper can tarnish to a luminous yellow-green; this tarnish is copper carbonate, a mix of carbon, oxygen, and hydrogen taken from the air. It can even become a vivid green called *verdigris*, but that level of change is unusual in a metalpoint drawing (Figure 2.2). Copper may be the second most interesting metal in metalpoint drawing; along with silver, copper (pure or as an alloy) tarnishes most noticeably. Copper is inexpensive and widely available as wire, hardware items, and coins.

Gold produces a warm, gray-brown line on a white ground, and, in spite of its reputation for being a very soft metal, it draws lighter in tone than silver (Figure 2.3). On a black ground gold shows its true color, appearing as a very light ochre. Using different pigments in the ground can bring out the yellow of gold; natural materials like bone ash, marble dust, and zinc white can "warm up" a goldpoint line, compared to a ground made from titanium white. Gold metal is highly prized for its stable, bright luster and is highly resistant to corrosion; when used in a

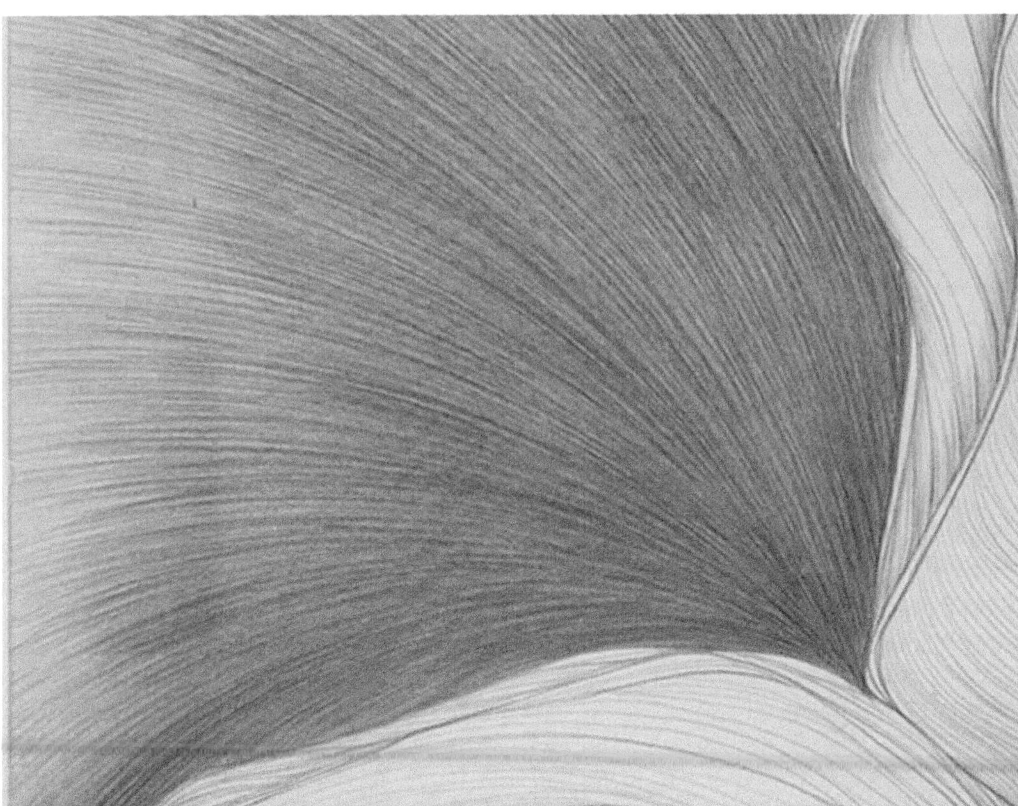

FIGURE 2.2 Detail of a metalpoint drawing showing *verdigris* tarnish in an area of copperpoint

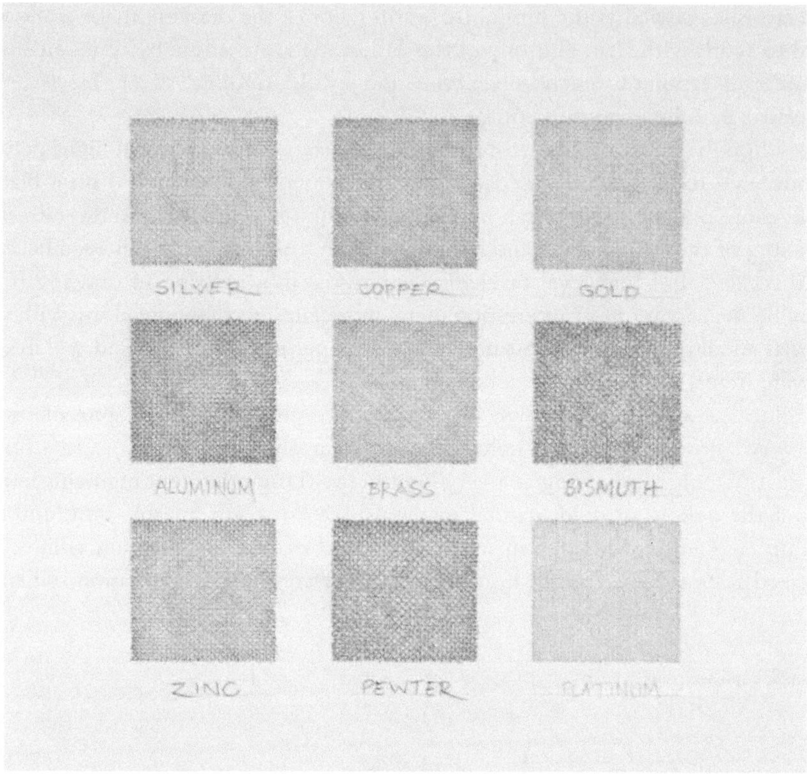

FIGURE 2.3 Examples of metalpoint colors: silver, copper, gold, aluminum, brass, bismuth, zinc, pewter, and platinum

drawing, marks made in goldpoint will retain their original quality while other metals age around them. Goldpoint is becoming more popular with each passing year; it may now be the second most often-used metal for drawing after silver. The availability of goldpoint tools is still slim, however, even though some specialty metalpoint retailers are selling them. In the larger world gold is certainly easy enough to come across as coins and jewelry. Adding gold to a metalpoint drawing can create contrast with silver and copper, especially after they tarnish, and the lure of seeing "24-karat goldpoint" as part of an artwork's description is a considerable draw.

Platinum and Palladium

Less common metals such as platinum and palladium, along with industrial metals like lead, bismuth, aluminum, zinc, magnesium, and stainless steel and alloys like brass and pewter are also used for metalpoint and have distinct lusters and ways of tarnishing.

Platinum and palladium are jeweler's metals, similar to gold in how lightly they mark and in how well they retain their luster. Platinum, which is a silvery metal, appears as a very light gray line on white grounds, and draws much lighter than gold. It is not exceptional, as its lightness does not offer much graphic punch, nor does it tarnish. It has uses, however, for very subtle tonal effects, where a pale gray field of marks, barely darker than white paper, is desired. Palladium is a silvery precious metal used in technical manufacturing and has seen growth as a jeweler's metal in recent years, due to its low density when compared to platinum. Palladium draws just a little darker than platinum, and the mark is similar in its coloration to silver – a warmish gray mark – but, unlike silver, it resists tarnish. Both platinum and palladium are available from specialty supply companies[2] as half-hard wires for metalworking.

Lead and Bismuth

Lead, which is the softest of drawing metals, gives a warm, dark line. It was used in the past for writing tools, and many unspecified metalpoint works from the medieval period are possibly lead-point drawings (graphite replaced lead in pencils starting in the sixteenth century, but we still refer to "lead" when speaking of the pencil point). Lead is a relatively unreactive metal and is quite soft, so its lines can soften and blur as the drawing is handled throughout its life. Lead can oxidize,[3] forming a soft white powder on the surface, which dulls and grays the metal, but the only reaction likely to happen to lead in a drawing is a subtle graying of the darkest areas. Lead is the easiest metal to erase and, along with bismuth, is the only metal that marks well on plain papers.

Though similar in many ways to lead, and now often used in its place, bismuth is quite distinctive. It is a metal that is very brittle, commonly found as rainbow-colored cubic crystals and as shiny, heavy, crumbly ingots from specialty metals suppliers. Not toxic, and with a low melting point, it can be cast by metalworkers into rods that point easily for drawing. When used to provide a mark on white paper, it makes a gray line with a cool cast, slightly violet. Very smooth to draw with, it blunts quickly, giving a dark, lively line that has a lot of variation and responds well to pressure. In terms of darkness it is similar to the mark silver makes before tarnishing, but bismuth is very stable and doesn't tarnish. The bismuth tool is quite fragile – the point can break if the tool is dropped, and a rod of bismuth will easily snap if flexed.

Aluminum and Zinc

A lackluster metal with which to draw, aluminum is quite soft and makes a gray mark a little darker than that of silver. In its natural state aluminum has a tendency to form an invisible, powdery-white aluminum oxide on the surface of the metal, and it is the presence of this oxide that protects aluminum from tarnish, allowing it to retain its gray luster over time. Aluminum can get very dark, especially in heavily worked areas of the drawing. Because it is a very soft metal, aluminum tools will blunt quickly, but with so little weight, it also has a subtly different "feel" from many of the harder, heavier metals.

Zinc is a common metal used in many alloys, including brass, bronze, and nickel silver, and is very similar to aluminum in the way it oxidizes. Zinc wire is very soft and flexible, which makes it easy to point, but it will also bend easily in the holder and lose its point rapidly. Zinc marks on white grounds with a cool, dark gray line that looks similar to that of silver.

Brass, Bronze, Pewter, and Type Metal Alloys

Brass (an alloy of copper and zinc) and bronze (an alloy of copper and tin) are interesting metals because they retain their yellowish quality when marking on white ground, especially in comparison with copper. Each has a different cast from plain copper, which is useful for adding color contrast to a metalpoint work. Brass, although similar in its luster to gold as a solid metal, is less yellowish and more grayish on dark ground, halfway between silver and gold. Brass is a fairly heavy, hard metal that holds a point, and can turn light green as it tarnishes. It is easy to find common items, such as keys and hardware, made of brass. Bronze draws darker and less yellow than brass and is commonly found as jewelry and decorative objects.

Pewter is another common alloy, made of up to 85 percent tin and other metals such as antimony, copper, bismuth, and sometimes silver, but pewter is historically known as an alloy of tin and lead. Being made mostly of tin, it will not tarnish, is highly resistant to corrosion, and is quite soft, making a fairly dark, warm-colored mark. Pewter is commonly found as costume jewelry but can also be purchased as wire. Found in antique stores as small metal printing blocks, type metal is another alloy made of lead (50 percent), antimony (30 percent) and tin (20 percent). It produces a dark, bluish mark that is very stable in terms of tarnish and oxidation, but because it contains lead, wearing gloves or thorough hand-washing is recommended after handling type metal.

Steel and Magnesium

In addition to the relatively common metals listed above, there are some metals that are almost never seen as drawing tools, because they do not work well. Steel[4] is generally too hard to use for drawing, but stainless steel, which has up to 10 percent chromium added, can leave a mark on very tough grounds. Stainless steel wool, screws, paperclips, and the like will make very pale gray marks that retain their luster over time. Stainless steel marks look similar to marks made with platinum, but the hardness of steel means that the tool will scratch through softer grounds after a few strokes. Magnesium is an industrial metal that is less dense than aluminum and very strong. It is bright silver in its metallic state, and it will draw a smooth, dark line that may fade very quickly. A test drawing of magnesium crosshatching on Golden Silverpoint Drawing Ground faded from 80 percent black to 10 percent black after a week, then disappeared completely.

The diversity of different metals available for drawing provides contemporary metalpoint artists with the opportunity to achieve subtle tone and color variations in their work, and many metals show their distinct lusters only when seen in context or when used in a way carefully chosen to exploit their characteristics (Figure 2.4).

More About Tarnishing

The metals used in metalpoint drawing all have different qualities when first used, but they can change their appearance in a process called *tarnishing*, a form of oxidation that is a reaction to various compounds in the air, the paper, and the ground, as well as from handling (Figure 2.5). Since metalpoint is made out of a very thin layer of metal, the effect of tarnishing is very mild, but many metals used in metalpoint will change to one extent or another. Tarnishing usually begins as a drawing is being made and continues for a short while after the drawing is complete. It can be hastened, but the process of artificially aging a metalpoint drawing is somewhat unpredictable and potentially harmful. A drawing may tarnish immediately or not at all, and once it tarnishes it is unlikely to change further as it ages.

There are ways to accelerate and ensure tarnishing. Jewelers use liver of sulfur to blacken silver, and a silverpoint drawing will tarnish in the presence of its fumes. Liver of sulfur is a mix of various potassium sulfides and is available as crystals or as a gel to be mixed with water and applied directly to metals. This solution is not intended to be applied directly to metalpoint tools

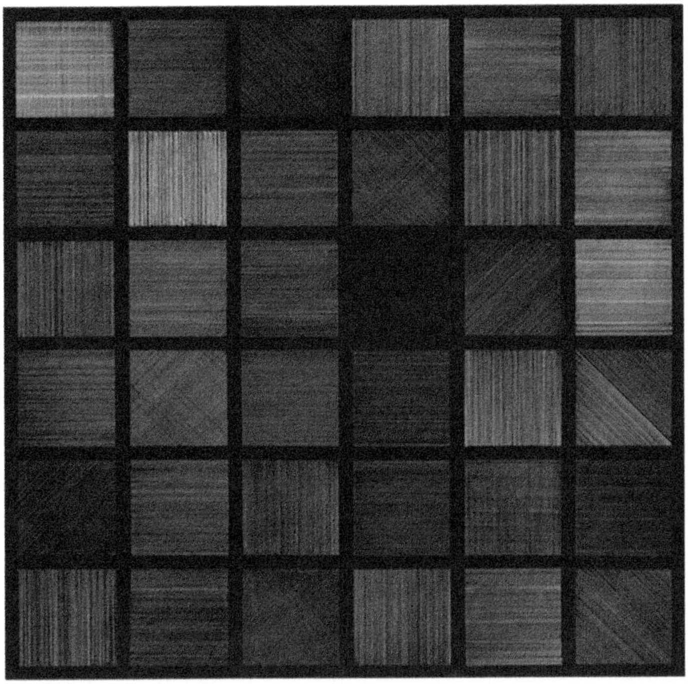

FIGURE 2.4 Susan Schwalb, *Harmonizations VIII*, 2017, silver, gold, aluminum, copper, brass, tin, platinumpoint, black gesso on museum mount board on panel, 24 × 24 × 2 inches (61 × 61 × 5.1 cm), courtesy of the artist

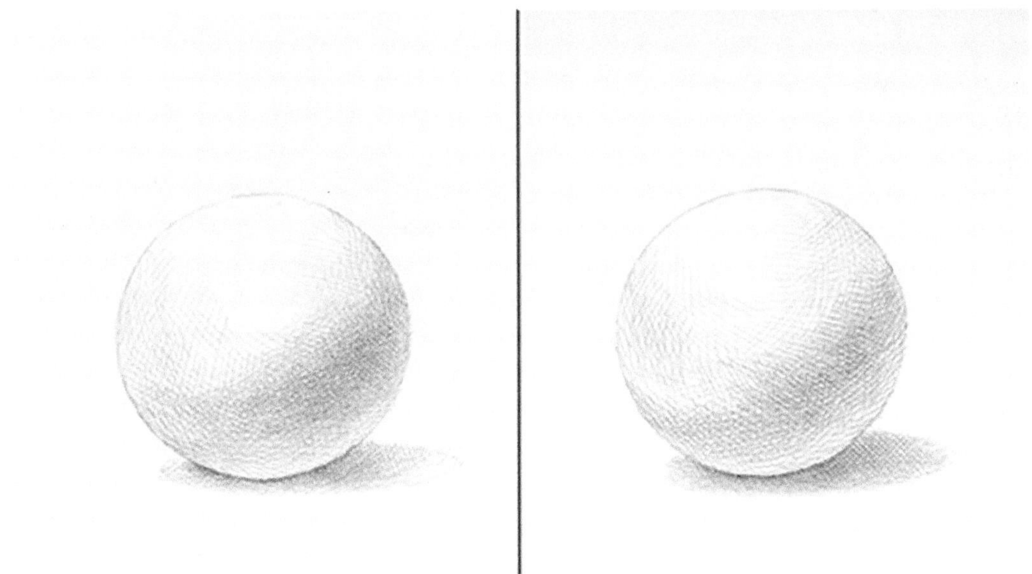

FIGURE 2.5 A fresh drawing in silverpoint (left) and one that has tarnished (right), done on the same paper and ground three weeks apart

or drawings or mixed with metalpoint grounds. It has a tremendous odor, a bright yellow color that stains easily, is toxic, though not acidic, and should be mixed and disposed of according to the manufacturer's instructions, using recommended precautions[5]. Tarnishing tests were conducted with XLGel Liver of Sulfur Extended Life Gel. The mix was placed in a sealed plastic container with a drawing done in sterling silver on zinc white/rabbit-skin glue ground applied to acid-free paper (Figure 2.6). The drawing was exposed to fumes of liver of sulfur solution for 12 hours, after which a fresh mix of the fluid was supplied before the drawing was exposed to fumes for another 12 hours. After 24 hours, there was a gentle "browning" of the silver, more a warming effect than a perceptible color change. The effect was uniform over the entire sheet, unlike the result of natural tarnish and aging. There were also some disturbing results – the formerly flat paper cockled in the humid environment and the ground softened; the paper retained a notable sulfurous smell even after drying in the open air, and it also yellowed slightly and tested positive for acidic pH.[6] Hastening the tarnish of silver with liver of sulfur works, but perhaps at the cost of deteriorating the drawing (Figure 2.7).

Adjusting the composition of the metalpoint ground can also affect tarnishing. Adding egg yolk to the liquid preparation can hasten tarnishing of silver, because yolk contains sulfurous amino acids. Egg yolk is actually quite transparent when added to paint and will impart only a slight yellow cast that fades quickly. Carefully clip the sac of a fresh egg yolk and add half a teaspoon of the fluid to a few ounces of liquid ground. Use it right away – the preparation can spoil if left to sit. Metalpoint grounds, especially casein and gouache grounds, have a tendency to flake and crumble over time, and adding yolk offers an extra binder that gives strength and sheen to the

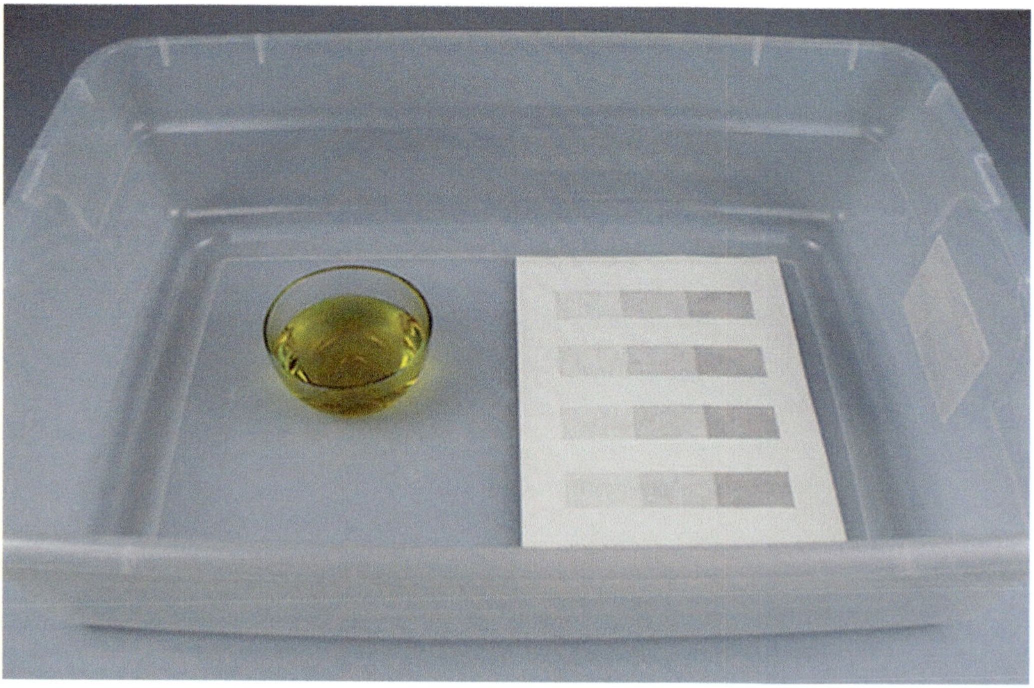

FIGURE 2.6 A silverpoint drawing and a dish of liver of sulfur in a container with the lid off

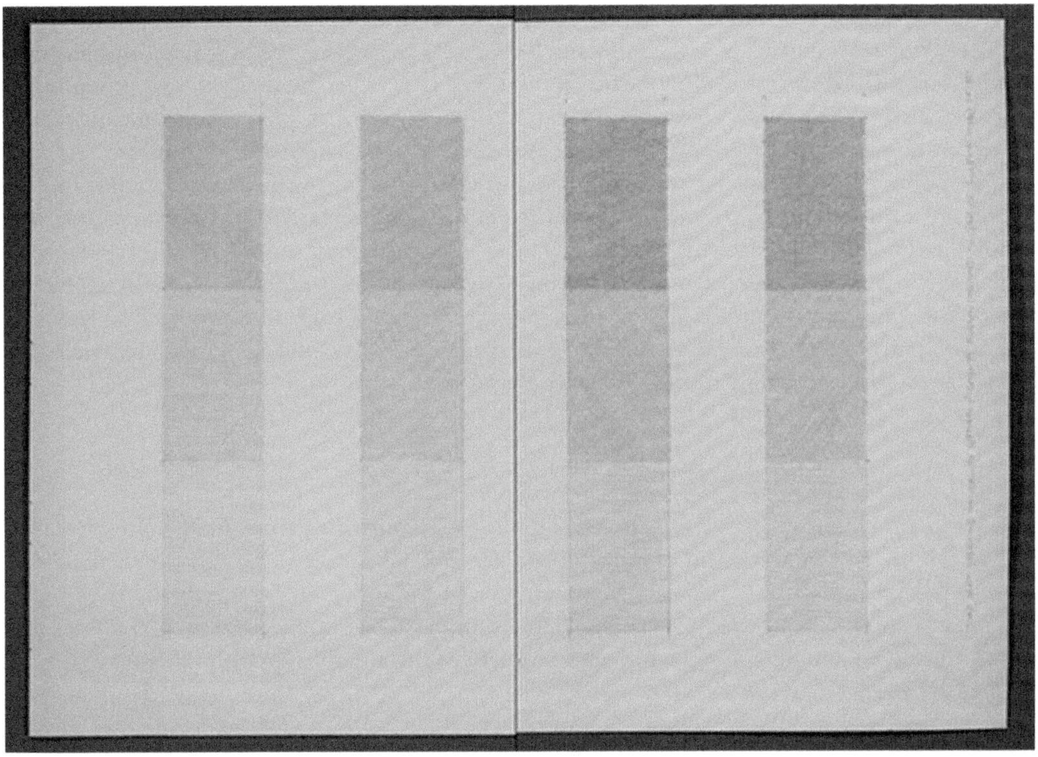

FIGURE 2.7 The fresh silverpoint drawing (left) and after 24 hours of exposure to liver of sulfur (right)

preparation. However, too much yolk is harmful and can cause the ground to flake even more, so the desire to hasten tarnishing with egg yolk should not be met with the temptation to add more yolk than necessary.

Adding coloration to the ground in the form of pigment can also affect the way metals age. Green or blue pigments, when mixed into a white preparation, can hasten the tarnishing of silver and copper. In tests where sterling silver marks were made on plain white ground and then on white ground with Winsor Green watercolor added, the green-tinted ground showed a distinct tendency to tarnish the silver more rapidly. Winsor Green is made from pthalocyanine, a copper-based pigment found in green and blue paint. It could be the copper's reacting with the silver that causes the rapid tarnish. Also, the overall composition of the white ground affects different metals differently. While titanium white grounds are common, some artists prize zinc white for the way it warms silver and shows off the yellow quality of gold. Non-metallic abrasives, such as marble dust and bone ash, can supplement white pigment in the preparation to bring out the cast of gold more sharply as well.

The composition of the paper also affects tarnish, and sulfite papers can cause rapid change of copper and silver. The sulfite process uses sulfurous acid to extract cellulose from wood pulp, allowing a tough paper to be made. Some of the sulfur remains in the paper, causing the paper to yellow and turn brittle (as compared to rag paper), and it will hasten tarnish even with an application of ground. Papers made from stone, such as TerraSkin, will cause silver to tarnish very rapidly, possibly because the manufacturing process leaves sulfur in the finished sheet. One further way to tarnish a drawing is by changing the humidity level in the area where the drawing is stored. Metalpoint drawings can tarnish quickly, within hours sometimes, when humidity is high. It is possible to accelerate tarnish by placing a metalpoint in a bathroom filled with warm, moist air. But bear in mind that humidity can adversely affect paper as well as some non-waterproof grounds.

The tarnishing of metals is not guaranteed and is inconsistent from one metalpoint tool to another of a similar type, or from one ground to another, or among different supports under the ground. Even when the materials are the same, the aging of metals varies depending on the area of the world where metalpoint drawings are made. Many factors contribute to tarnish, including whether the drawing is handled a lot or how long it is exposed to air. Care must be taken when combining metals that at first look similar on the paper, as each could age differently, changing the character of the drawing noticeably and irrevocably.

Tools: The Metalpoint Stylus

The most common tool for working in metalpoint is a holder with a metal tip, commonly called a *stylus*. In the past, it was a rod of metal alloy like lead and tin, or silver and copper, one end tapered to a fine point, and often decorated with carved designs. Today, a metalpoint tool is usually a mechanical pencil or pin vise into which a thin piece of pure, soft metal wire is inserted. Many artists have multiple tools, some with a variety of metal points or with different shapes or sizes of tips for different ways of drawing.

There are some metalpoint styluses that can be purchased ready-made, such as the Cretacolor Silverpoint Pencil. Available from Dick Blick Art Materials for roughly eleven dollars[7], it looks like a quarter-inch of thin silver wire fused to a black plastic pen holder. These tools do not have replaceable points, and do not last very long. Two kinds of silverpoint, goldpoint, and copperpoint styluses can be purchased from SilverpointWeb.com,[8] along with complete drawing kits, paper, and ground. Replacement wire is also sold, along with a "New Traditional" thin point stylus, which is a plastic mechanical pencil with 0.9mm silver or gold wire, and a "Modern" stylus with 2mm pure silver wire shaped to a cone on one end and a smooth bevel on the other. Naturalpigments.com,[9] a retailer of Old Master and specialty art materials, also sells a double-ended pin vise from Aurum Metallic Arts that holds their wide and thin sterling silver, fine silver, nickel silver, copper, yellow and red brass, lead, and aluminum points. The wide metalpoints of Natural Pigments also come in two shapes: a conic point and a beveled point. In addition to tools, metal wools are also available, along with a metalpoint ground preparation. The London, UK, art supply store L. Cornelissen & Son sells a similar metal pin vise holder along with a large selection of metal wires in two-inch lengths and many thicknesses, including silver wire, yellow and rose gold, brass, copper, bronze, nickel, and aluminum. Cornelissen also sells a "Silverpoint Pencil" – a wide-diameter (1.6mm) silver wire held in a wooden handle that can be trimmed to expose more of the 50mm length of wire as needed. Zecchi, in Florence, Italy, sells a traditional leadpoint stylus and a lead-tin alloy tool. More like crayons, these thick, stumpy tools are very soft and will not hold a fine point. Metalsmiths, artists, and artisans also make metalpoint tools to sell. Joanne Hopper, based in Hawaii, sells metalpoint tools in a wide, 4-gauge width polished to a soft chisel point. She also offers a narrower, 16-gauge platinumpoint.

Many contemporary metalpoint artists use a mechanical pencil or lead holder fitted with metal wire (Figures 2.8 and 2.9). Common holders are the 2mm and 0.7mm mechanical pencils

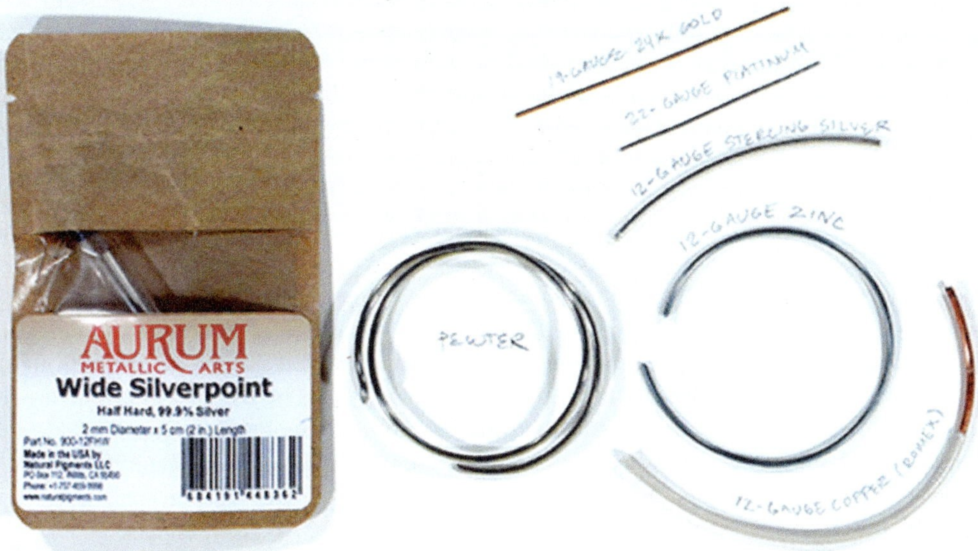

FIGURE 2.8 Wire for metalpoint (left to right): Natural Pigments "Aurum Metallic Arts" Wide Silverpoint, 12-gauge pewter wire, 19-gauge 24-karat gold, 22-gauge platinum, 12-gauge sterling silver, 12-gauge zinc, and 12-gauge Romex copper wire

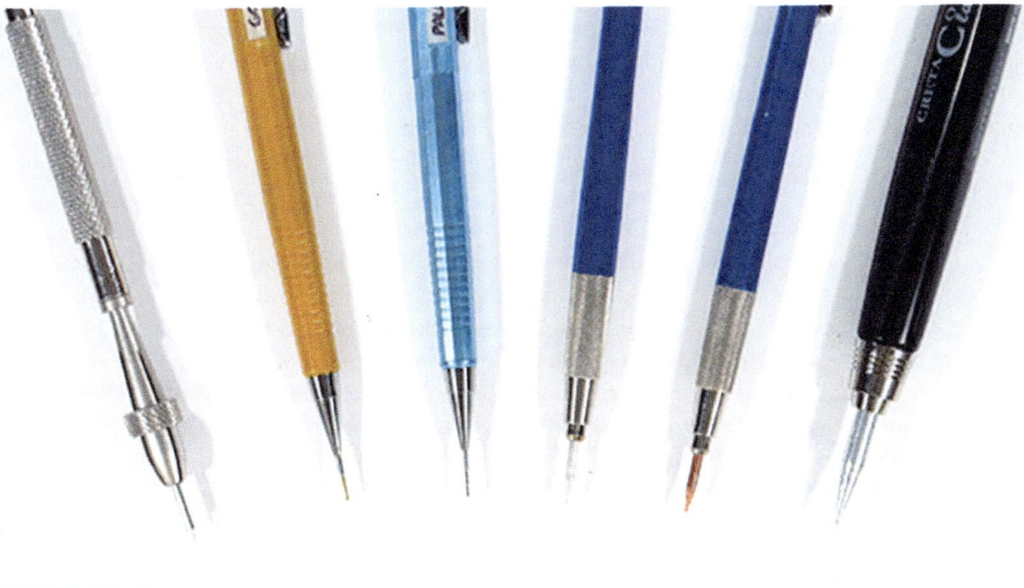

FIGURE 2.9 Metalpoint styluses (left to right): a pin vise with wide silver wire, a 0.9mm lead holder with gold wire, a 0.7mm lead holder with palladium wire, 2mm lead holders with silver and copper wire, and a wide lead holder with aluminum rod

that have a push-button feed for thin graphite "leads." Mechanical pencils from manufacturers Staedler, Pentel, and Pilot are available from a variety of sources, including art supply and office supply stores. 12-gauge wire fits in the 2mm lead holder, and 22-gauge wire fits in a 0.7mm lead holder. The reason to use wide or thin wire is both stylistic and economical; a wide wire can be pointed to a fine point, an oval chisel point, or a wide round point, whereas thinner wire is less expensive for the same length but gives fewer options.

Wire suitable for use with mechanical pencils can be ordered from jewelry supply stores, wholesalers of precious metals, craft stores, local metalsmiths, and jewelry-repair stores or can even be found in hardware stores. Myron Toback Inc. or Ross Metals in the jewelry exchange are popular metal retailers for New Yorkers. Another source for metalpoint wire is RioGrande.com,[10] a popular online jewelry supply company based in New Mexico, which sells, by length or weight, both sterling and fine silver, platinum, and gold. Silver is economical and easy to obtain from many retailers. Fine and sterling silver, in many gauges of wire, are sold by length and priced at market price. Gold wire is available in different karats, for example, 24-karat pure gold and 22-karat gold alloyed to make it harder.[11] Lower karat alloys can contain copper, silver, titanium, silicon, and zinc, all increasing hardness and altering color. 14-karat gold is only 58 percent pure gold, for example, and 18-karat rose gold is an alloy of 75 percent gold, 21 percent copper, and 4 percent silver. Almost all the gold wire one can easily purchase will be an alloy and will make a pale mark. 24-karat quarter-hard gold wire is available in 22-gauge thickness from Rio Grande and is probably the most economical means of producing a substantial line with pure gold. The best way to obtain 24-karat gold in large gauges is to find a metalworker and ask that a gold coin be melted, rolled, and drawn into a short length of wire. 22-gauge, dead soft platinum and half-hard palladium can also be purchased as wire and are almost always alloyed with 5 percent ruthenium.

There are other sources for metal wires, especially less precious metals and alloys. 12-gauge, 99.9 percent pure annealed soft copper electrician's wire[12] is available from most hardware stores for a few dollars by the foot. Brass and aluminum rods can be found at hobby shops, with 0.072-inch and 5/64-inch solid rods useful for the 2mm holder. Solders, typically alloys of tin and lead, can be used for drawing; they come in spools of wire in 12-gauge size, perfect for the 2mm mechanical pencil. Amazon.com is a great site to search for unusual metal wires.

Two inches of metal wire will be enough for a metalpoint tool. Wide wire is typically pointed to a long cone by using a file or sharpening stone. To file a long, tapered point, place the wire into the mechanical pencil, exposing roughly half an inch of wire, then hold the metalpoint tool using a fingertip to support the wire from underneath. In the other hand, hold a mill bastard file against the wire at a very shallow angle, and work the file in one direction while rotating the stylus (Figure 2.10). It will take a few dozen strokes to get a fine point, and the flatter the file is held, the more tapered the point will be. Periodically brush off the metal filings and check the tip for evenness and length. Once the point is filed to shape, the tip will need to be polished with a piece of emery paper to remove the metal burr; rub the point of the stylus across a fingerprint and if it catches on the ridges, it is too sharp. Blunt the point just slightly by using a sheet of emery paper (Figure 2.11), then test the point on a sheet of prepared paper. Once the point is polished, the tool is ready for use and will last for hours of drawing.

A sharpening stone can also be used to point a metal tool (Figure 2.12). Silicon carbide whetstones come in various grades for pointing and polishing; some have two grades bonded together in one block and come in both large and pocket sizes. Work the tool against the stone in small circles at a shallow angle until a fine tip is ground into the wire. Remove any rough areas with the finer side of the stone.

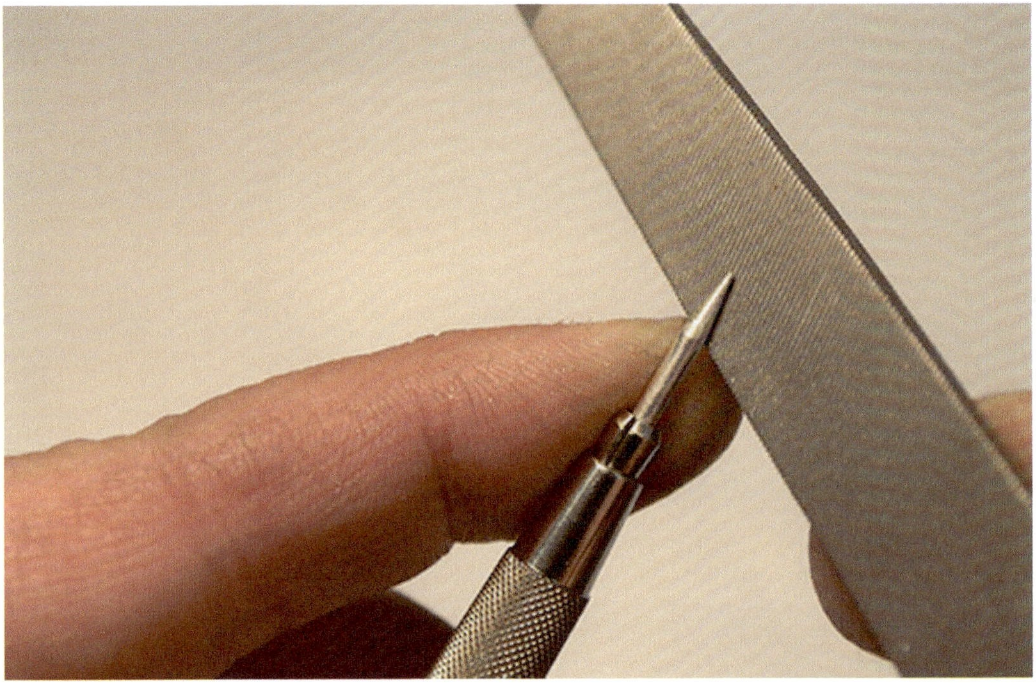

FIGURE 2.10 Pointing the metalpoint stylus with a file

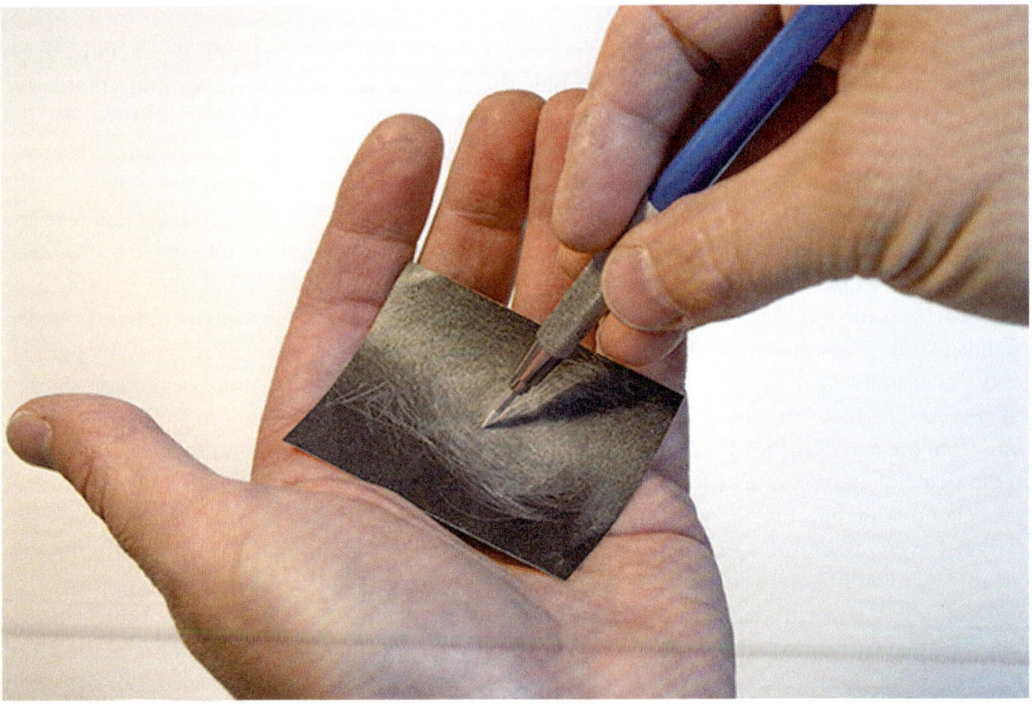

FIGURE 2.11 Polishing the point with emery paper

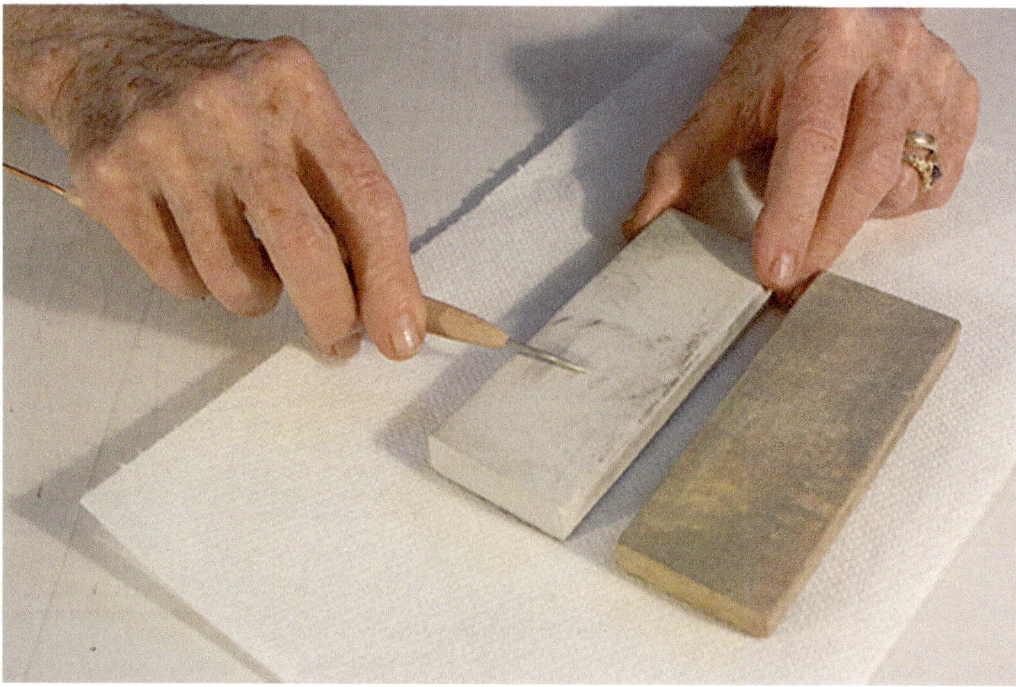

FIGURE 2.12 Pointing the metalpoint stylus with a sharpening stone

It is also possible to use a rotating lead pointer intended for 2mm mechanical pencils to shape the point of 12-gauge wire. The device holds the stylus at a precise angle around an abrasive drum. At first, pointing metal will offer quite a bit of resistance, so expose just a little metal at a time to the grinder. The rotary lead pointer will grind a very sharp point, so even using this tool, clean up and polish the point with a file and emery paper before using the tool.

Wide metal wire offers the possibility of two different points, one on either end, for different line qualities. In addition to the fine point for drawing thin, light lines, the other end can have a rounded point for tonal work and for drawing thicker, bolder lines. To make one end blunt, move the file back and forth in an arc over the very tip of the wire while rotating the tool. Take care to produce a regular, rounded "dome" on the end of the wire. Polish with a piece of emery paper to remove any burrs.

Another point shape, and the most interesting stylistically, is the bevel point, which produces a calligraphic line that varies in weight (Figure 2.13). To file a bevel point, expose half an inch of cut wire from the end of the lead holder and file at a 30-degree angle to the wire until there is a flat area in the shape of an oval. A sharpening stone is easier to use; simply work the wire back and forth at an angle until the bevel is smooth. Polish the sharp edge of the point with emery paper.

When using 0.7mm lead holders with 22-gauge wire, shaping the point is very easy. Freshly cut thin wire will be very sharp – too sharp to draw with – so polish it to a round point with a piece of emery paper. Even with regular, frequent use, once the burr has been polished off of a thin wire metalpoint tool, it is likely that it will never need to be smoothed out again, as the act of drawing will keep the tool ready for use. Thin wire can also be tapered or beveled, but the effect will not be as dramatic as with wider wire.

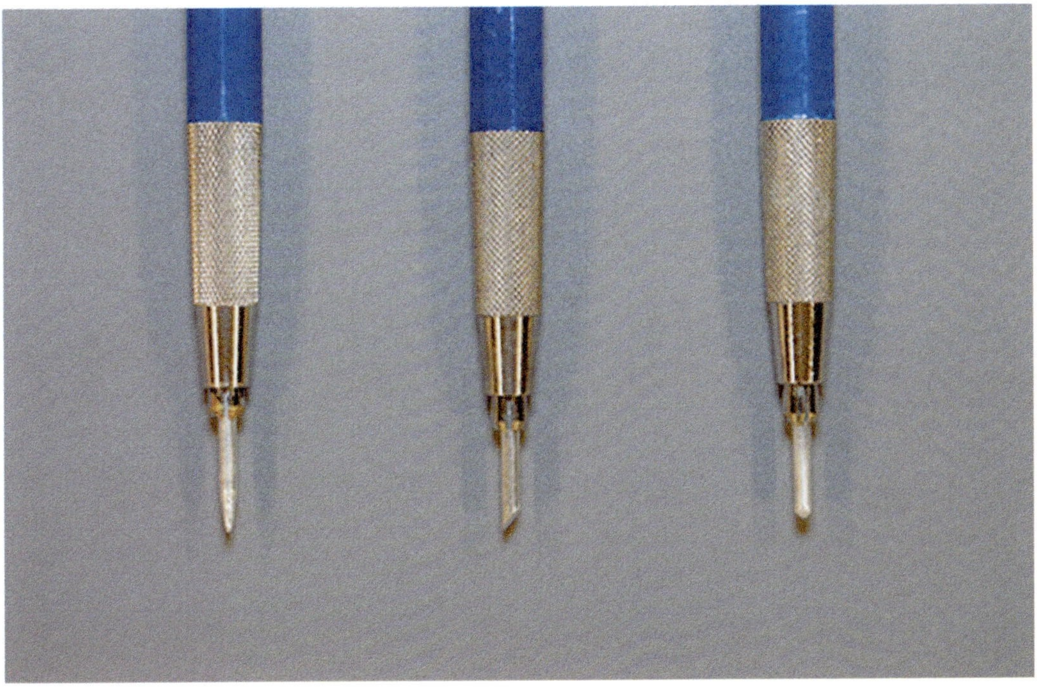

FIGURE 2.13 Metalpoint tip shapes (left to right): fine taper, bevel, round

After shaping the metal wire, most artists will occasionally need to repoint their tools as they draw. Soft metals blunt quickly, especially on coarse grounds, and the "perfect point" will change over time as it is used. Compared with graphite, however, a tool will hold its point for a long time, which is one of the benefits of working in metalpoint.

Other Tools for Metalpoint Drawing

In addition to using the wire-and-mechanical-pencil tool, some metalpoint artists customize their own tools or employ metalsmiths to make custom tools (Figure 2.14). Simply modifying a mechanical pencil with an ergonomic rubber grip will allow for longer, more comfortable drawing sessions. Artists also find a use for common metal items like silverware, jewelry, or wire brushes, either with modifications or as they find them. For example, the back of a sterling silver spoon will give a soft, diffuse, wide mark, skipping over small depressions in the prepared paper surface, focusing the mark toward the center because of its curved profile. The tines of a silver fork will act like a comb, producing parallel marks, and the finer serrated edge of a butter knife will produce a linear, tonal pattern. An antique type metal block can produce a variety of marks: the corner will give a dark, calligraphic mark, the flat sides will produce tonal marks, and even the raised letterform will imprint if firmly pushed onto the prepared surface. A flat bar of soft metal, when dragged across the prepared paper, will create a tonal area that reveals much of the texture of the paper and ground, similar to the marks made from a rubbing (Figure 2.15). A smooth, flat bar cut with many regular notches, called a *comb*, will create a field

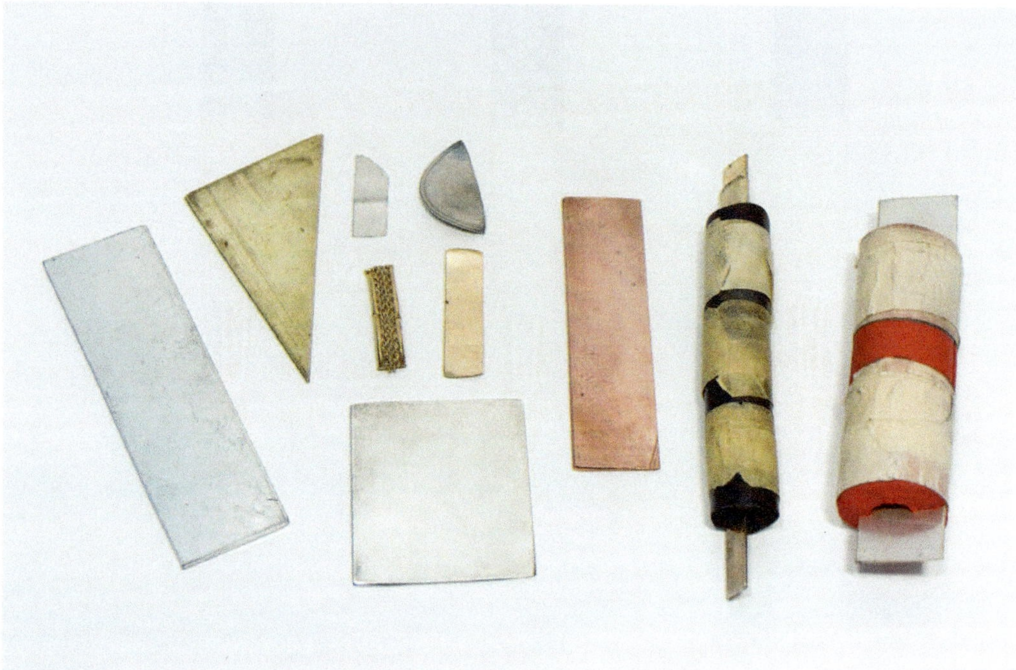

FIGURE 2.14 Unique metal tools, including sheets of silver, copper, and brass

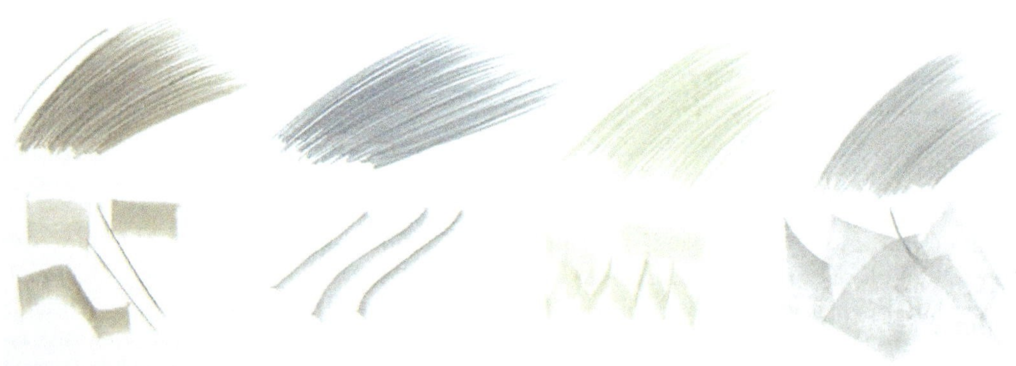

FIGURE 2.15 Marks made by uniquely-shaped tools (left to right): silver, gold, copper, brass

of lines when dragged across the paper, similar to cross-hatching, but with more mechanical, artificial regularity. Flat bars of metal, whether notched or smooth, can be rotated while drawing to create a calligraphic mark.

Metal wools are also useful, and bronze wool, sold at hardware stores and used for finishing wood and metal, can be used on prepared paper to make soft, diffuse fields of tiny, curly marks (Figures 2.16 and 2.17). The online art supply store Natural Pigments sells aluminum, brass, and copper wool pads just for drawing. These pads come in several types, from fine to coarse, with fine

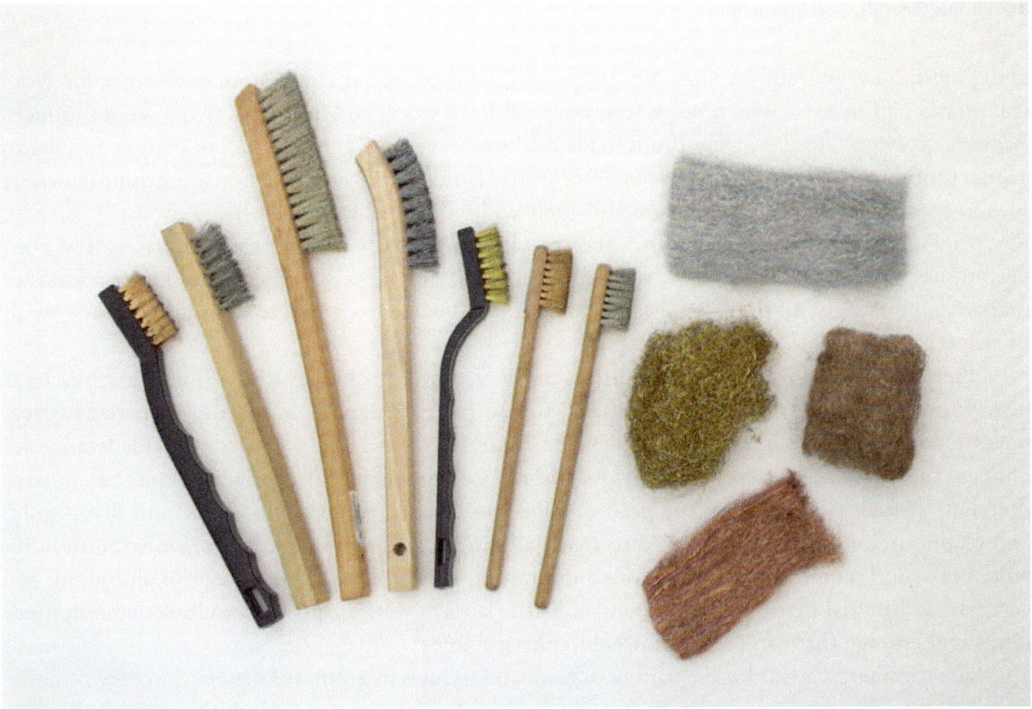

FIGURE 2.16 Wire brushes and wools

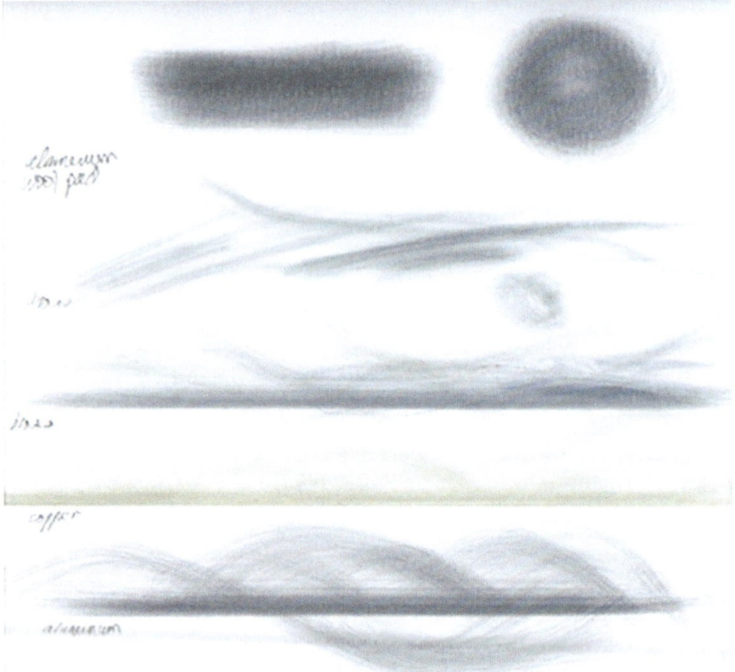

FIGURE 2.17 Marks made by wool and wire brushes

being the most practical for metalpoint drawing. The most comprehensive store for metallic wool is Lustersheen Online,[13] which offers four types of metal wools and dozens of metal wool products. Another wonderful tool is a wire brush made of aluminum, brass, nickel silver, or copper. Similar to a large toothbrush, it usually has a wooden or plastic handle, and the metal portion is approximately one to two inches in length and one-half inch wide. Nickel silver brushes are available through Kremer Pigments, and aluminum and brass brushes can often be found in hardware stores; copper brushes, used for cleaning guns, can be found in sporting goods stores. Many different kinds of marks can be made with these brushes, from light parallel lines to a variety of tones and large swirls or shapes.

Other metal items are interesting to investigate as drawing tools. Antique silver thimbles have been used by several artists, whose thimble-tipped fingers "dance" across the prepared surface, making dots or parallel lines (for examples, see Figures 4.11 and 7.38). Old coins made from gold, copper, and silver, and even brass and aluminum, are wonderful for producing loose, expressive sketches. The posts from silver and gold earrings can be used to make fine lines, and silver, gold, and platinum jewelry can be adapted to make all kinds of marks. Even nails made of aluminum, zinc, brass, and stainless steel can produce interesting marks. A crumpled piece of aluminum foil can give an unusual mark as it is pushed across the surface. Once one starts to look around, more items will emerge that can create unusual marks and lines.

Many metalpoint artists keep a variety of tools and styluses in a variety of metals, so they can produce marks of different color, texture and shape depending on the demands of the artwork. Finding a preferred metal or a uniquely shaped tool can inform creativity and inspire new work, as well as allowing artists to perfect the type of work they have in mind. And understanding the way each of these metals tarnishes can also lead to new discoveries. Making one's own tools has the double satisfaction of providing unique drawing implements and being a creative endeavor on its own.

Notes

1 Binnion, James. *Jewelry Metals: A Guide to Working with Common Alloys* (Attleboro, MA: MJSA Press, 2015), 20.
2 www.gsgold.com/metals/palladium-mill-products.html. Accessed 19 October 2017.
3 Guardian Industries Goole Ltd, Yorkshire-UK, www.atcglass.co.uk/pdf/TS-TH-05a.pdf. Accessed 31 October 2017.
4 Steel, while generally too hard to mark on prepared paper, comes in many varieties. Stainless steel contains chromium, which is soft enough to mark, and many small steel objects, such as nails and staples, are galvanized, or coated with zinc, which also marks. There are soft steel alloys used for almost every conceivable manufacturing application. Carbon steel, on the other hand, is the hardest type of steel, and has difficulty marking on almost any ground without chipping the surface.
5 MSDS Authoring Services, XLGel, Birmingham, Alabama, 2015, https://media1.riogrande.com/Content/331033-SDS.pdf. Accessed 19 October 2017.
6 A Lineco pH testing pen was used on the margin of the sulfured sheet and made a purple mark, as compared to the colorless mark made by the pen on a fresh, unused piece of Arches watercolor paper cut from the same sheet.
7 www.dickblick.com/products/cretacolor-silverpoint-pencil. Accessed 7 May 2018.
8 http://silverpointweb.com/shop. Accessed 7 May 2018
9 www.naturalpigments.com/catalogsearch/result/?q=silverpoint. Accessed 7 May 2018.
10 www.riogrande.com. Accessed 19 October 2017.
11 Binnion, *Jewelry Metals*, 4–8.
12 www.southwire.com/ProductCatalog/XTEInterfaceServlet?contentKey=prodcatsheet6. Accessed 19 October 2017.
13 https://lustersheenonline.com/product-category/metallic-wools/bronze-wool. Accessed 27 December 2017.

3

GROUNDS, PREPARATION, AND SUPPORTS

Introduction: What is Prepared Paper?

Metal is too hard to mark on plain paper, so metalpoint is typically done on what is called a *prepared* surface. A coating, called a *ground*, needs to be applied that is abrasive enough to grab particles of metal from the drawing tools. There are many types of grounds, from commercial paints to antique recipes made from traditional components. Before a ground is applied, it is called a *preparation*, and the preparation is applied to a *support*, either traditional paper and panel or sometimes new materials. In addition to supports prepared by the artist, there are commercially prepared papers ready for drawing without extra preparation, such as clay-coated papers and stone papers. Each artist prefers a particular method and materials, but there are common starting points for preparing surfaces for metalpoint drawing.

Metalpoint Grounds

The types of metalpoint grounds used are as varied as all the types of paint (Figure 3.1). Some artists swear by their own recipe, or a particular brand of paint, while others use whatever is at hand, or choose a ground to realize specific artistic intentions. Almost all metalpoint preparations are *aqueous* paints using water as the vehicle, a binder such as acrylic, gum arabic, casein, etc., an abrasive body such as marble dust or bone ash, and pigment as coloration. In general, fluid preparations are brushed on the surface, but they can also be sprayed or rolled. Many preparations are commercial paints like acrylic gesso or gouache, and there are a few products specially made for use as metalpoint grounds. Some artists make their own preparations from scratch. And each ground will yield different results according to the materials used, how they are mixed, and how they are applied.

Commercial Grounds

The simplest way to make prepared paper is to use a commercial paint. Many types of paint – acrylic gesso, gouache, casein, latex house paint – will work as metalpoint grounds. Paint right from the jar or tube is often too thick to spread evenly on paper and must be thinned with water to brushing consistency.

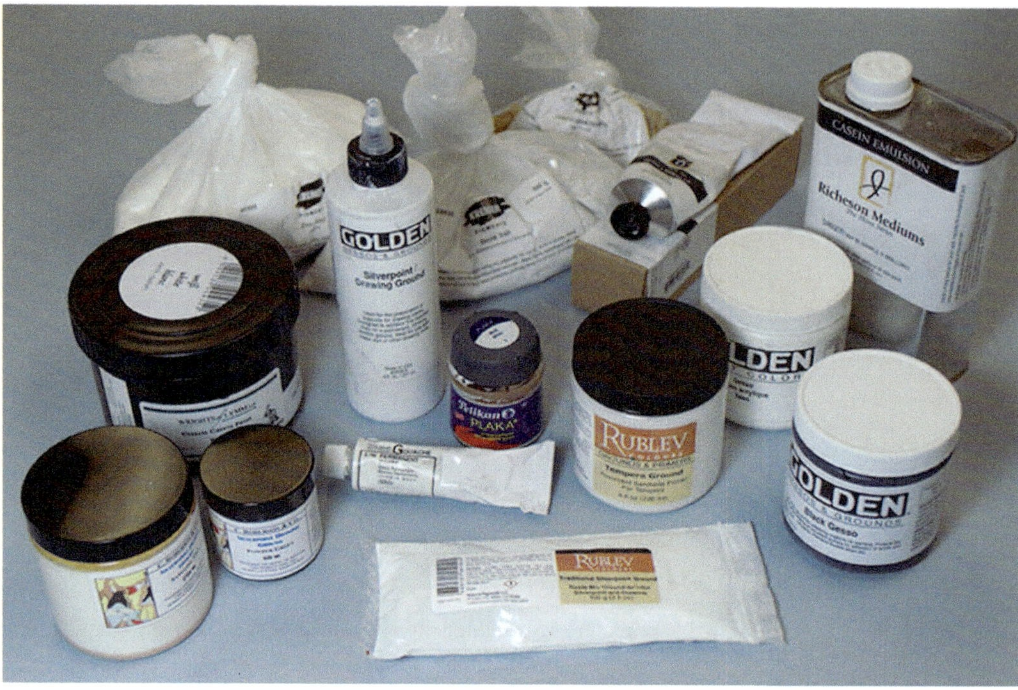

FIGURE 3.1 A selection of paints and preparations including Roberson Ground, casein paints, zinc white pigment, bone ash, gouache, Golden Silverpoint Drawing Ground, Natural Pigments grounds, Pelikan Plaka, rabbit-skin glue crystals, and black and white gesso

Acrylic gesso is by far the most common preparation, and is comprised of titanium white pigment, calcium carbonate (marble dust), and acrylic medium. Better quality gesso generally has a higher concentration of pigment. Golden Artist Colors Gesso is a good quality primer, with a high ratio of titanium dioxide pigment for excellent opacity. Golden recommends three coats of gesso,[1] but many artists use four to six and sand between coats to ensure a smooth surface without brush strokes or bubbles. Liquitex Acrylic White Gesso is a preferred primer, because it dries to a matte finish that takes metalpoint superbly. Liquitex also manufactures a clear gesso, which can be used overtop existing artwork or printed supports to allow other imagery to be seen under the metalpoint. Art Boards Panel Gesso is another good metalpoint ground. Acrylic-based paints also seal the support and are less susceptible to flaking and cracking but will sometimes cause paper to curl unless both sides are primed. Most acrylic gessoes work well on board and panel as a metalpoint ground.

Gouache and Chinese white watercolor are traditional paints used for metalpoint grounds; both are made from pigment and gum arabic, and gouache has chalk added to make it opaque. Winsor & Newton Designer Gouache is recommended as a top brand, and the zinc white hue is preferred as a metalpoint ground, "warming up" gold and other yellow metals. Other colors are also useful as dark grounds or for mixed-media metalpoint work. Chinese white is a nearly opaque watercolor paint historically made with a high percentage of zinc oxide pigment. Winsor & Newton is a recommended brand. When applying gouache or Chinese white, two thin coats are recommended, and the second coat should be lightly brushed on before the first coat is completely dry, so that the two layers bond. Care should be taken not to disturb the first coat with vigorous brushing; adding a little more water helps the second coat flow. Wait 24 hours for the ground to harden before drawing. Caution is needed when working with gouache and opaque watercolor, as they remain soluble even when dry. Both are also prone to flaking, chipping, and cracking on almost any surface, especially when heavily applied.

Casein paint is similar to gouache but has the advantage of being water-resistant when dry. It is made with denatured milk protein as a binder, which will cause it to spoil, so commercial caseins usually have a small amount of linseed oil added as a preservative, which adds several days of curing time after the paint dries. Plaka, sold in 50ml jars from the Pelikan company, is becoming harder to find in colors, but is still available in white and black. It is quite thick and viscous, with outstanding opacity, and a velvety matte finish when dry, perfect for metalpoint. Richeson Shiva Series Casein is available in tubes, large and small, and is softer and more water-soluble than Plaka. Other commercial casein paints are available from specialty manufacturers Sinopia of San Francisco and Wrights of Lymm in London.[2] Sinopia produces hand-crafted "Milk Paint" in many custom colors as well as Casein Gesso and Black Casein Gesso, all of which are quite fluid and need only a little added water for brushing. Sinopia's Absorbent Chalk Gesso and Silverpoint Ground give good results, especially after drying and sanding between coats to smooth the surface. Sinopia casein paints, when used as metalpoint grounds, produce a line that seems to "spread" and soften, possibly due to the relatively soft surface of the paint. Also notable is a distinct yellowing of their white paint, likely because of the linseed oil in the mixture. Wrights of Lymm Classic Casein is available in a variety of colors in large, 500ml jars. Thinner and not as heavily pigmented as Richeson or Plaka, making it less ideal as an opaque ground, it dries to a velvety surface with perfect abrasive qualities.

In addition to artist paints, commercial interior latex paint can also be used as a preparation. "Flat finish" paint is recommended, as it has a higher pigment to binder ratio (binder is called *resin* in the context of commercial interior paints). Multiple coats are needed, as wall paint tends to be thin when compared to artist colors, and sanding is recommended between coats to minimize brush or roller marks. Because of their thin consistency, latex paints work better on boards than on paper.

There are now several metalpoint-specific grounds being produced by both large and small manufacturers. Golden Artist Colors, Inc., has produced a metalpoint ground which is very white, nicely chalky, and sold in a squeeze-bottle. Golden Silverpoint Ground contains finely ground abrasives with a high concentration of titanium dioxide pigment and is pre-mixed to brushing consistency. Because it is a very fluid acrylic paint, Golden recommends using a board or a heavyweight watercolor paper as a support to minimize buckling. Taping medium- or lightweight paper to a rigid surface while the preparation dries will also minimize buckling, and painting both sides of the paper will keep the paper flat. One drawback of Golden Silverpoint Ground is that the abrasives tend to settle to the bottom of the bottle, so that the mixture requires vigorous shaking before use.[3]

London art supply stores sell a metalpoint preparation by C. Roberson & Co. called "Silverpoint Drawing Ground," which comes in three colors: "Traditional Off-White," "Sanguine Tint," and "Powder Green." Roberson ground is described as "a natural bone ash primer" with an acrylic emulsion.[4] The pigment ratio of Roberson ground is low, making the preparation very transparent in the style of historic rabbit-skin glue grounds. The consistency is also very thin, requiring two coats or more, and for this reason, a very soft brush is needed to minimize streaking. Bone ash makes for a coarse ground, but the final coat can be lightly sanded when completely dry. Roberson ground is sold in two sizes, 60ml and 250ml wide-mouth jars, and the manufacturer recommends using the ground within six months. With both Roberson and Golden ground, abrasives settle out of the mixture, and while shaking or stirring the ground is often enough to make it usable, mulling the solids back into the liquid with a mortar and pestle can return the product to a uniform consistency.

In addition to fluid metalpoint grounds, Natural Pigments sells Rublev Traditional Silverpoint Ground in powdered form based on Cennino Cennini's recipe, made of chalk, silica, titanium dioxide, talc, and finely ground rabbit-skin glue. Follow the directions for mixing on the packet and the ground will have a consistency perfect for brushing; satisfactory results were obtained using one coat. Leftover preparation should be capped tight in the jar and refrigerated, as this product is made with materials that will spoil.

Homemade Grounds

Some artists seek to make metalpoint grounds like those the Old Masters used (Figure 3.2). Cennini describes a ground made from bone ash and spit,[5] quickly brushed on, after which the extra particles are whisked off to produce a rough-and-ready ground. Similar results can be achieved by simply rubbing the surface of the support with a pastel, which deposits gently abrasive pigment

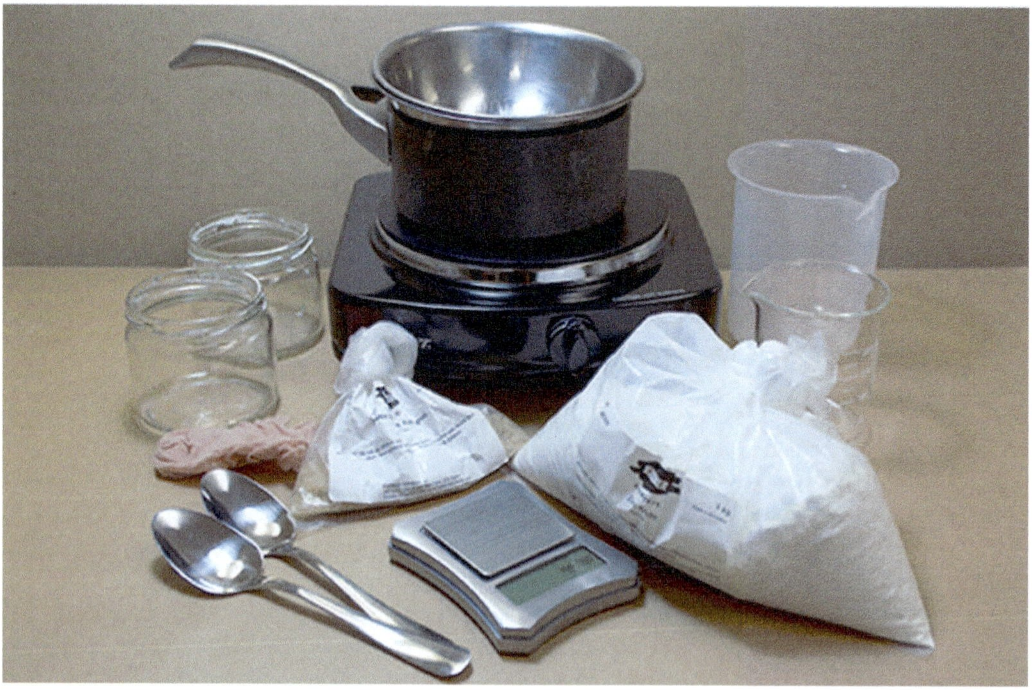

FIGURE 3.2 A selection of materials needed to make homemade ground, including a double-boiler, fine-measure scale, rabbit-skin glue crystals, zinc oxide pigment, and nylon for straining fluid preparation

with a tiny amount of binder. Neither is an ideal ground, as there is little adhesion of the powdery ground to the support, and the stylus itself removes a bit of ground while drawing.

Here is a recipe for a metalpoint ground made with zinc oxide and rabbit-skin glue; this ground has no extra abrasives such as bone ash or marble dust, as the powdered pigment functions as the sole abrasive, giving a smooth, chalky, matte surface.

Ingredients:

- 1/8 oz. (3.5g) rabbit-skin glue crystals
- 4 oz. (114g) zinc oxide or titanium white pigment
- 5.75 oz. (170ml) water

Equipment:

- Two clean glass jars with lids
- Double boiler or bowl of water nested into a pot of water
- Burner for warming pot of water
- Liquid thermometer
- Spoon for stirring
- Scale for measuring weights to the half gram or fraction of an ounce
- Measuring cup or graduated cylinder for measuring fluid to the milliliter or fraction of an ounce
- Patches of clean nylon stocking for straining, with rubber bands for fastening

Preparation:

- Sprinkle the rabbit-skin glue crystals into the measured water; stir, cover, and let sit for one hour.
- Heat tap water in the top of a double boiler to a temperature no higher than 120° F (49° C) (Figure 3.3).
- Place the jar with the water and rabbit-skin glue crystals into the water bath, stirring to melt the gelatin.
- When the temperature of the glue reaches 120° F (49° C), remove from heat and sift the white pigment into the jar with the glue, stirring constantly.
- Work quickly to incorporate all the pigment from the sides and bottom of the mixture. The ground will be the consistency of light cream and a little frothy from stirring.
- Strain the mixture by stretching two thicknesses of nylon over another clean glass jar and pour the warm mixture through the nylon into the clean jar (Figure 3.4).
- Spoon large lumps back into the original jar and break them up before continuing to strain.

The preparation will remain fluid for several minutes and may be thinned with an additional tablespoon of warm water. Any extra should be refrigerated until needed again, to prevent spoilage. The preparation will thicken when it cools, so immerse the jar in a bowl of warm tap water to return it to brushing consistency. Rabbit-skin glue grounds dry quickly and need to be brushed on rapidly, and the ground should be completely dry before additional coats are applied.

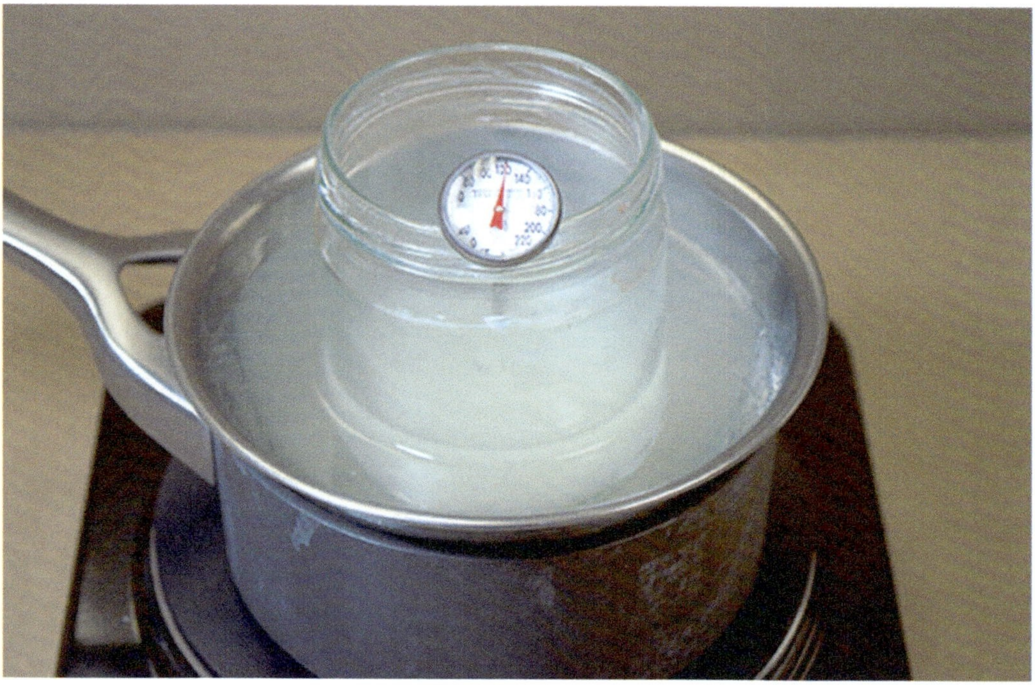

FIGURE 3.3 Heating rabbit-skin glue to 120° F (49° C) in a double boiler

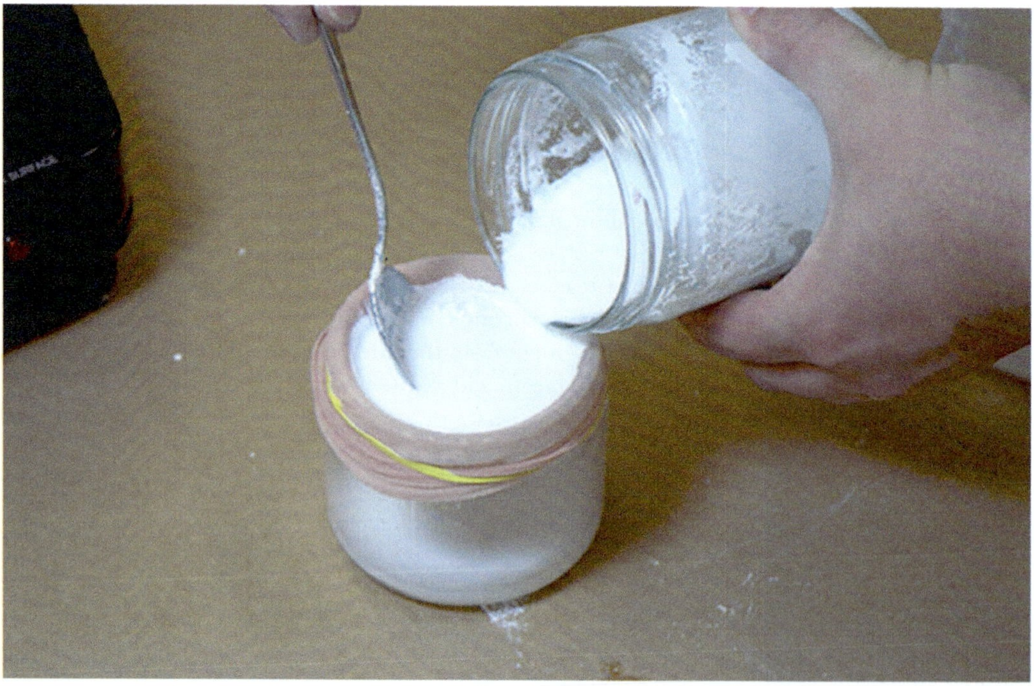

FIGURE 3.4 Straining fluid preparation through layers of nylon

The result is a tough, smooth-textured ground; although not waterproof like casein, it is among the most ideal surfaces for metalpoint drawing. In fact, because rabbit-skin glue ground remains water-soluble, erasing or removing the drawing from the ground is as simple as rubbing a damp cloth over the surface of the drawing.

Mixing Preparations

An ounce of paint and an ounce of water, in general, is a good initial measurement for a fluid preparation; use a little less water with gesso and a little more with gouache. As a rule of thumb, thin the paint to the consistency of whole milk. Wide-mouth jars are used to mix preparations, and the opening should be large enough to fit a large, flat brush to apply the ground (Figure 3.5). A tight-fitting lid will keep any extra preparation fresh for several days.

Mix the ground with a small, disposable brush that can dig into the recesses of the jar and incorporate the big lumps that cling to the sides. Half-inch bristle brushes from the hardware store are cheap and work perfectly for this task. Some paints will foam when mixed – acrylic and casein emulsions will form lots of frothy bubbles that should be left to settle for a moment before preparing the paper. Some artists *screen* their paint through nylon to remove large particles and thoroughly incorporate the solid materials.

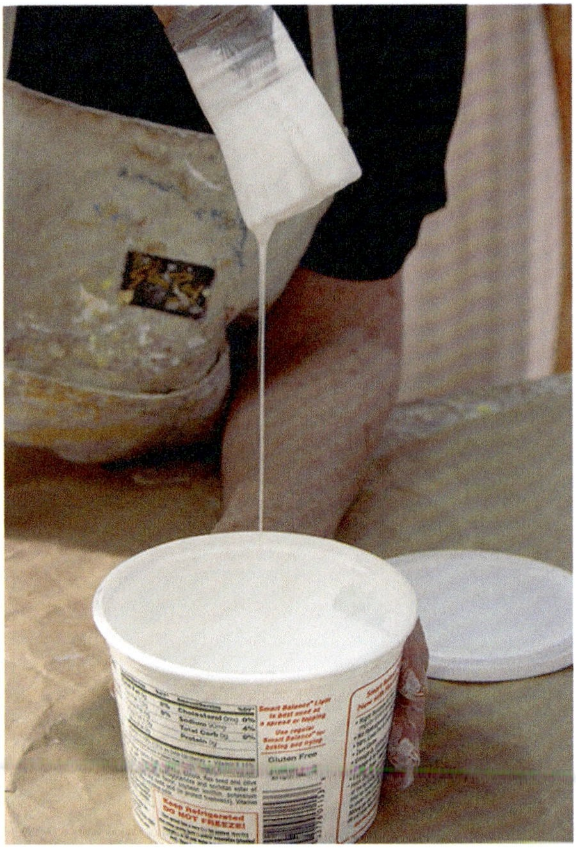

FIGURE 3.5 Thinning paint with water to make ground preparation

Test the preparation on a scrap of paper or other support to check color, flow, and consistency. Once the ground is mixed, it can used right away; if it needs to be stored, be sure to thoroughly remix the fluid before use, as the grittier elements will settle out of the mixture. Casein paints, rabbit-skin glue preps, and grounds with bone ash should be used as soon as possible.

Making Tinted Grounds

As far back as the mid-fifteenth century there were *chiaroscuro* (Italian for "light-dark") silverpoint drawings done on medium-toned grounds and highlighted with white paint or chalk. In the twentieth century, Paul Cadmus (American, 1904–1999) produced a series of male nudes using the chiaroscuro technique, adding brushstrokes of white over loose, open silverpoint hatching on a variety of colored grounds (for an example, see Figure 7.2). Traditionally, colored grounds were created by mulling pigment together with bone ash before adding liquid and applying the mixture to the support. Today, adding a small squeeze of good quality tube watercolor to fluid white paint is an easy way to tint the ground. Better quality watercolor has more finely ground pigment, and synthetic-organic or synthetic-inorganic pigments tend to mix better than non-synthetic pigments. Acrylic paint colors should only be added to acrylic gesso.

Instead of watercolor, pure pigment can be added to any aqueous ground. Dry pigment is the most potent tinting agent; 1/8 teaspoon (0.5g) added to 2 oz. (60ml) of fluid white prep will produce a medium-tone ground. Make a paste of the pigment by mulling it with a few drops of water before adding it to liquid ground; otherwise the dry pigment will clump, and the paint will streak when it is applied (Figure 3.6).

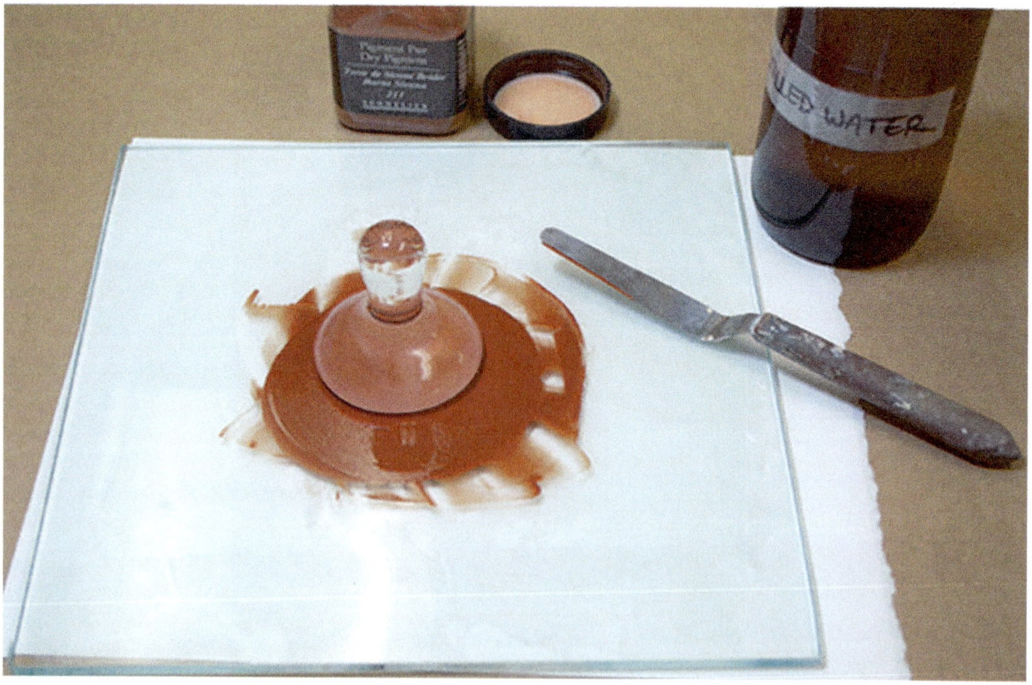

FIGURE 3.6 Mulling pigment

One caution when using tinted grounds is to make sure that the mixture is opaque enough, or else the colorant will exaggerate inconsistencies in the thickness of the ground, whereas white ground on white paper is much more forgiving. In any case, mix up enough of the tinted preparation to cover all the sheets with as many coats as needed, because it is nearly impossible to mix identical tinted grounds every time.

Lastly, it is possible to use commercially made color paint to provide a tinted ground for metalpoint. Colored gesso, black gesso, store-mixed acrylic latex interior flat paint, color gouache and casein can be mixed to the proper consistency and applied to the support, but multiple coats may be necessary to achieve a flat color. Opaque silk-screen inks, pulled through a blank screen onto sheets of almost any paper or board, will give a smooth, chalky, and flat color ground that is wonderful for metalpoint. For colored gesso, Holbein Acryla Colored Gesso, which comes in a variety of hues, is excellent quality and makes a better ground for metalpoint than does regular acrylic paint.

Application of Preparations

Metalpoint artists prepare supports with one result in mind: a smooth, chalky surface that allows the metal tool to make a mark and also bonds well with the underlying material.

To apply the preparation, use a wide, flat, soft-haired brush such as a two-inch golden Taklon, squirrel, or white nylon short-handled brush (Figure 3.7). Softer brushes produce smoother grounds; bristle brushes leave brushstrokes; and foam brushes leave a "pile" of ground at the

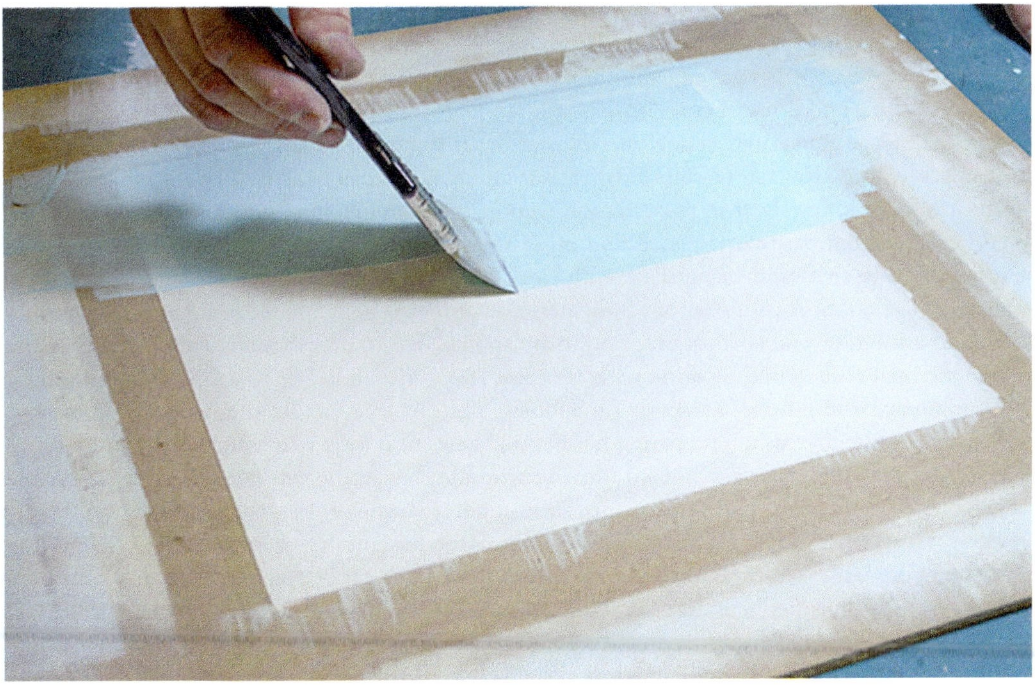

FIGURE 3.7 Preparing light-weight paper taped on all sides to a rigid board

edges of each brush stroke. For smaller supports, a one-inch brush or watercolor mop will also work well. Apply the preparation rapidly from side to side with a loaded brush, refill the brush, and cover the paper with a second layer of perpendicular overlapping strokes. Observe the support in bright light to be sure there are no bare spots. While the first coat is still damp, work over the sheet with an empty brush to smooth out the ground. If the paint begins to dry, mist the ground with a little water from a spray bottle or reload the brush with preparation to smooth out the ground. One coat is rarely enough with most paints; two or more are necessary to provide a good metalpoint ground. Thin the subsequent coats slightly by adding a little more water. Between coats, allow several minutes for the ground to "soak in" – if too little time passes, the second coat will dissolve the undercoat, and if too much time passes, the top coat will not bond with the undercoat and may flake off later. Depending on the type of ground, let the paint "cure" for a period after it is dry. Commercial casein can take a week or more to harden, depending on how much linseed oil is in the paint. Even acrylic needs to harden, overnight or longer.

If light- or medium-weight paper is being prepared, it will need to be taped on all sides to a rigid board. The paper can be misted with water on the reverse and allowed to grow slightly before it is taped, dry side up. This is called *stretching* the paper, and it is similar to preparing paper for watercolor painting. Paper will absorb a lot of liquid and become wavy (called *buckling*). As the paper dries, it will flatten. Use a wide, waterproof tape such as packing tape, and be sure a half inch or more of the paper is underneath the tape. Large sheets may need to be stapled or tacked on all sides to a heavy board. Allow the prepared paper to fully dry before removing the tape from the board. Remove the tape by pulling it away from the paper, level with the paper surface and at a right angle to the margin; this will prevent the tape from tearing the paper as it is removed. Packing tape can leave a sticky residue on the margin of the finished paper, which can be rubbed off later with a rubber cement pick-up. Heavy papers and paper boards can be prepared without taping them down, but an "X" of paint should be applied to the reverse to prevent the paper from curling as the ground dries (Figure 3.8).

Other thin supports, such as polyester film or other synthetic papers, will not absorb water in the same way as cotton rag or sulfite paper, but taping these materials to a board will provide a clean margin, hold the sheet in place, and prevent paint from creeping under the edges.

When preparing hardwood panels and other smooth, rigid supports for metalpoint drawing, it is common to first sand the surface with fine, 220-grit sandpaper to create enough tooth to grab the preparation. A thin coat of acrylic gesso or primer is next applied and sanded when dry. Onto this primer, several coats of preparation are applied, left to dry, then sanded as well. Sanding before the final coat should be done with very fine, 800-grit sandpaper to achieve the smoothest possible surface without any marks or air bubbles. The last coat can be thinned with water to a very light consistency. When preparing hardwood panels, it is only necessary to secure the board to the work surface to prevent it from moving around. Elevate the support off the work surface to be able to neatly brush preparation out to the edges (Figure 3.9).

Many artists sand their final coat of ground to provide the smoothest surface. After the ground is dry and cured, use very fine, 800-grit sandpaper folded or attached to a sanding block, making sure the sandpaper is perfectly flat. To sand prepared paper, tape the paper to a very flat, rigid surface first. Move the sandpaper gently, without much pressure, in circles over the entire surface (Figure 3.10). Small, nearly invisible scrapes may appear as the surface is sanded, but they will be difficult to see except in raking light.

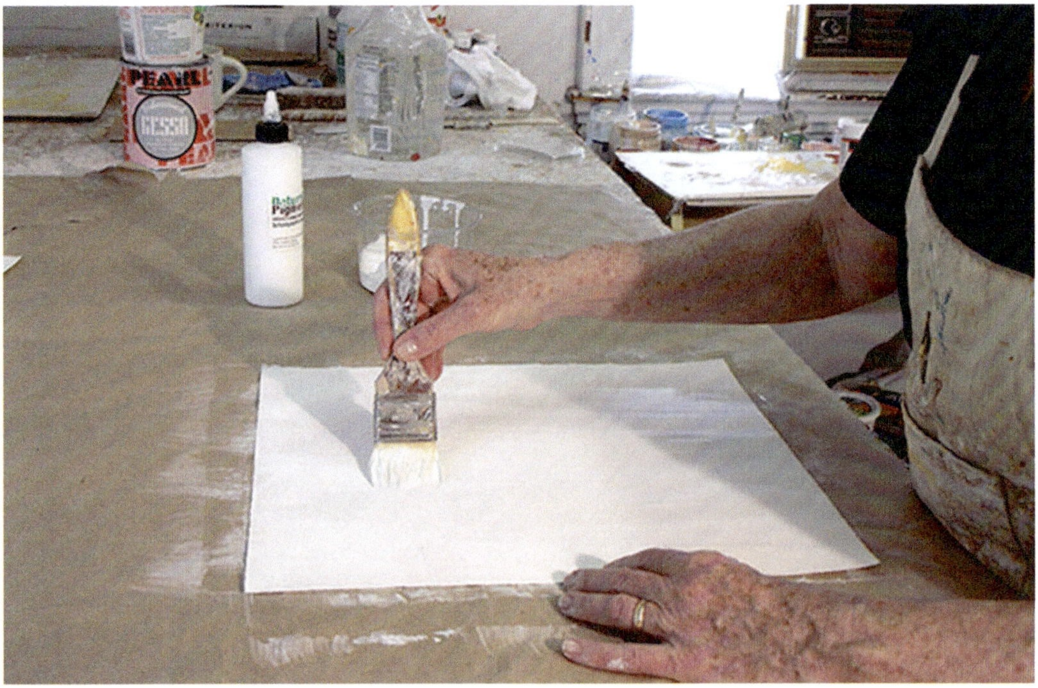

FIGURE 3.8 Preparing heavy-weight paper with a pre-mixed ground and a wide, soft brush

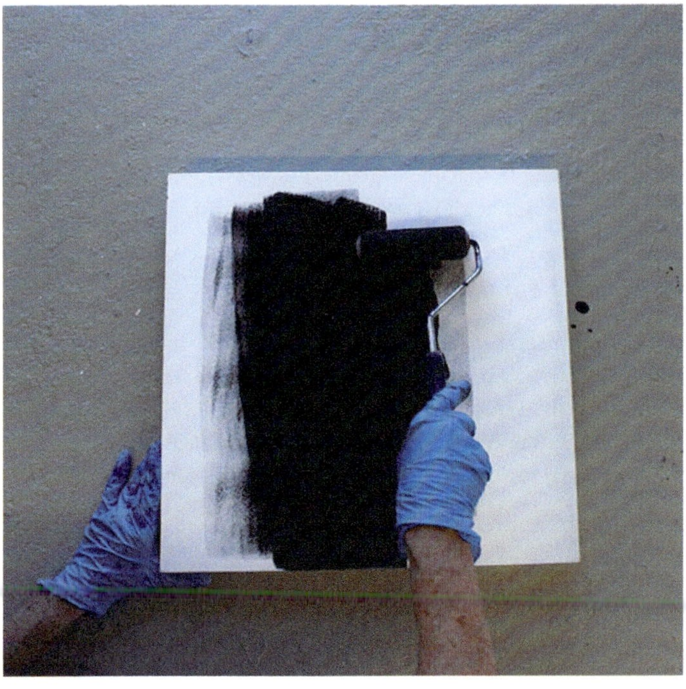

FIGURE 3.9 Preparing a cradled panel

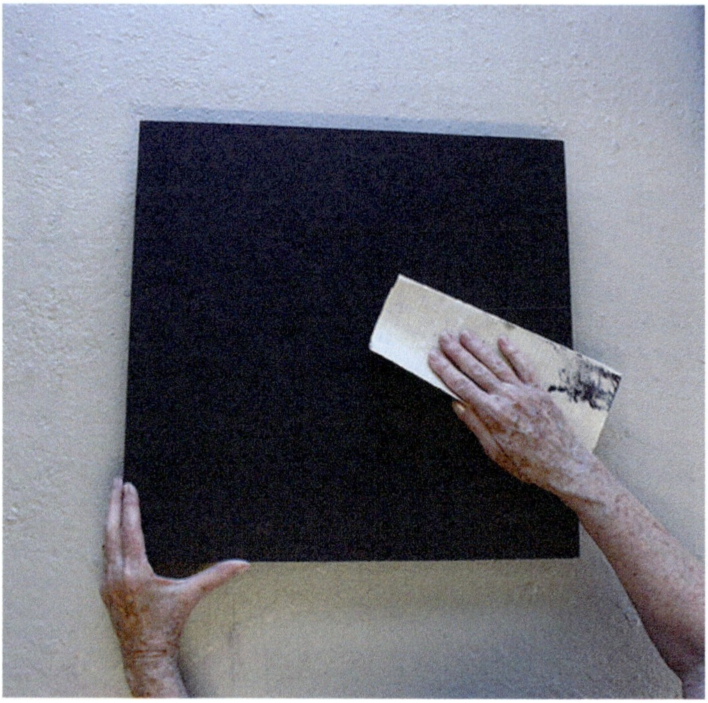

FIGURE 3.10 Sanding a finished panel

Metalpoint Supports

Paper, paperboard, and hardboard panels are the most often used supports for metalpoint grounds, but new materials as well as fabricated and found objects are also used. In addition, there are commercially prepared papers available that have grounds already applied to them, and several kinds of paper that do not need grounds at all to work for metalpoint.

Papers and Other Flexible Supports

Paper has been the most common support for metalpoint work since the sixteenth century, when it overtook wood and parchment as a general drawing surface. There are many types of paper that will work with metalpoint, but a smooth, heavyweight paper like watercolor paper, printmaking paper, or drawing paper is generally preferred (Figure 3.11). Most paper is *sized*, meaning it has glue added during the manufacturing process that affects how long fluids remain movable on the surface before they begin to "set in." 140lb. paper is a medium-weight paper that will absorb a lot of liquid, and, if taped down on all sides to a firm board before applying preparation, will dry flat and rigid. Lighter weight 90lb. paper has a tendency to buckle when a lot of liquid is applied and, even when dry, is somewhat transparent and flimsy. A lot of artists prefer heavyweight 300lb. paper because it is rigid enough to prepare without needing to tape the paper to a board while it dries.

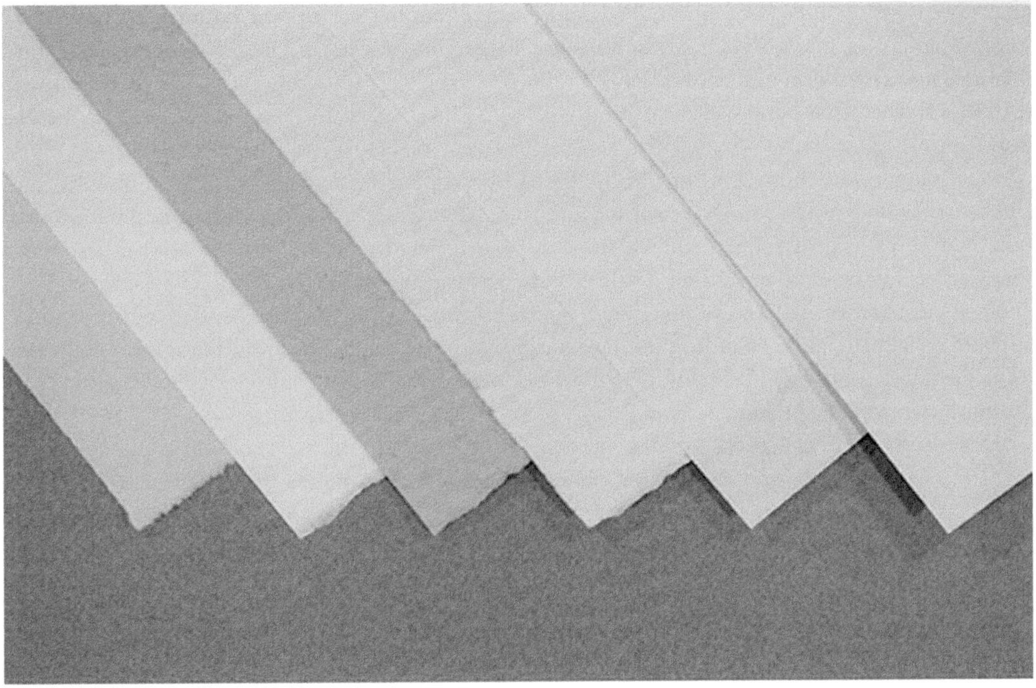

FIGURE 3.11 Paper, paperboard, and paper-like metalpoint supports (left to right): Ingres Antique Laid, 140lb. hot-pressed watercolor paper, handmade linen paper, Arches Cover White, frosted Mylar, and 4-ply Bristol board

Drawing paper is heavily sized to enable clean erasing; watercolor paper is lightly sized, and printmaking papers have less sizing than watercolor papers. Good quality, heavyweight rag papers are recommended, as sulfite (wood pulp) papers tend to deteriorate quickly both in the presence of moisture and normal environmental conditions.

Papers have different textures, usually *wove*, or even-textured, and *laid*, meaning textured with a linear grid. There is a further distinction of *hot-pressed*, *cold-pressed*, and *rough* surface papers. Hot-pressed means a smooth paper, and it is preferred by metalpoint artists who work in hatching, because preparing a ground on hot-pressed papers provides a very smooth surface for making fine lines. Cold-pressed paper has a subtle, grainy texture, which becomes less pronounced after preparation, especially if the ground is sanded. A metalpoint tool will mark the high points of the texture, skipping over small depressions, leaving minute patches of light within the darks. Rough papers are rarely used for metalpoint work, as the application of a preparation would exaggerate the texture and require more coats and more sanding to achieve an even ground.

Among the paper-like supports metalpoint artists use, there are new materials such as Dura-lar, as well as traditional materials like parchment and vellum, and even linen and canvas. Dura-lar (Mylar) is polyester paper and is available in both clear and white transparent sheets and rolls of different sizes and thicknesses. Matte finish, white, transparent Dura-lar, sometimes called "frosted Mylar," is manufactured to have a vellum-like surface for direct drawing with ink and watercolor, markers, and some types of pencils. Mylar takes some painted metalpoint grounds very well and has the benefit of being stable and lightweight in very large sheets. These papers are very flexible and not absorbent, and traditional grounds like gouache can easily flake and chip from the surface. On the other hand, acrylic grounds have good flexibility and work well when applied to polyester paper.

Parchment and vellum are historically the earliest supports used for metalpoint drawing, and some artists still use them. Both are natural animal products; parchment is made from the stretched, untanned skins of goats, sheep, and calves and has many natural imperfections both in color and texture. Vellum is made from young calves, kids, and lambs and has a smooth, even surface. Both vellum and parchment, commonly called *animal membrane*, will swell and soften when liquid is applied, so it is advisable to mount them to a rigid support before preparing them for metalpoint. When mounted this way, the resulting flat, smooth, mildly absorbent support is superb for preparing with thin layers of traditional gesso for a perfect metalpoint surface.

Linen and canvas can also be used as supports for metalpoint drawing, provided the material is first stretched over a frame or mounted on a rigid support. Because of the porous nature of both linen and canvas, they are typically sized after stretching, then primed with layers of gesso that are sanded smooth to provide a paper-like surface. Acrylic gesso can also be used and does not require the linen to be sized. Linen is often the preferred substrate of the two, as it has a much finer texture for metalpoint drawing. Both are excellent choices for large works in metalpoint, as the size of the drawing is only limited by the size of the roll of fabric.

Boards, Panels, and Other Rigid Supports

The general term *board* includes illustration boards, Bristol boards, and mat boards; *panels* refers to sheets of hardboard and plywood (Figure 3.12). In addition to unfinished boards and panels, there are products available made from watercolor paper sheets mounted on hardboard supports or panels of hardboard pre-primed with gesso.

Illustration board, which is available in a range of qualities, is paper, laminated to a 4-ply substrate, which may be rag or wood pulp. It is sold as hot-pressed, cold-pressed, or rough, and has only one workable side. Illustration board made from 100 percent cotton rag paper is the best choice for metalpoint work. Some artists attach illustration board to a wood cradle for exhibition. Another type of paperboard is Bristol board, a multi-ply support frequently used for watercolor painting and that has both sides available for drawing. Bristol board is sold by ply, and the thicker version is better for metalpoint work. It typically comes in two surfaces: *plate*, which is extremely smooth and intended primarily for ink drawing, and *vellum*, an even, matte surface that will hold the metalpoint ground nicely. Preparing Bristol board is similar to preparing 300lb. watercolor paper; there is no need to tape it to a rigid support to prevent it from buckling, and most artists simply paint an "X" from corner to corner on the back of the board to make it dry flat.

Working on board is one of the oldest ways of doing metalpoint, and there are fourteenth-century "sketchbooks" made of thin sheets of boxwood. The benefit of working on board is that a ground can be applied without curling or stretching the support, and several coats of ground can be applied and sanded smooth to achieve a perfect surface for drawing. Untempered hardboard, or high-density fiberboard (HDF), which is commonly used in egg-tempera painting, is the ideal support; it is smooth on both sides and does not contain harmful chemical stabilizers,

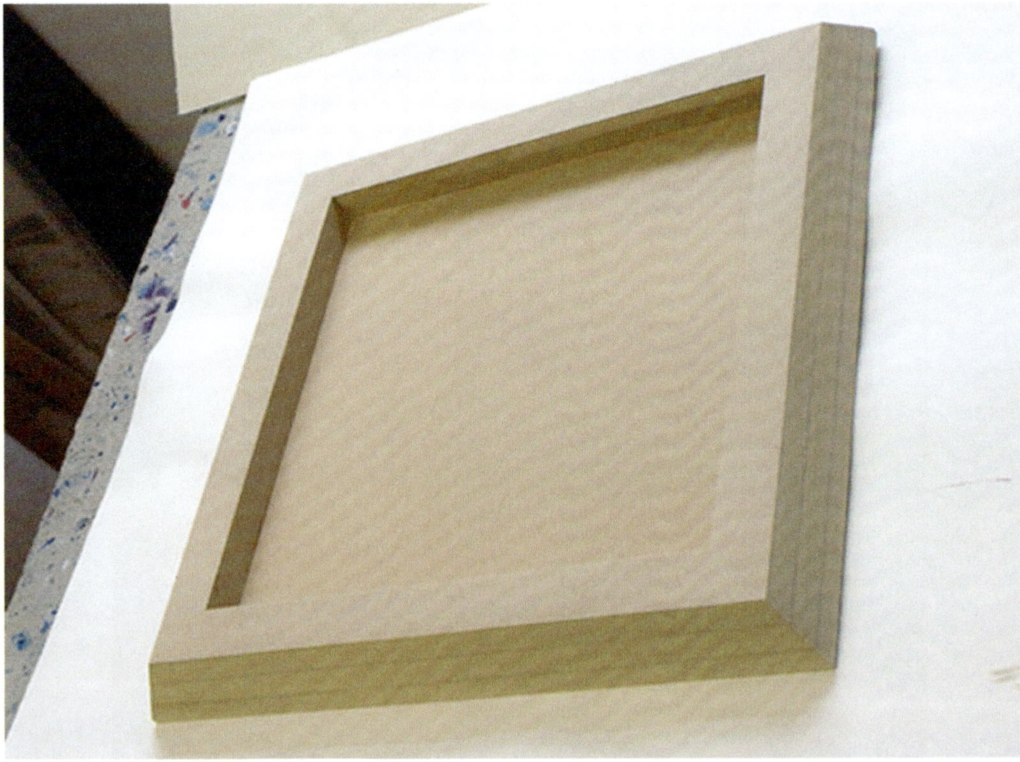

FIGURE 3.12 A cradled hardwood panel

which can affect the longevity of the board. Tempered hardboard, commonly called "Masonite," is impregnated with oil to waterproof the board. Once thought inferior as an artists' support, modern tempered hardboard uses less oil in its manufacture and is more stable. Medium-density fiberboard (MDF), found in home-supply stores, is essentially a thick cellulose panel, but it contains formaldehyde, is prone to off-gassing even when sealed, and is not as durable as a product specially made for artists. The process of making hardboard panels leeches nearly all the acids from the wood, but artists who use hardboard of any kind will seal the board first with layers of primer before applying metalpoint ground.

There are artists who have expanded the vocabulary of metalpoint drawing to include unusual supports such as three-dimensional plastic forms, found objects, and large wooden shapes. Carol Prusa (American, b. 1956) has done metalpoint drawings over sanded and primed Plexiglas spheres and domes (Figure 3.13). She uses layers of Weber Prima Acrylic Gesso to provide a sturdy ground, and a thin layer of Guerra Titanium White Acrylic to create a brilliant cool white surface or Golden Black Gesso for dark surfaces. She hatches with silverpoint to create her drawings and deepens values with ground graphite applied with acrylic binder, then heightens with Titanium White acrylic paint.[6]

In addition to fabricated plastic forms, shells, spoons, shaped plywood, and even walls have been prepared and worked on by metalpoint artists. Each will take grounds well or poorly depending

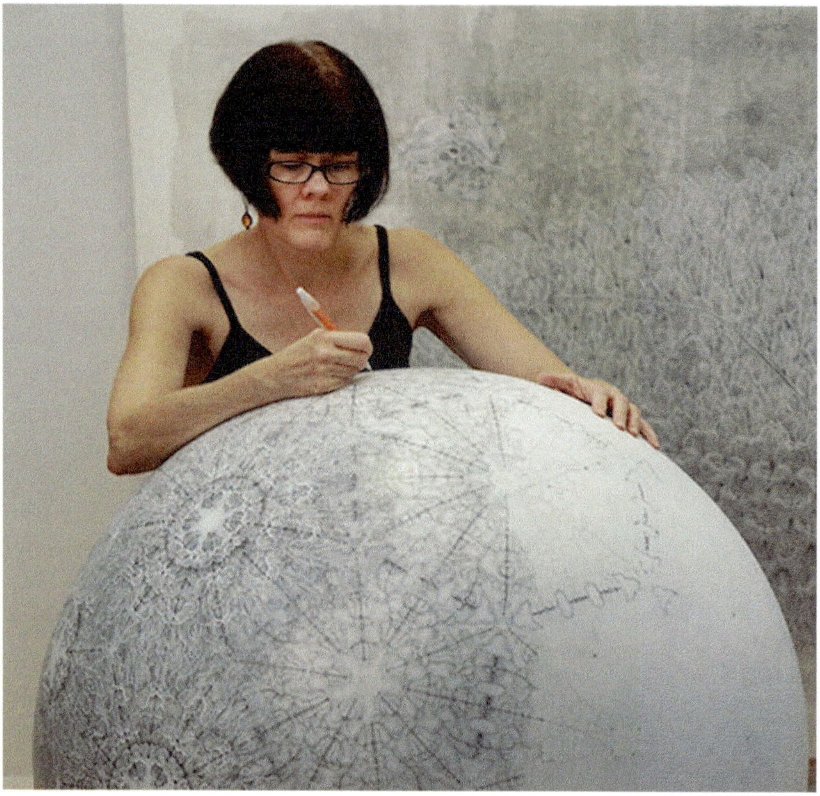

FIGURE 3.13 Carol Prusa drawing with silverpoint on a custom-made acrylic sphere, sanded and prepared with Weber Prima acrylic gesso. Photo courtesy of the artist

on its composition, but in general acrylic polymer grounds bond well with most surfaces if they are first sanded to provide a *tooth*. Once the metalpoint artist begins to realize they are drawing on paint on top of a support, the desire to experiment with all kinds of rigid supports becomes part of the visual and conceptual possibilities of metalpoint artwork.

Commercially Prepared Papers

There are several "ready-to-go" papers that will work for metalpoint without the need to apply a preparation (Figure 3.14). Commercially prepared clay-coated papers have been widely used by metalpoint artists since the late nineteenth century, both for sketching and for highly finished works. A few types of these papers are still available from several manufacturers, though they are getting harder to find with each passing year, since these papers are made for commercial printing and are generally not retailed as art supplies.

Coated paper is a machine-made paper "imprinted" on both sides with a polymer that contains compounds like kaolinite, leading to the term *clay-coated paper*. The resulting surface is very smooth and regular, with a lustrous white sheen. Metalpoint marks well on these papers, giving a fine, clear line and showing the distinct lusters of different metals. Coated papers do not take correction well,

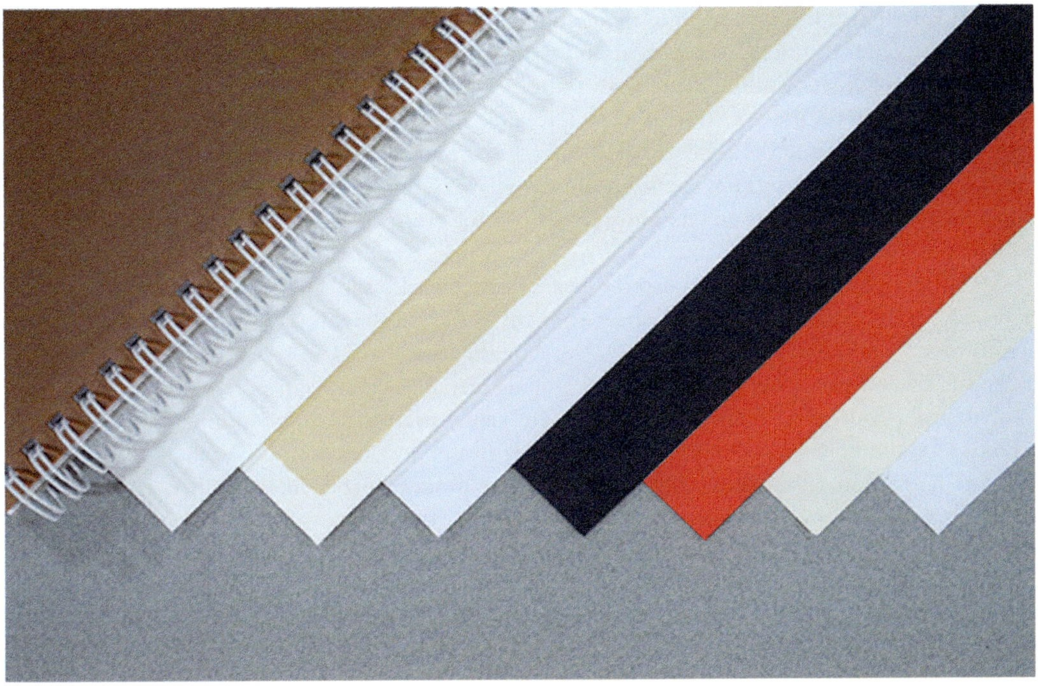

FIGURE 3.14 A selection of metalpoint-ready commercial papers (left to right): A spiral-bound pad of Sennelier Papier Pointe-d'Argent, TerraSkin stone paper, Art Spectrum Colourfix pastel paper, McCoy Clay Coated paper, black and red medium-weight Plike, and buff and white light-weight Plike

since erasers buff the coating, preventing the clean adhesion of new metalpoint marks. Also, many clay-coated papers are sulfite papers; they are made with wood pulp treated with sulfurous acid, and despite their coating they can deteriorate when exposed to the elements.

McCoy Clay Coated Cover is a popular brand of this type of paper, which was once available from New York Central Art Supply before it closed. It was sold in very large sheets for a low price, and was a medium-weight, very white, matte-finished paper, coated on both sides. McCoy also holds up well over time, resisting the deterioration of most sulfite papers. Silverpoint marks well on McCoy, but gold, copper, and other metals do not mark as well. Legion Art Coated Cover, a white, matte, heavyweight paper made in the USA, is also coated on both sides. It contains a high alpha cellulose buffered with calcium carbonate and is pH neutral and acid-free. Silver works very well with a nice strong line on this paper, but other metals mark slightly lighter and do not seem to tarnish. Like McCoy paper, Legion was once sold at New York Central Art Supply but is now only available directly from the manufacturer in large quantities for industry. One early favorite commercial paper was Video Media Paper, a heavyweight paper with a thick clay coat on one side. The ground contained approximately one part kaolinite to three parts silica, with an acrylic binder. This paper was used for special printing techniques, and it was possible to carefully scrape off the surface to correct mistakes. The clay coating was unusual, since most metals showed up in their "real" colors, copper as a reddish brown, gold as warm brown, and silver as grey. In any case, Video Media paper has been unavailable since 1985. Another paper widely used for metalpoint but no longer available is Cameo paper, a very thin, light yellow paper with clay coating on both sides that is only useful with silver.

Plike paper is a 100% sulfite paper with a smooth, rubbery, "plastic-like" surface; made in Italy, it is available in several colors (including white, cream, black, blue, brown, graphite, and red) in very large, 95lb. text and 122lb. cover sheets. The heavier weight cover stock is the preferred choice. While metalpoint lines show up quite well, they tend to tarnish quickly. Plike also does not erase well, as even soft erasers remove the coating from the surface, thereby preventing the paper from taking corrections.

Sennelier in Paris offers a clay-coated paper called Papier Pointe d'Argent Furioso, sold in sheets and pads. A 200gsm (about 140lb.) sheet is 45cm × 65cm (roughly 18 × 25 in.), and there are spiral-bound pads containing 21cm × 29.7cm (roughly 8 1/2 × 11 in.) sheets. Workable on both sides, the sheet is very smooth and shiny. It is acid-free, pure cellulose paper, is soft, and embosses easily but does not give a full range of metalpoint values even with soft, dark metals. It is available to order only in France as of this writing, and only from Couleurs du Quai Voltaire in Paris.[7]

Mitz TerraSkin Multimedia Art Paper, another modern paper-like product, is made from calcium carbonate and high-density polyethylene[8]. Designated as an "eco-friendly" paper by the manufacturer, it is sometimes also referred to as *stone paper*. It is sold in pads, sheets, and rolls of many weights, from 8pt (roughly 120lb.) to 16pt (roughly 200lb.), and in many sizes, from 9 × 11-inch pads and sketchbooks to 40-inch by 5-yard rolls. It is water-resistant and tear-resistant, takes pencil, ink, printmaking ink, and paint equally well, and works with silverpoint without any preparation. The paper is quite soft and flexible, giving a dark metalpoint mark that tarnishes quickly. The paper is described as 100 percent acid-free and is intended to be recycled with plastics, as it is commercially compostable and photo-degradable. The rapidity with which metals tarnish on this paper suggests a fairly high sulfur content, and its archival longevity is not well-documented.

Working on sandpaper is another option for metalpoint artists. Although non-traditional, the inherent colors of the metals used in drawing show up beautifully on sheets of very fine, 2,000-grit black sandpaper. Gold looks yellow, copper looks red, and silver looks light gray. Similar to working on a black gesso ground, but with more abrasive quality, a drawing can be worked "in reverse," adding the lights and achieving a remarkably full range of values. One drawback is that the grit takes a lot of metal off the tool; another is that there is no adhesive property to the sandpaper – good quality sandpaper is manufactured to resist clogging, and so the drawing easily smears and must be handled with extreme care. It is also not evident how long a drawing on sandpaper will last, as archival information about different brands of sandpaper is not well-documented. Similar to sandpaper is pastel paper, such as Art Spectrum Colourfix Paper, a 140lb. smooth watercolor paper coated with a textured acrylic primer and available in over a dozen colors. Pastel paper is designed to grab pastel and hold it, so it is very toothy.

Many metalpoint artists prepare multiple supports in advance to have them ready for any drawing projects that come up. Preparing papers, boards, and panels takes time, and depending on the ground, drying and curing can take days. Also, many metalpoint artists use a variety of supports, papers, and preparations, so that labeling the back of the sheet with the name of the paper or ground used allows the artist to keep track of which materials work well. Surfaces can be kept safe from scratches by storing the finished supports in a cardboard folio, a file drawer, or a box, with an interleave between them to protect their surfaces. But even with all the different types of paint, paper, boards, preparations, applications, and colorations available, many artists have one preferred preparation or one preferred support that they love to use to the exclusion of all others.

Notes

1 Golden Artist Colors, Inc., www.goldenpaints.com/technicalinfo_gesso. Accessed 18 October 2017.
2 Wrights of Lymm, Ltd., www.stonehouses.co.uk/index.php/signwriting-pinstriping/signwriting-paints/classic-casein-paints/500ml-classic-casein-white.html. Accessed 18 October 2017.
3 Golden Artist Colors, Inc., www.goldenpaints.com/technicalinfo_silverpoint. Accessed 18 October 2017.
4 Paul V. Snowdon, C. Roberson & Co. Technical/Manufacturer, email correspondence with the author, 23 August 2017.
5 Broecke, Laura. *Cennino Cennini's 'Il Libro dell'Arte': A New English Translation and Commentary with Italian Transcription* (London: Archetype, 2015), 27.
6 Carol Prusa, email correspondence with the author, 15 July 2017.
7 www.magasinsennelier.com/papier/p_speciaux.html. Accessed 18 October 2017.
8 "Stone paper," Wikipedia, https://en.wikipedia.org/w/index.php?title=Stone_paper&oldid=800605327. Accessed 18 October 2017.

4

DRAWING WITH METALPOINT

Introduction: Drawing with Metalpoint

There are many reasons to work in metalpoint – its ties with the Renaissance, the luster and the way it tarnishes, the fact that it is still rare, or because it is done with precious materials on special surfaces – but at its core metalpoint is a drawing medium. Techniques used with charcoal, graphite, crayon, pen and ink, marker, and colored pencil all work to some extent with metalpoint, but expecting metalpoint to do the same things as those other media undervalues its unique qualities. A metal stylus glides across a hard, prepared surface with a feel unlike that of any other medium, producing a gray line that maintains its evenness and delicacy even after many strokes. Custom styluses, metal wools, and shapes of metal will make a variety of interesting and expressive marks with a range of values. Increasing pressure and overlapping strokes will allow a very gradual buildup of tones to create subtle, elusive gradients that can mimic the finest of transparencies and the effects of light. And metal implements like thimbles, coins, wire brushes, and notched wedges of soft metal will make unique marks that expand the expressive range of drawing beyond line and tone. Before tarnishing, a traditional metalpoint drawing is a gray line on a white or pale-colored ground; adapting to or overcoming tonal limitations of this kind is part of the practice of metalpoint. Many artists treasure the paleness and precision of traditional metalpoint, while others exploit the subtle variations of different metal tones or push boundaries by using different tools, grounds, supports, and techniques.

Planning, Sketching, and Preliminary Work

Some planning is essential before work in metalpoint begins. Having a prepared support ready is absolutely necessary; otherwise work stops while materials are gathered, and paper or board is coated with a ground and allowed to dry. Many metalpoint artists prepare dozens of sheets in advance to have them on hand for any drawing purpose, while others prepare just enough for specific works of art. Often work begins with the barest of ideas, and as the work changes one needs to stop and prepare more supports, sometimes in other colors or different sizes to accommodate the new scope of the project. Unlike working on an oil painting or a charcoal drawing, starting on the wrong foot with metalpoint usually means more than wiping down the surface and starting again.

While most artists begin directly with metalpoint, some artists start a complex drawing with a sketch they intend to transfer; with metalpoint this can be a tricky process because the prepared surface is sensitive to every mark and unforgiving to correction. Transferring an image means that a drawing or photograph is simplified into a line drawing; the line drawing is copied onto tracing paper; graphite is applied to the back of the tracing paper; and a stylus is used to transfer the outline onto the ground as a light graphite mark. The graphite mark can be carefully removed using a kneaded eraser after the outline is reinforced with metalpoint. Artists working in the traditional method of medieval illuminators will transfer the drawing without graphite by using a *blind stylus*, which means that the tracing is placed over the prepared paper, and the metal stylus is then pressed along the outlines through the tracing paper, leaving a colorless incision in the ground. This incised line can be seen in raking light and worked over in metalpoint. Other artists will transfer the image from below with a light table or from above with a projector (Figure 4.1). Working up a detailed drawing as a study is another way to gain a sense of the overall design before beginning in metalpoint. The contours of the study can be transferred as described, and then the "key" drawing or group of studies can be referred to as the artist begins laying in metalpoint. Contemporary figurative artists will often have a group of photographs of their subjects on hand for just such purposes. The most direct, spontaneous method is to work from the subject or idea directly on the ground without any preliminary studies, developing the composition as one allows "mistakes" to become part of the process. Many of these artists begin drawing with the

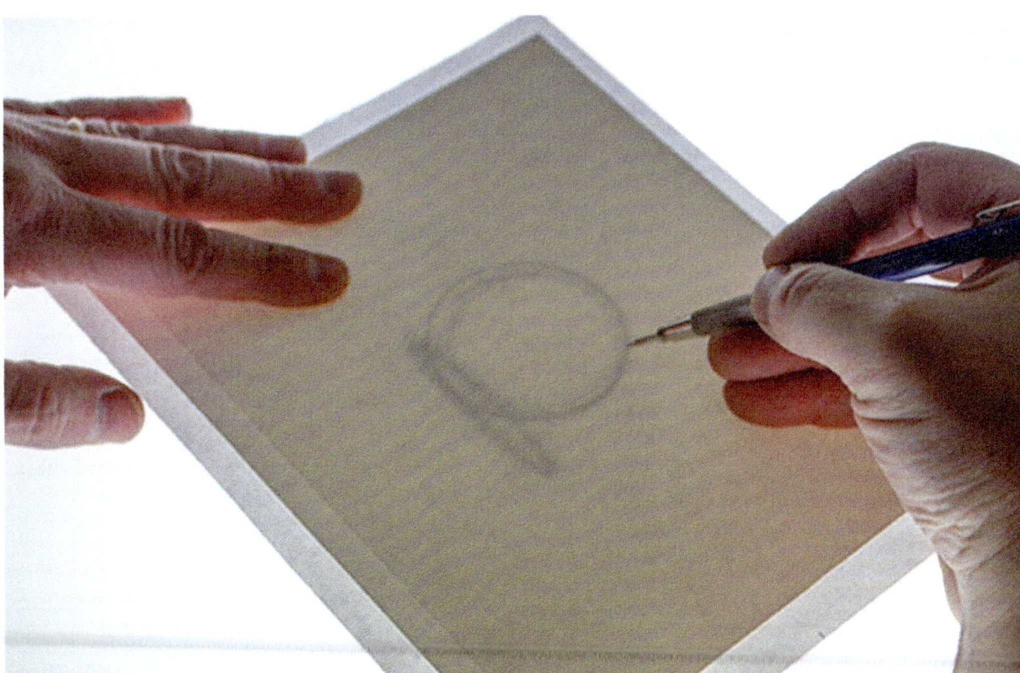

FIGURE 4.1 Transferring a sketch to prepared paper with silverpoint using a light box

primary metal (i.e. silverpoint), but some will begin with a lighter metal, such as gold or platinum, before working in silver.

No matter how the drawing is planned and transferred, metalpoint drawing is best done *additively*, working from light to dark, beginning simply and adding marks as necessary to build the darks while leaving light areas untouched. A heavily worked area can sometimes be lightened with an eraser, but building up the darks gradually ensures smooth gradations.

Working from light to dark over a large sheet means that metalpoint can be a slower drawing process than that of other media, and there are two main approaches to a complex composition. The first is to focus on one area and bring it to completion before moving to another area. This method works especially well with reference photos, where each area of the photograph is defined by shapes and gradations of tone that can be closely copied to achieve a high degree of photorealism. Figure and ground can be worked independently, and sections from different references can be inserted into the composition where needed. Working slowly and methodically, the artist fits the entire drawing together like a jigsaw puzzle. A similar approach can be used for complex abstract works, where repeating patterns are worked up, one area at a time, until the entire composition is completed.

The other approach is to work over several areas of the composition simultaneously, giving elements equal, but incomplete, attention, responding to the work as it develops. Leaving the work "open" in this way offers a great degree of integration, because all the elements can be developed to relate to one another as the work is completed. Choosing what to develop is as much an aesthetic and emotional reaction as it is one of process and planning.

Tonal Drawing: Hatching, Tonal Layering

After all the preliminary work is done, the metalpoint drawing needs to be developed. A few artists, such as Joseph Stella (American, 1877–1946) and John Storrs (American, 1885–1956), have produced finished works in metalpoint using a minimal line, but many more artists develop a full value range. When working with a metalpoint stylus, there are really only two methods of tonal development: *hatching*, and *tonal layering*. Beyond these, there are methods of working with unusual metal tools to produce lively lines and areas of tone.

Hatching

Hatching, the term that describes a field of linear marks that create an illusion of volume and tone, is a technique best-suited to a fine-point stylus. Each line is carefully placed parallel to another line, perhaps at a distance of a millimeter or less apart. The finer the hatching, the easier it is to create soft gradations of tone. A smooth board or hot-pressed paper, prepared with ground that is also sanded smooth, is the best surface for fine hatching with a metalpoint tool; a rough uneven ground can cause the hatched marks to skip or change direction in unexpected ways. The type of point the artist uses makes a difference as well. A metalpoint stylus with a long taper will allow the artist to make fine lines that are barely darker than the paper color to build up a field of tone extremely gradually. A long point also allows the artist to see each mark more clearly as the tool is positioned for the next line. Hatching is best achieved working flat, with the hand resting on the drawing surface. A clean sheet can protect the paper from transferring skin oils or *burnishing* the ground with the side of the hand. Many metalpoint drawings are small, and working flat is

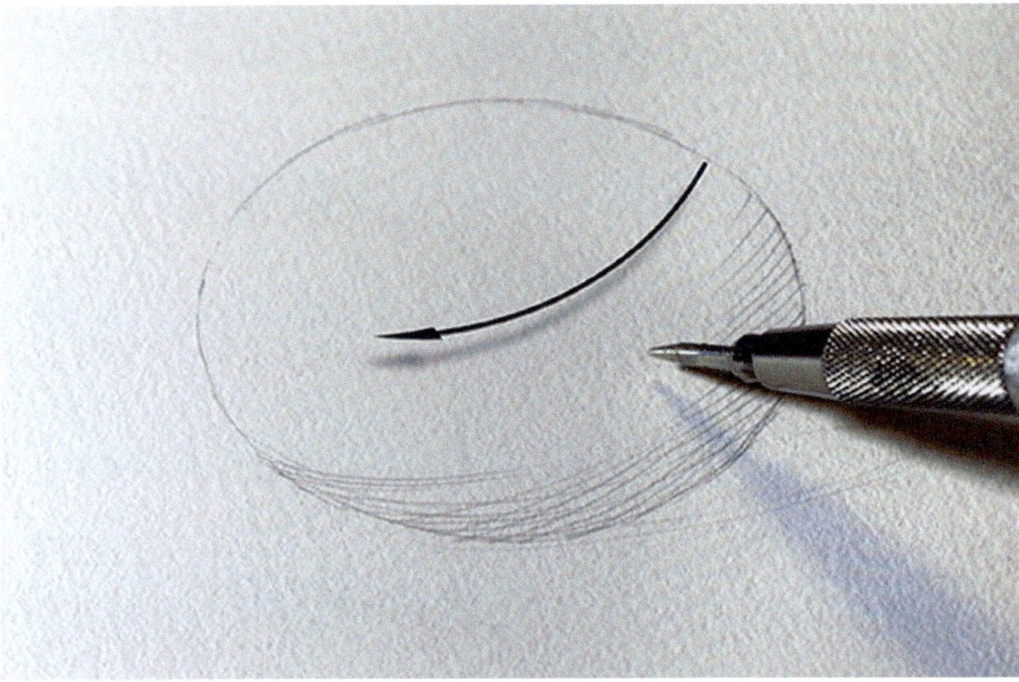

FIGURE 4.2 Hatching away from the contour to "feather" strokes into the paper tone

easiest when the drawing is attached to a small, movable board that can be rotated to make marks in any direction. Working larger, one must contort the hand, arm, and body to produce marks of multiple directions, and it is difficult, while standing up, to lay down even and fine hatching. A mixture of hand-eye coordination and repetitive muscle control is needed to make fine hatching. Also, the artist should draw *away* from the contour, rather than *up to* the contour. It is easier to repeatedly place the point on an edge and draw the tool inwards than it is to end the mark on the same line every time (Figure 4.2). This will help to maintain a smooth edge where the hatching does not extend beyond the boundary of the object being drawn. Some artists also use a slip of paper as a template to create a clean edge in their drawings. To produce a soft edge to the field of hatching, lift the point at the end of each stroke to create a natural taper to the line. This also gives the group of lines staggered endpoints, forming a natural feathered edge that blends the field of hatching with the paper color.

Cross-hatching is the technique of adding a field of marks at an angle over the marks just created and is used to create a gradation of tonality while also indicating surface contour and form. Metalpoint is superb at this type of mark-making. For very subtle cross-hatching, a long, thin line that follows the external contour will give a softer, more naturalistic-looking tonality to the shades and shadows of the object. Right-angle hatching will look like a grid rather than a volumetric tone; a shallow angle to the hatching creates a softer surface. Cross-hatching is seen most often in Renaissance art and has a very antique look, but the contemporary sculptor Tom Otterness (American, b. 1952) uses a very free cross-hatching technique with much more space between his lines in a series of humorous metalpoint drawings (Figure 4.3).

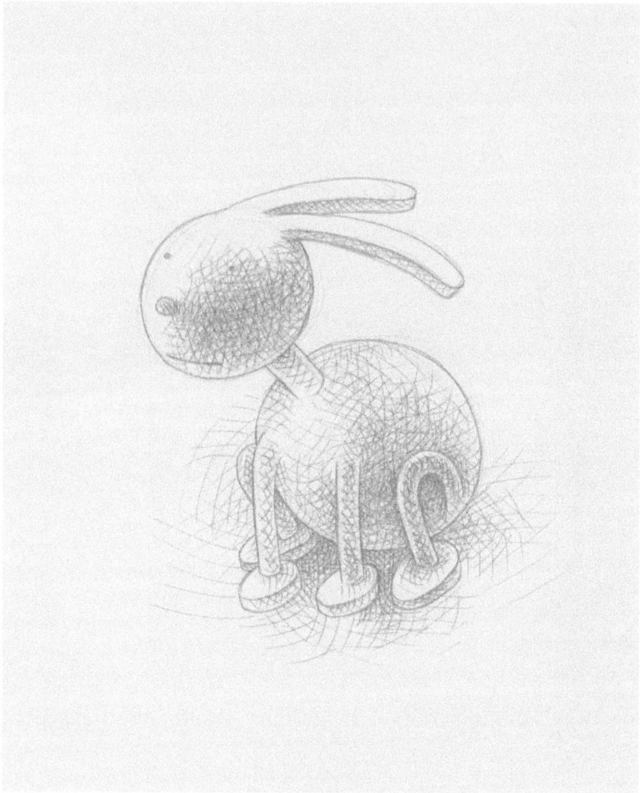

FIGURE 4.3 Tom Otterness, *Rabbit*, 2015, silverpoint on prepared and toned paper, 24.5 × 21 inches (62.23 × 53.34 cm), © Tom Otterness, courtesy Marlborough Gallery, New York

Hatching can also change direction and length within a field to achieve the effect of varying form. This *cascading* cross-hatching is often seen in drawings by artists like Albrecht Dürer and is used to show an area of shadow over a flowing surface like skin, fur, or drapery. Cascading hatching is one way of adding motion and variety to tonal areas while suggesting underlying form.

Overlapping multiple directions of hatching will create gradations, blending tone from the ground color all the way to the darkest gray that metal will give. Black is difficult to achieve with cross hatching, because there will always be some spots of ground color showing through the *weave* of hatched lines. Creating very dark tones with hatching involves making lines that follow several directions, sometimes at only slight degrees of difference. Work from light to dark rather than from dark to light, adding new directions of faint lines until the desired tone is achieved. Also, for a very smooth transition, try to hatch over the entire surface area with light marks, rather than just hatching near the edges (Figure 4.4). One or two layers of hatching over a highlight, when done faintly in metalpoint, will still "read" as a light tone and will indicate the form of the surface.

How the tool is held can greatly affect the quality of hatching (Figure 4.5). Holding the stylus as if for writing, with the fingers near the point, will produce short, straight hatching of

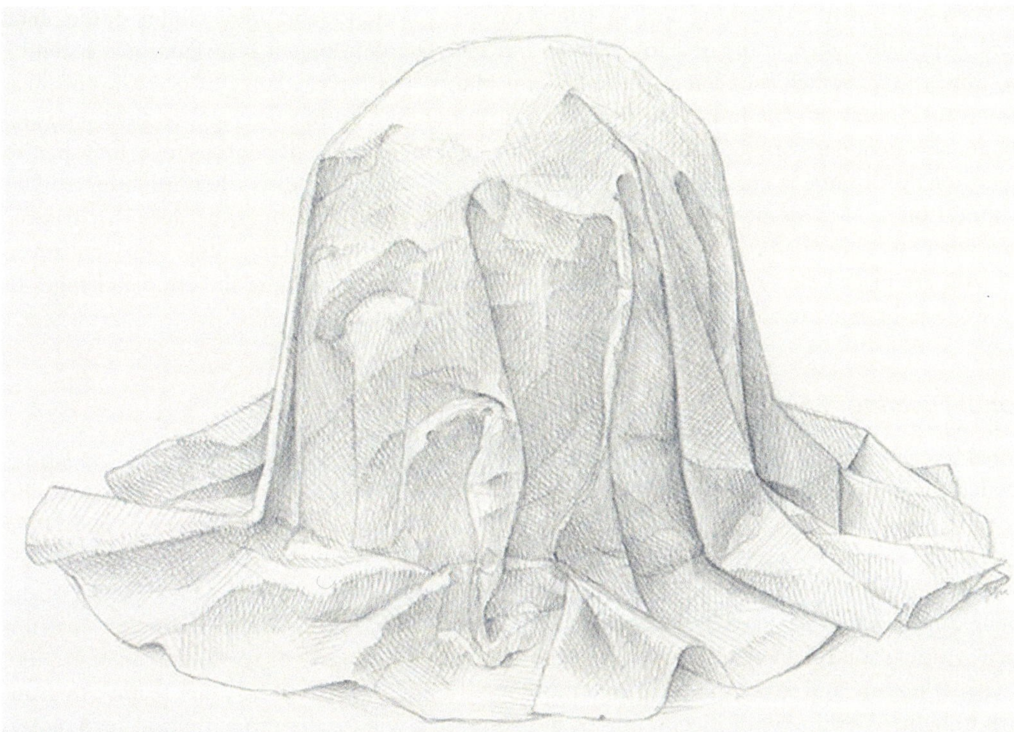

FIGURE 4.4 Tom Mazzullo, *Lily of the Valley* (detail), 2014, silverpoint on prepared paper, 9 × 12 inches (22.86 × 30.48 cm.), courtesy of the artist

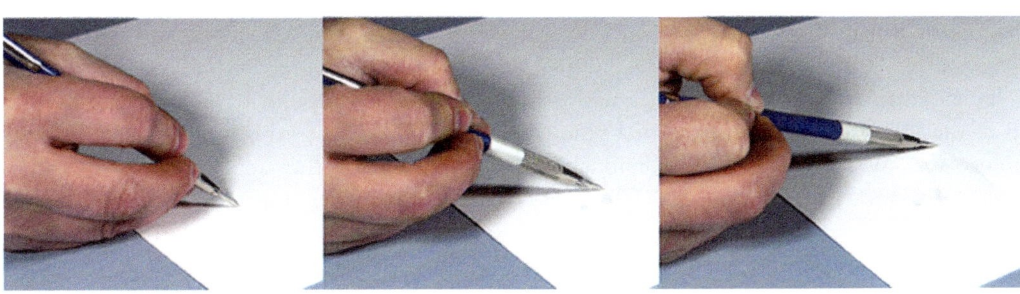

FIGURE 4.5 Holding the stylus in different positions for different marks (left to right): near the point, center, and opposite end

about a quarter-inch in length. Pressure is easily applied and control over the spacing between lines is easy to maintain with this grip. Holding the stylus further back will give longer, more curved marks, better for contour hatching. Holding the tool all the way back will produce the longest and most curved line, and without any extra pressure, the weight of the tool is enough to create a mark.

The main benefit of hatching with metalpoint is the consistency and predictability of the metal mark, especially when compared to graphite and ink. Graphite pencil is a traditional hatching tool, but the mark will broaden as the soft point blunts, and the tendency of graphite to smear can create blooms of tone in light areas and a blurring of lines within the hatched field. Pen and ink are also frequently used for hatching, but with fluid ink there is the opportunity for a pen to blot as one damp line is crossed by another, and this can also be the case when using markers or technical pens. Metalpoint is possibly the best tool for fine crosshatching, because the material stays where it is intended to go, and the fine line is excellent for producing subtle tonal gradations as marks are placed closer and closer together or multiplied over minute directional changes to achieve a full range of values within a drawing.

Tonal Layering

Tonal layering is perfect with metalpoint, and this technique provides the continuous gradations needed for photorealistic artwork. The technique will be immediately familiar to people who work in pencil, charcoal, crayon, and colored pencil. With these media, gradations from light to dark are created by varying the pressure of the tool as it moves on the paper while controlling the amount of paper color that shows through. When using soft media, the texture of the paper can help to grab particles of drawing material from the stick, and that creates variation even within a solid field of tone. Rubbing the material with fingers or tortillons can overcome the paper texture and make the tonal area more consistent, even blending tones seamlessly from dark to light. Working with metalpoint creates issues that will be alien to people accustomed to working with soft tools. With metalpoint, pressure is only moderately responsible for creating tone, as the mark made by a metal tool is either "not there" (paper color), "barely there" (light gray), or "fully there" (dark gray). Metal does not smear like graphite or crayon does, where gently rubbing with a fingertip or stump will easily soften edges and blend tones. Also, rubbing a metalpoint mark after it is applied will likely remove the metal particles from the sensitive ground, or it can burnish the ground, discolor it, or remove both the metal and the ground altogether.

Tonal layering can be done either with a sharp or blunt metalpoint tool, but polishing the tip of the stylus to a smooth, rounded point is the best approach to this type of mark-making (Figure 4.6). Wider, soft-edged, individual marks blend well together and are less distinct than marks made with a sharp point. The length of the mark is determined by the natural movement of the fingers as they flex when holding the tool or of the whole hand as it flexes back and forth to move the fingers holding the tool. Generally, the length of tonal marks is shorter and more controlled than the length of hatched lines, and the marks often change direction to fill the area with tone.

Different tones can be created with one metal tool somewhat by modifying pressure and more by controlling how much ground shows through the marks. The farther back one holds the stylus, the lighter the mark, and the closer to the point the stylus is held, the more control one has by bearing down to create darker marks. A textured paper will show through metal marks much more than a very smooth ground, because the tool will skip on a toothy paper, depositing metal on the high points (Figure 4.7). Even if care is taken to fill the texture with metal, the irregularity of the ground on a toothy paper will add some nice variation to the fields of tone. At some point, however, the ground will become completely covered in metal, and no tooth will be exposed that

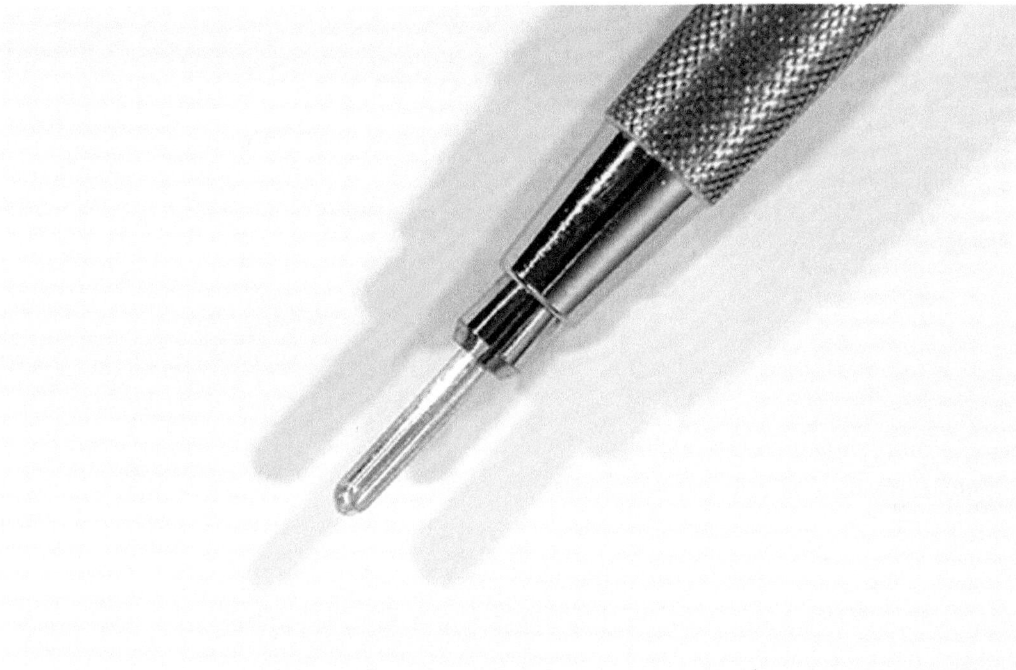

FIGURE 4.6 A smooth, round point for tonal layering

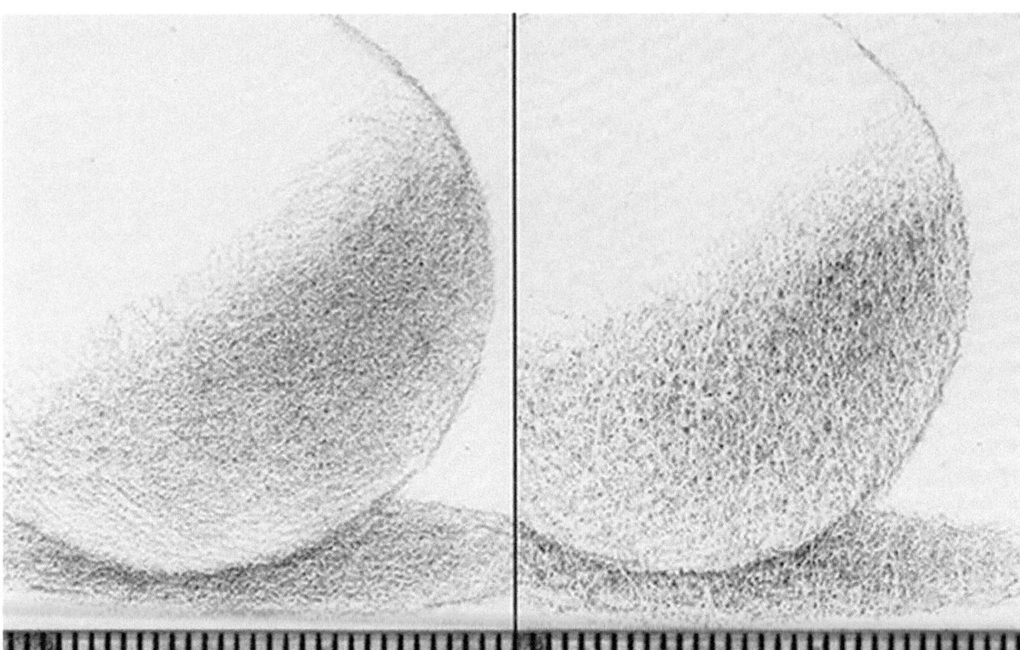

FIGURE 4.7 Tonal drawing of a sphere on smooth (left) and rough (right) papers

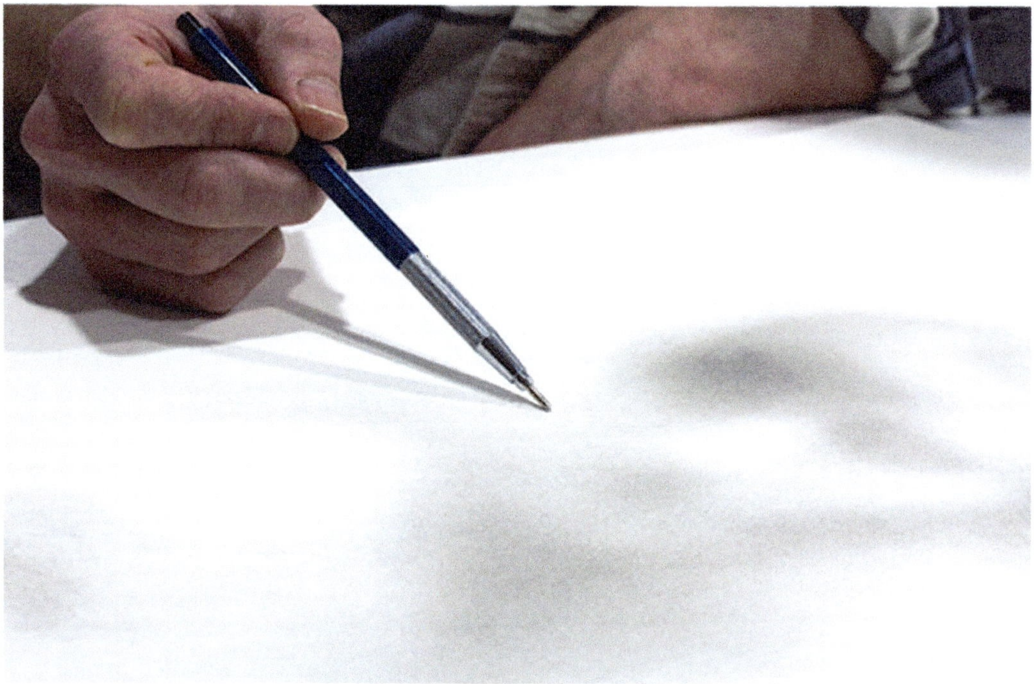

FIGURE 4.8 Artist Michael Nichols demonstrating his tonal metalpoint technique

FIGURE 4.9 Michael Nichols, *Smaze*, 2013, silverpoint on paper, 9 × 12 inches (22.86 × 30.48 cm), courtesy of the artist

can grab metal particles. This *saturation* of the ground is one of the reasons that even the darkest metalpoint drawings appear gray.

The metalpoint work of Michael Nichols (American, b. 1973) has a unique, soft appearance that relies on a particular method of tonal layering to achieve its carefully controlled gradations (Figures 4.8 and 4.9). His art "features classic materials," and he uses traditional chalk gessoes as well as Liquitex Acrylic Gesso, clear gesso, and Golden Silverpoint Drawing Ground. He writes,

> As an alternative to hatching and cross-hatching to create value, I use a lineless approach. . . . I distribute the weight of the tool by holding the stylus loosely from the end to make wispy marks. By gently shading in circular motions, I create faint veils of tone that darken slowly through successive layering. . . . For my style, which is softly blurred, it is important that values and gradients are evenly applied. In an almost surgical manner, I fill in light spots and draw around dark spots until the values are perfectly uniform. The result leaves an airbrushed-like appearance.[1]

Application of Unique Tools and Unusual Techniques

Since pressure has little effect on the darkness of the metalpoint line, some artists use different point shapes to produce a variety of marks in their work, while others blend different metals to achieve subtle color variations. One way to create variety is with an assortment of metal objects that make unique marks. The corner of an antique printing block made of type metal will draw a dark, variable contour; the edge of a coin will create a calligraphic mark. Finding unusual metalpoint tools can be as simple as crumpling a piece of aluminum foil for groups of free and abstract marks or folding foil into a point to draw a wide line. Metal wool pads rubbed lightly on the ground can create a beautiful toned area around an already carefully drawn form, and applying the pad firmly gives you a wider range of tones. Using the pads against a template creates tonal areas with sharp contours. Dragging or rotating a metal brush on the surface produces swirls of parallel lines that can be very subtle or built up to a much darker color (see, for example, Figure 2.17).

Flat, rigid pieces of metal are another alternative tool. The metal can be dragged across the surface, making fine, tonal marks similar to watercolor washes, and the edges will make a crisp contour. All kinds of metal scraps, jewelry or objects can be explored to make free forms and shapes. Susan Schwalb (American, b. 1944) uses flat shapes of multiple metals in her *Strata* series (Figure 4.10), which exploits the subtle differences in metal luster to create luminous, linear abstract works. Other possible tools include silver spoons and silver thimbles. The back of the spoon will glide across the ground making tones, lines, and circular forms. Several artists have used antique silver thimbles worn on their fingers to make marks, including Linda Hutchins (American, b. 1957) who wears thimbles on both hands to record her movements directly on the wall (see Figures 4.11 and 7.38).

Drawing on Tinted Grounds

The subtle differences of metals show up nicely on white grounds, but a color ground can affect the cast of metals as well (Figure 4.12). Tarnished silver looks particularly warm against pale blue or pink grounds and blends more subtly on ochre grounds. A medium-tint ground

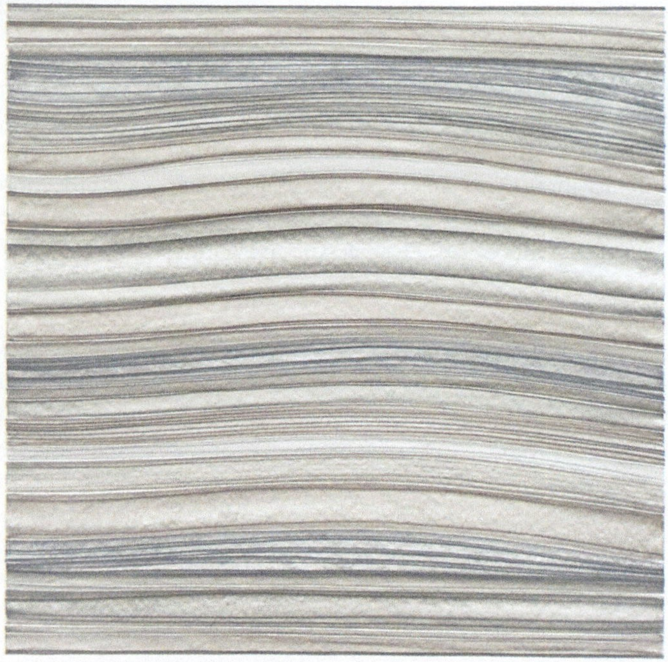

FIGURE 4.10 Example of areas of different metals in one drawing: Susan Schwalb, *Strata #295*, 1998, Silver, gold, copper, aluminum, brass, and platinumpoint on Video Media paper sheet: 24 × 24 inches (60.96 × 60.96 cm). Collection of Eric Chafe, Newton, MA

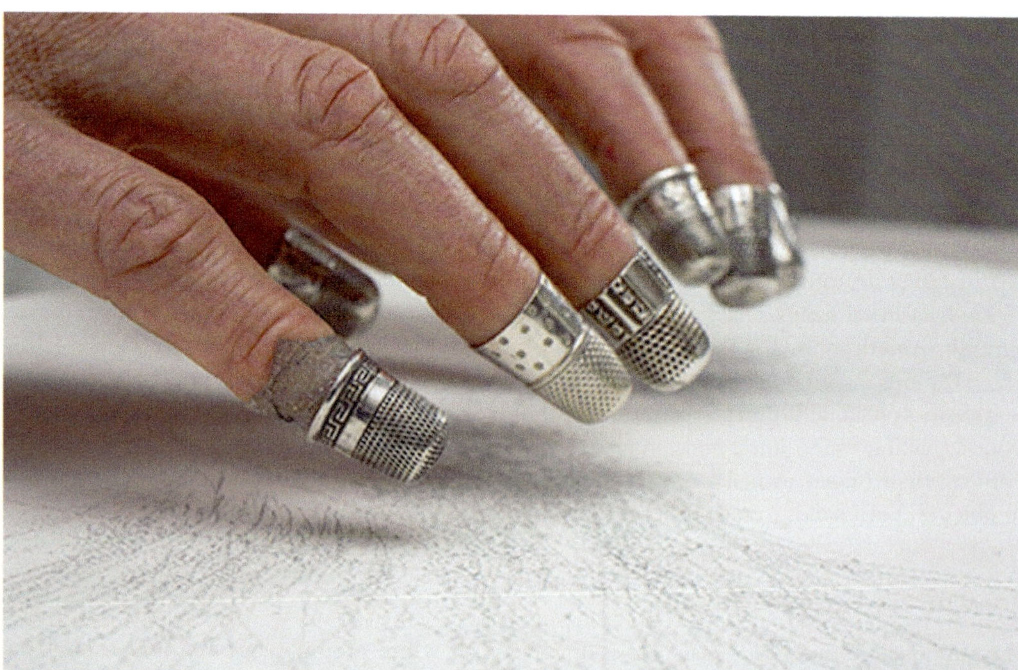

FIGURE 4.11 Artist Linda Hutchins using silver thimbles on all fingers to mark on prepared surfaces. Photograph by Dan Kvita.

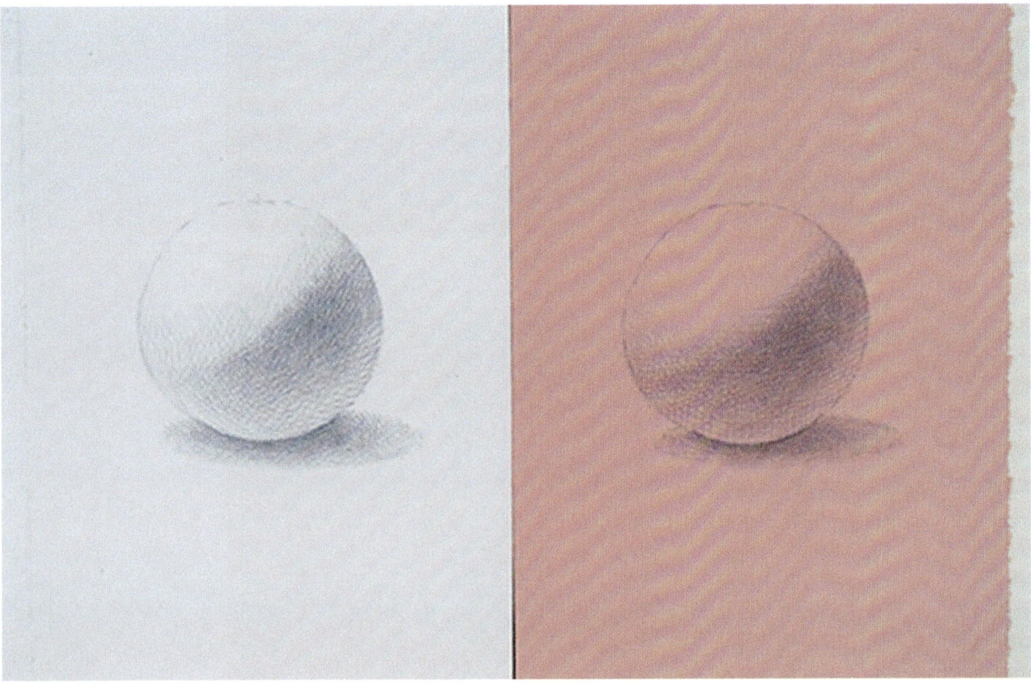

FIGURE 4.12 Example of metalpoint hatching on white vs. toned ground

allows the gradation of tones to be controlled more gradually, because it reduces the contrast between metal and ground.

When using very dark grounds, the metals look quite different than they do on pale grounds. On black, metals are lighter than the ground and show their true colors; artists can work in a "negative" manner and achieve great control over a very large range of values. On dark color grounds, each metal will react to each ground's hue and value differently. For example, aluminum looks bright white on dark blue grounds, while silver has less contrast difference. Similarly, silver, gold and copper look warm and bright on dark violet grounds, whereas those same metals look gray on dark red grounds. Susan Schwalb's recent work investigates these color relationships; she prefers Holbein Acryla colored gessoes and uses them in their pure form or mixes her own colors (for an example, see Figure 0.3, Susan Schwalb's *Currents I*).[2]

Artists can introduce light into tinted grounds by removing the ground selectively, using a sharp blade to scrape the ground down to the white substrate. Large areas of light can be introduced by erasing through the ground down to the white paper below, but control is hard to maintain, as the eraser needs to be rubbed with great pressure over the surface of the ground. This technique creates a "bloom" of light near the center of the erasing, with a diffuse blending of light back into ground color near the edges. A beautiful example of this technique is seen in a 1987 drawing by Charles Schmidt (American, b. 1939), *Ms. Hunter: Sibyl* (Figure 4.13), a figure study done on a red ochre-tinted ground that has been worked up in silverpoint with highlights added by means of an electric eraser for a luminous, modern twist on the chiaroscuro technique. In addition to scraping, strokes of white paint or crayon can be added to metalpoint drawings on tinted grounds to enlarge the tonal range. More on combining metalpoint with other media is covered in the next chapter.

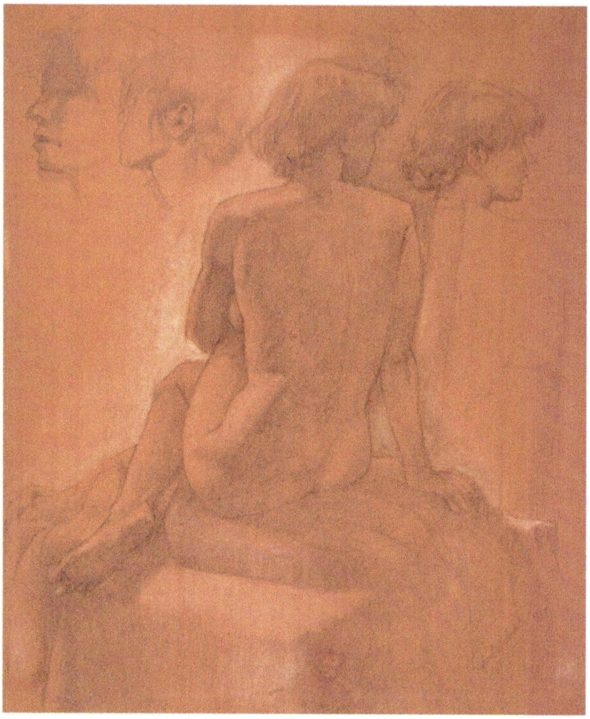

FIGURE 4.13 Charles Schmidt, *Ms. Hunter: Sibyl*, 1987, silverpoint on prepared paper, 14 × 11.5 inches (35.56 × 29.21 cm), collection of Tom Mazzullo

Erasing and Correcting

Contrary to popular belief, metalpoint erases. A white plastic eraser will clear an area of metalpoint work, and a kneaded eraser can "lift" and lighten patches of metal (Figure 4.14). Blades and sandpaper will also remove metal marks, but there are some consequences of removing metal applied to painted ground that are not desirable, and which reinforce the idea that metalpoint is only an "additive" medium. Removing metal from the ground will also alter the abrasiveness of the prepared support, preventing new metal from adhering in the same way as in the uncorrected areas. If no new marks are added, an eraser will leave a shiny spot on the otherwise matte paper, visible at an angle or in raking light.

To correct metalpoint work with an eraser, erase gradually, with very little pressure. There are two ways this works: with a sliver of white plastic eraser cut to a flexible *wedge* or with a morsel of kneaded eraser.[3] The white plastic or vinyl eraser, if applied lightly, will leave the ground and surrounding metal mostly undisturbed. One can use this method for removing single lines of light hatching, with the intention that the area will be re-worked with more hatching. Done carefully, the corrections will be almost invisible. Worked in the hands until soft and sticky, then shaped to a blunt point, a clean, new, kneaded eraser can pick up small areas of metal by *daubing*, or pressing gently and releasing. This method is excellent for lightening tonal layering, contour lines that are too dark, or areas of hatching at the edges of shadows that should properly blend invisibly into the color of the ground. Care should be taken when using a kneaded eraser in this manner, as too

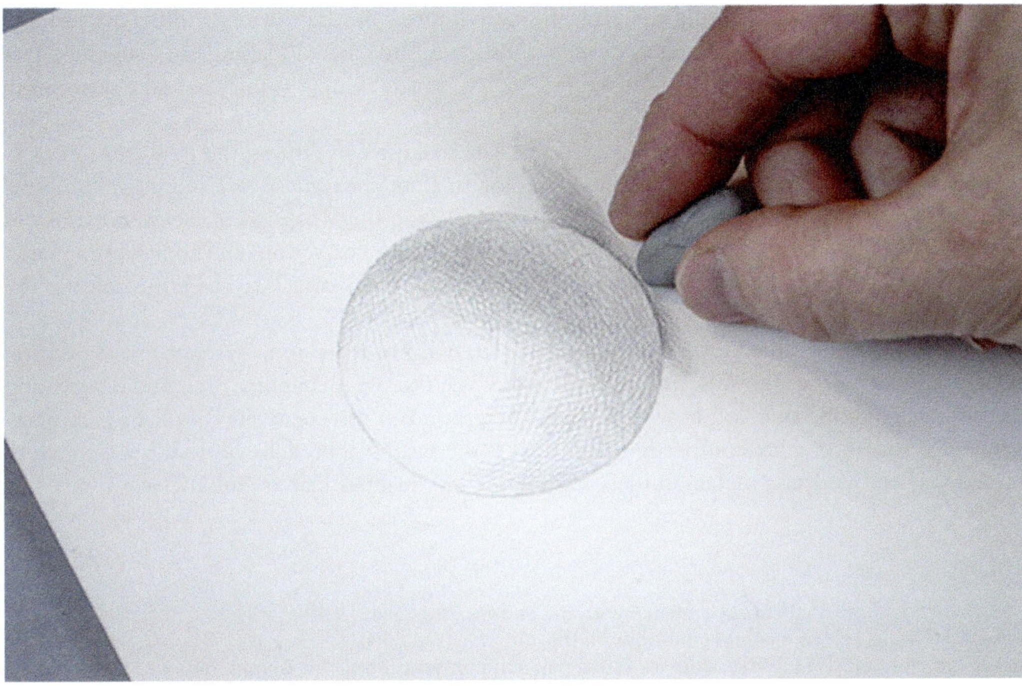

FIGURE 4.14 Carefully lifting metalpoint marks with a kneaded eraser

much or too vigorous daubing can actually lift the ground off the support, revealing the substrate underneath.

It is also possible to abrade a drawing to make corrections. A fine-bladed knife or a razor blade will chip away the metal and some of the ground, exposing either a fresh layer of ground or the white substrate, to remove a single, errant line or as an effect to reintroduce light into a tonal area. Care should be taken to drag the blade very, very gently over the area, so as not to create a "furrow" that cannot be drawn over. Some artists will use a small piece of sandpaper to remove metal marks, revealing a fresh area of ground that may or may not retain a residue of metalpoint work; this works best if the ground was sanded before making the drawing, so that the newly sanded area matches the rest of the ground in texture. Lightly sanding an initial sketch can reduce the visibility of the sketch so the sketch does not interfere visually with later work. This effect, if used purposefully, can create a palimpsest of effaced layers of drawing and sketching, adding meaning and memory to a work of art.

When working on prepared paper, there is a temptation to add more ground to cover a mistake, but repairs to a ground are usually visible – the addition of preparation can mean a patch that does not blend into the background, and working on a thicker patch of ground can produce a darker line in that one area compared to the adjacent areas. There is also the chance that the stylus will chip through the new ground if the patch does not adhere well. If it must be done, patch the ground in very thin layers, feathering the patch into the previous layers. This works best on water soluble grounds like rabbit skin glue or gouache, as the edges of the patch will melt a little into the ground. When working with tinted grounds it is next to impossible to patch an area, even if using leftover preparation, because the new layers will often dry to a different opacity. Creatively adding ground to an area is the best solution in this case – blocking out a whole shape, then redrawing over the new patch or using the correction as an opportunity to add a contrasting tint of ground or even mixed media.

The tarnishing of some metals is also an issue when making corrections; the new area of drawing may not match the area that has changed color, at least not right away, and possibly never. One way to force additions to tarnish quickly is by placing the work in an enclosed bathroom where hot water has created high humidity. In general, getting corrections and additions to match earlier work in metalpoint involves just waiting for the metal to tarnish to the same color as the original marks.

Overcoming the limitations and exploiting the strengths of metalpoint are part of the exciting process of using this medium. Learning all the many ways to use metalpoint tools and discovering the subtle relationship of colors between metals and grounds is also creatively stimulating. Expecting metalpoint to do what another medium does is the wrong approach; while it is adaptable to familiar ways of working, metalpoint has capabilities and qualities that are uniquely its own.

Notes

1 Michael Nichols, email correspondence with the author, 29 January 2018.
2 Susan Schwalb, telephone conversation with the author, 30 May 2018.
3 It has to be mentioned in the context of materials and conservation that it is unknown whether the plasticizers in erasers will adhere to prepared papers, leaving a residue that will contaminate or discolor the ground over time.

5

MIXED MEDIA

Carol Prusa

Metalpoint has frequently been combined with other media from its early use to today. Historically, it was used as underdrawing for ink and wash; pale metalpoint drawings were sometimes reinforced with crayon or charcoal, and white "body color" was used with metalpoint on tinted grounds to provide a chiaroscuro effect. Today artists employ many different drawing media, so it is not surprising that they also reach for graphite, carbon, colored pencils, and pastels to add to their metalpoint drawings. Working in wash provides a bridge between drawing and painting and as a result, ink, watercolor, and gouache are often combined with metalpoint, particularly when the support is paper. Acrylic and oil paint are used with metalpoint, both as grounds and in mixed media fashion. Unusual metalpoint combinations include digital technology and constructed forms that bridge the fields of drawing, photography, and sculpture.

When using mixed media on a metalpoint ground, the qualities of the ground need to work for all the media being used. Experimentation and testing become essential, since there are many brands and products that can produce viable grounds for metalpoint, and often some compromises must be made when combining several media on one ground (Figure 5.1).

Dry Media

Traditional dry media, including graphite, pastel, and colored pencil, are used in mixed-media metalpoint drawings to deepen the range of values, as well as to introduce color. Metalpoint grounds generally work well with these materials.

Graphite and Carbon

Discovered around 1550, graphite is a form of carbon that quickly superseded metalpoint as a drawing medium. Available in many forms, from pencils to sticks, powders, and liquids, graphite has the ability to provide a wide tonal range from pale fine lines to rich, reflective blacks. While graphite is traditionally used on plain paper, it also works well on chalky grounds but not on many

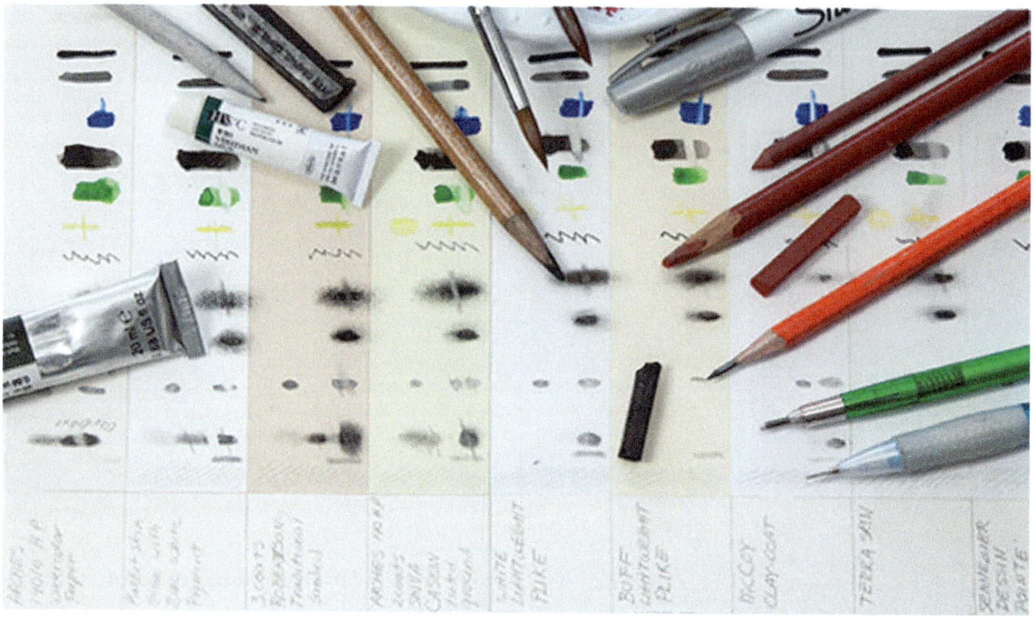

FIGURE 5.1 Test samples of various grounds and media

acrylic grounds or the clay-coated papers typically used for metalpoint. Marks in pencil are sometimes hard to remove from metalpoint grounds and so should be done very lightly.

Graphite and metalpoint both have a reflective sheen, and it would seem natural to combine them together, but graphite is very slick, and when used as an underdrawing, it will resist further metalpoint work. However, adding graphite to a completed metalpoint drawing can increase value range and contrast (Figure 5.2). In addition to direct application with a pencil, liquid and powdered graphite can also be applied with small brushes to deepen the tonal range.

Artist Robyn Ellenbogen (American, b. 1953) enjoys exploring different media combined with metalpoint and has used liquid graphite in her work (Figure 5.3). She states that

> Drawing on the surface of liquid graphite feels akin to burnishing and seems to deepen the reflective quality of the metalpoint. . . . I also incorporate liquid graphite as a discrete element in metalpoint paintings and this allows for a range of atmospheric mark-making. The tinted liquid graphite adds a subtle color relationship to metalpoint.[1]

Carbon art materials are made from soot, which has a looser chemical structure than graphite and is therefore very soft, smooth, and pure black in color. Carbon applies well and erases cleanly on traditional grounds like casein and rabbit-skin glue but adheres poorly on smooth commercial metalpoint papers. Supports prepared with most acrylic products also resist a dense application of carbon, but Weber Prima and Golden acrylic gessoes work well.

Carbon is dusty and dry and will not stick to dense areas of metalpoint, but metalpoint can be worked over carbon. The more abrasive and porous the surface, the more densely the carbon can accumulate and the darker it will get. A finer abrasive surface will allow for more subtle value gradations and cleaner erasing. A vinyl eraser can manipulate values and create sharp edges, and a

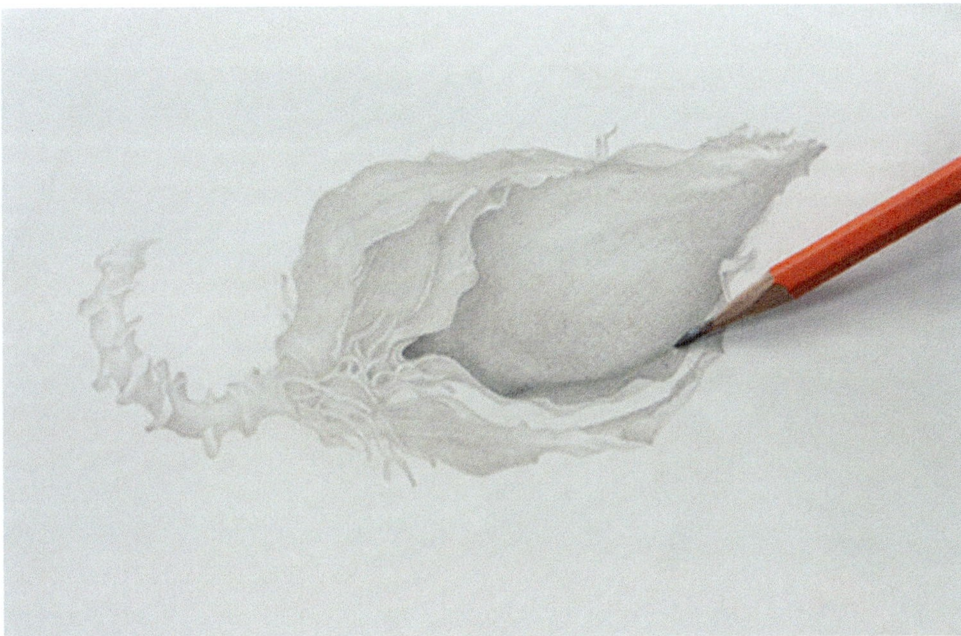

FIGURE 5.2 Deepening the value range of metalpoint with addition of graphite pencil

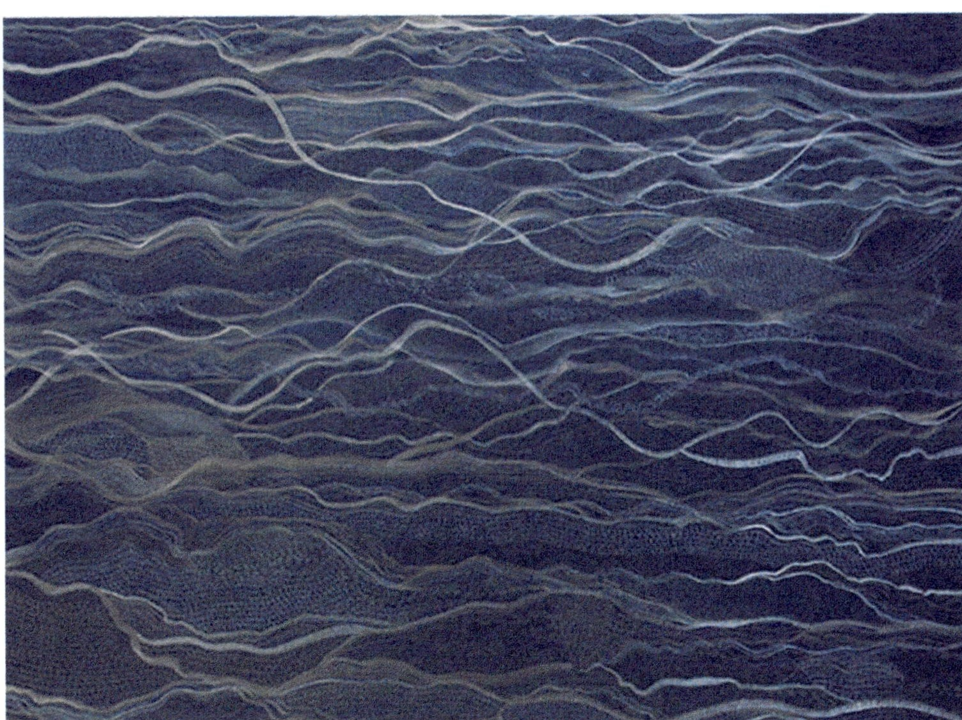

FIGURE 5.3 Robyn Ellenbogen, *On the Membranes of Mountains*, 2018, gold, silver, aluminumpoint, metal wire brush, liquid graphite, colored pencils, on colored gesso wood panel, 18 × 24 inches (45.72 × 60.96 cm), courtesy of the artist

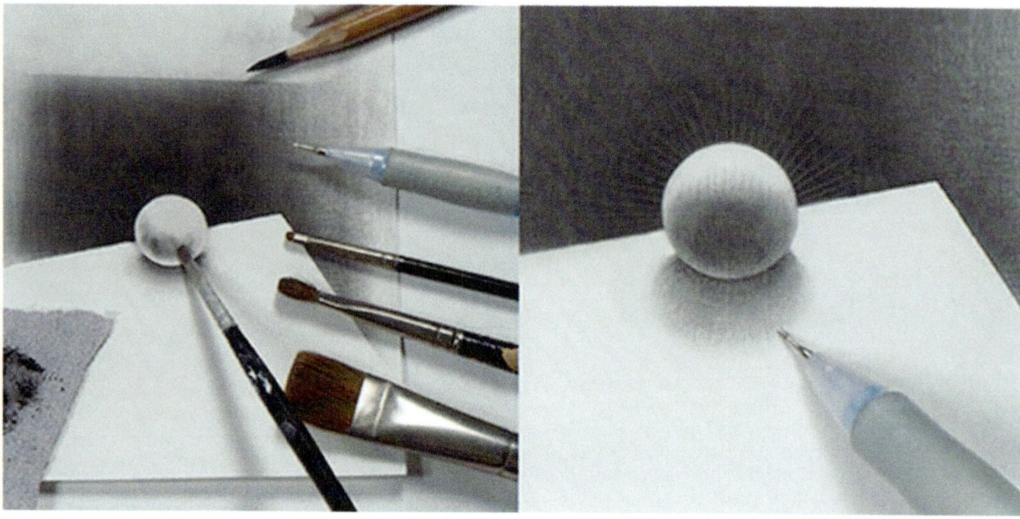

FIGURE 5.4 Silverpoint with carbon dust

kneaded eraser can soften areas of contrast. Fine value transitions can be achieved with powdered carbon and soft-haired brushes, and crisp edges are achieved by brushing the carbon onto the paper along a tape or paper mask (Figure 5.4).

Colored Pencil

Joseph Stella (American, 1877–1946) is well known for his precise and rigorous drawings that combine colored pencils and silverpoint in a series of nature studies focused on a singular form floating on the page (for an example, see Figure 7.1). A colored pencil is essentially a crayon made of pigment and wax, encased in wood, and sharpened like a graphite pencil. A higher pigment-to-binder ratio produces a better quality pencil, with preferred brands being Berol Prismacolor and Faber-Castell Polychromos. The two typical colored pencil techniques are *layering*, or lightly combining colors next to one another to gradate tones while still showing paper color, and *burnishing*, or applying colored pencil with enough pressure to mix all the colors to a uniform gradation.[2]

Colored pencils can be sharpened to a fine point to make marks that blend well with metalpoint, and the sheen of colored pencil is similar to the luster of metal. Colored pencil adheres well to most metalpoint surfaces, as long as they are not too slick; Plike and TerraSkin papers work well, as do Golden Silverpoint Ground and traditional preparations. Colored pencil produces a waxy surface resistant to further work in metalpoint and should be added last (Figure 5.5).

More traditional than colored pencil, conté crayons are also made from pigment and wax or clay and are synonymous with the sanguine, black, and white drawing sticks primarily used in *aux trois crayons* technique. Conté crayons work well on most metalpoint papers and grounds, but do not adhere well to Golden Silverpoint Ground. Some artists add soft white conté crayon into their metalpoint drawings on medium-toned ground to achieve a chiaroscuro effect, working from the paper color toward light with strokes of the crayon (Figure 5.6).

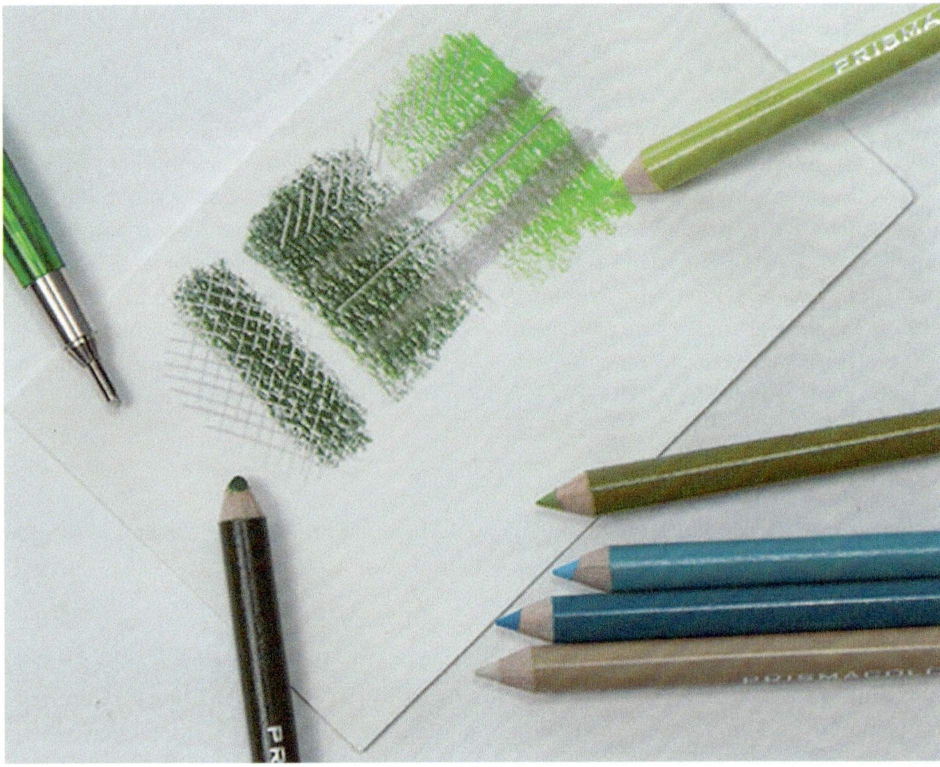

FIGURE 5.5 Example of metalpoint and colored pencil, showing the tendency of metalpoint to resist adhesion to colored pencil

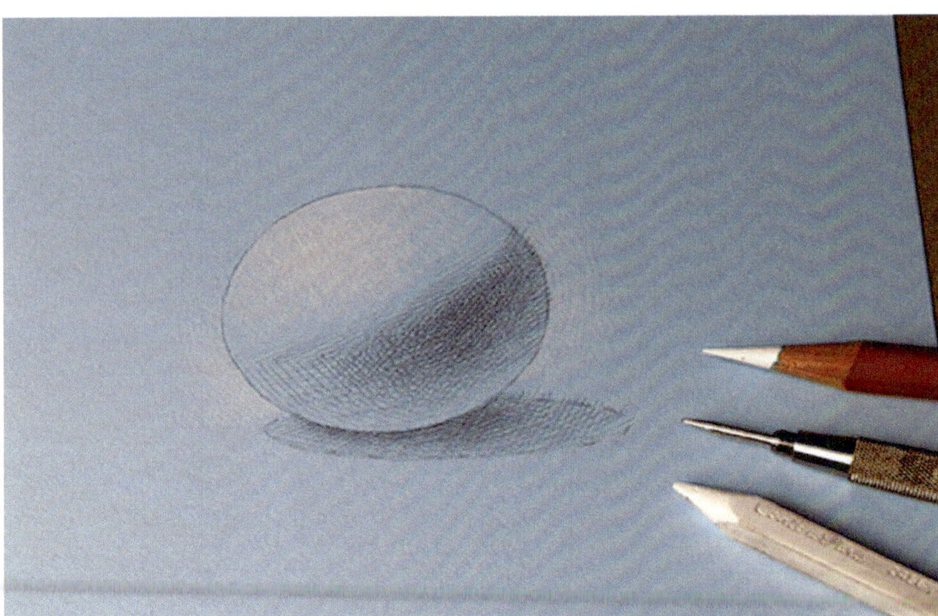

FIGURE 5.6 Chiaroscuro metalpoint drawing with white conté crayon

Soft Pastel

Soft pastel in its simplest form is a stick of pigment held together with gum arabic.[3] Good quality pastels are made by Sennelier and Schminke; Derwent produces the most preferred of pastel pencils. Pastels are offered in multiple tints of each hue, allowing precise application of color as needed. In addition to direct work, pastels can be applied to the ground with brushes for soft blooms of color that mix well with metalpoint marks (Figure 5.7). Soft pastels work particularly well on metalpoint grounds that have a moderately abrasive surface; Colourfix pastel paper and supports prepared with Roberson's Traditional Ground are particularly good for both, whereas acrylic grounds may be too smooth. Pastel has mixed results on commercial metalpoint papers; smooth transitions and minute detail can be achieved on Plike and TerraSkin, but not on most clay-coated papers.

Wet Media

Artists working in metalpoint have used paint to add color to their work for hundreds of years. Contemporary art sees these materials used together in surprising new ways.

Watercolor

Watercolor is one of the oldest painting mediums, using water as a vehicle for a mixture of finely ground pigment and gum arabic binder. When combining watercolor and metalpoint, the paper

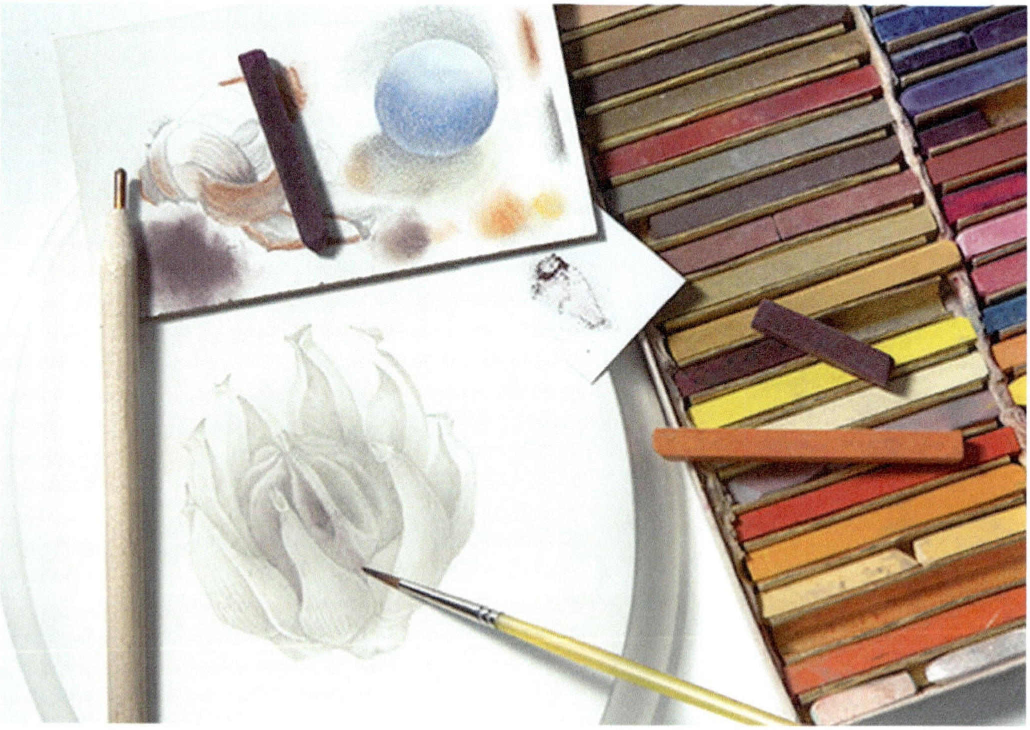

FIGURE 5.7 Soft pastel with metalpoint

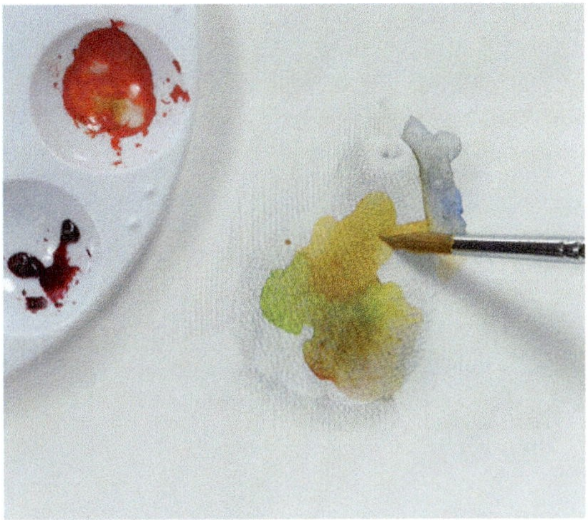

FIGURE 5.8 Example of watercolor over silverpoint drawing

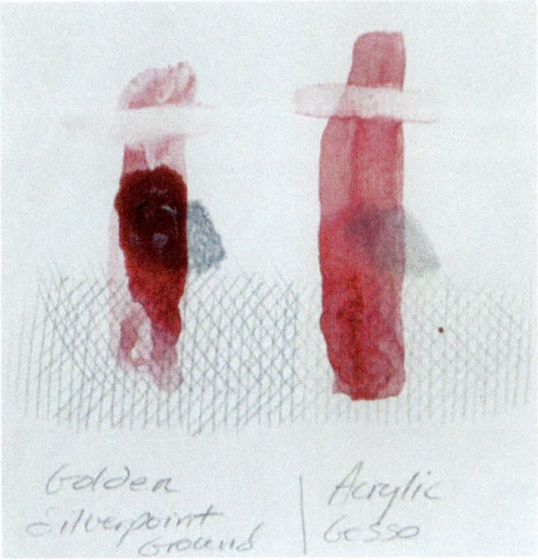

FIGURE 5.9 Watercolor over acrylic gesso ground and Golden Silverpoint Ground, showing *crawling* due to low absorbency

or board should be coated with an absorbent preparation that yields successful results with both, such as Golden Absorbent Ground (Figure 5.8). The less absorbent the surface is, the more the watercolor will *crawl* on the surface before drying. If the ground is too absorbent, however, the pigment is absorbed into the surface, dulling the color (Figure 5.9).

Watercolor on prepared papers often takes a long time to dry. Smooth surfaces, like Golden Silverpoint Ground and Plike paper, are resistant enough for the watercolor to cause crawling and beading, and once dry, areas could easily be lifted with water. Silverpoint combines well with watercolor on most acrylic gessoes. Weber Prima Acrylic Gesso offers the best adhesion while maintaining brilliance of watercolor and reception of metalpoint. Watercolor also works on papers coated with grounds, like Shiva Casein or rabbit-skin glue combined with zinc white; however, these grounds can lift when moistened, so delicate treatment is required.

Victor Koulbak (Russian, b. 1946) is particularly well known for his many works combining metalpoint and watercolor. He prepares his heavyweight deckle-edged paper (specially made for him at a mill in France, with a pronounced watermark bearing his initials) using marble powder mixed with rabbit-skin glue. His loosely applied ground makes the paper texture seem more physically present, although the ground sometimes appears scraped on, with the texture exaggerated. Silverpoint has an exquisite balance with watercolor in his work, providing subtle emphasis and precise delineation (Figure 5.10).

Ink

Like watercolor, ink is one of the oldest drawing mediums, dating back 5,000 years. Black ink is made from finely ground soot or from compounds leeched from oak galls or black walnuts. Modern inks come in all colors, using water either alone or in combination with volatile solvents. Inks can be applied with all types of pens, markers and watercolor brushes, and they can be thinned to produce washes similar to that of watercolor.

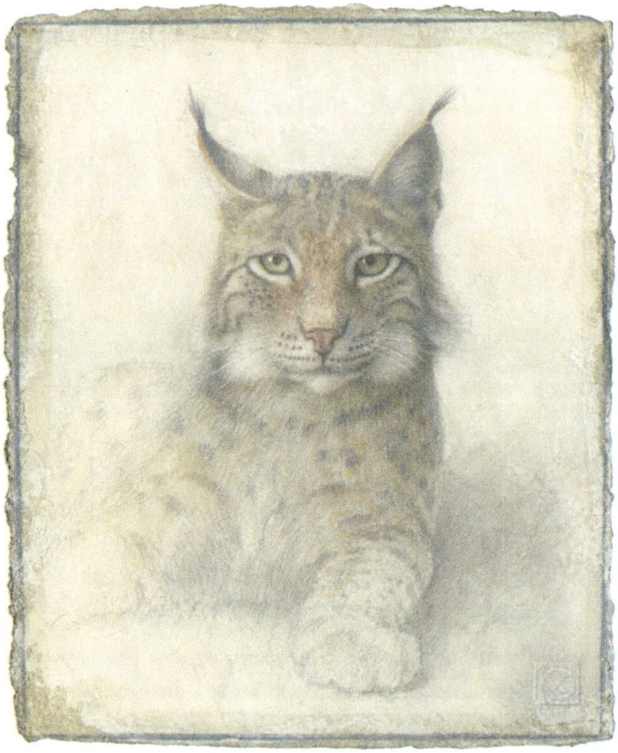

FIGURE 5.10 Victor Koulbak, *Lynx* 2014, silverpoint, watercolor on handmade paper, 12 1/2 × 10 inches (31.75 × 25.4 cm), © Victor Koulbak, courtesy of Didier Aaron Inc., New York

Plike, McCoy Clay Coat, TerraSkin, and Sennelier Dessin Pointe d'Argent papers all give good results with ink. Similar to watercolor, ink washes crawl on Golden Silverpoint Ground and on regular acrylic paint. Generally, grounds that support watercolor will support ink and ink wash, though they remain fluid longer on insoluble grounds, such as acrylic gesso. Care must also be taken if clear gesso is prepared on top of a completed ink drawing or ink jet print, as some of the solvents in acrylic preparations may dissolve even water-resistant inks. Sarah Sands, writing in the magazine *Just Paint* from Golden Artist Colors, suggests adding a layer of varnish over an ink drawing if an acrylic ground is to be layered on top.[4]

Someone who exploits the potential of combining metalpoint drawing with ink wash is Dale O. Roberts (American, b. 1959). In his work *Dissolving Sill Life*, Roberts used hatched lines of silverpoint in his still life drawing, then added loosely applied ink wash to toned casein ground on acid-free board. He employed the wash, in his word, "abstractly," allowing it to dissolve the underlying ground as well as overlaying it (Figure 5.11).[5]

Acrylic and Oil Paints

First used as industrial paints, acrylics for artists were developed by Golden in the late 1940s. Acrylic paints use a polymer emulsion as their binder and water as the solvent but become

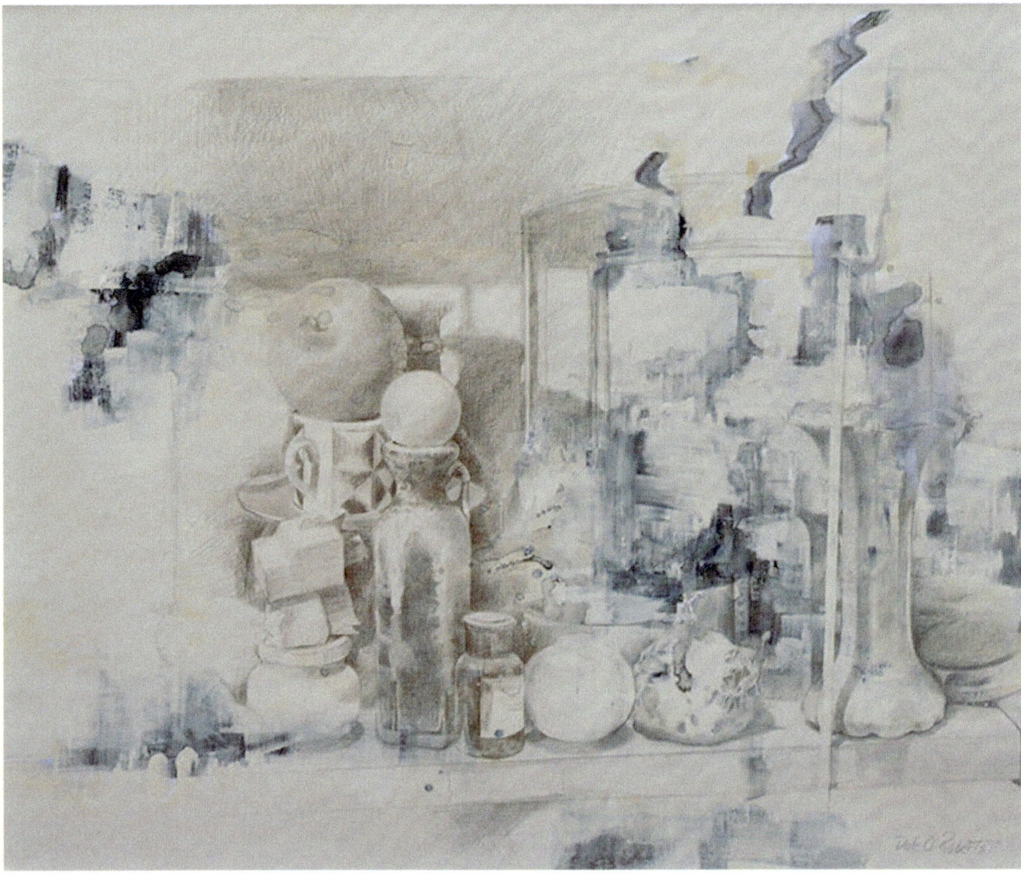

FIGURE 5.11 Dale O. Roberts, *Dissolving Still Life*, 2017, silverpoint with ink wash and toned casein ground on acid free board, 16 1/2 × 19 1/2 inches (41.91 × 49.53 cm), courtesy of the artist

waterproof when dry. Liquitex, Holbein, and M. Graham are also good quality brands. They are available as heavy body paints or as fluids and can be used straight, thinned, or as washes. There are many additives and modifiers available to increase the body, texture, drying time, and fluidity of these versatile paints. Acrylics are also available as many kinds of *mediums*, with gloss and matte finishes and as gessoes, pastes, and even varnishes. Unlike oil mediums, acrylic paints and gessoes dry quickly and are quite suitable for use on plain paper; they seal the surface and will not leech into the support and discolor it over time. Acrylic paint adheres well to most metalpoint grounds, but if the acrylic paint application involves overlapping brush strokes or a lot of watery paint, water-soluble preparations such as casein, gouache, or rabbit-skin glue will likely be disturbed.

Many acrylic paints are too slick to use with metalpoint, but the binder/pigment ratio of better brands offers more tooth to the surface of the paint. The metalpoint work of Susan Schwalb (American, b. 1944) relies both on the color of grounds as well as metals. After working on commercial papers, she eventually moved to acrylic gesso on Arches hot-pressed watercolor paper as she added more color into her work. Schwalb made a series of works titled *red/white/blue*, in

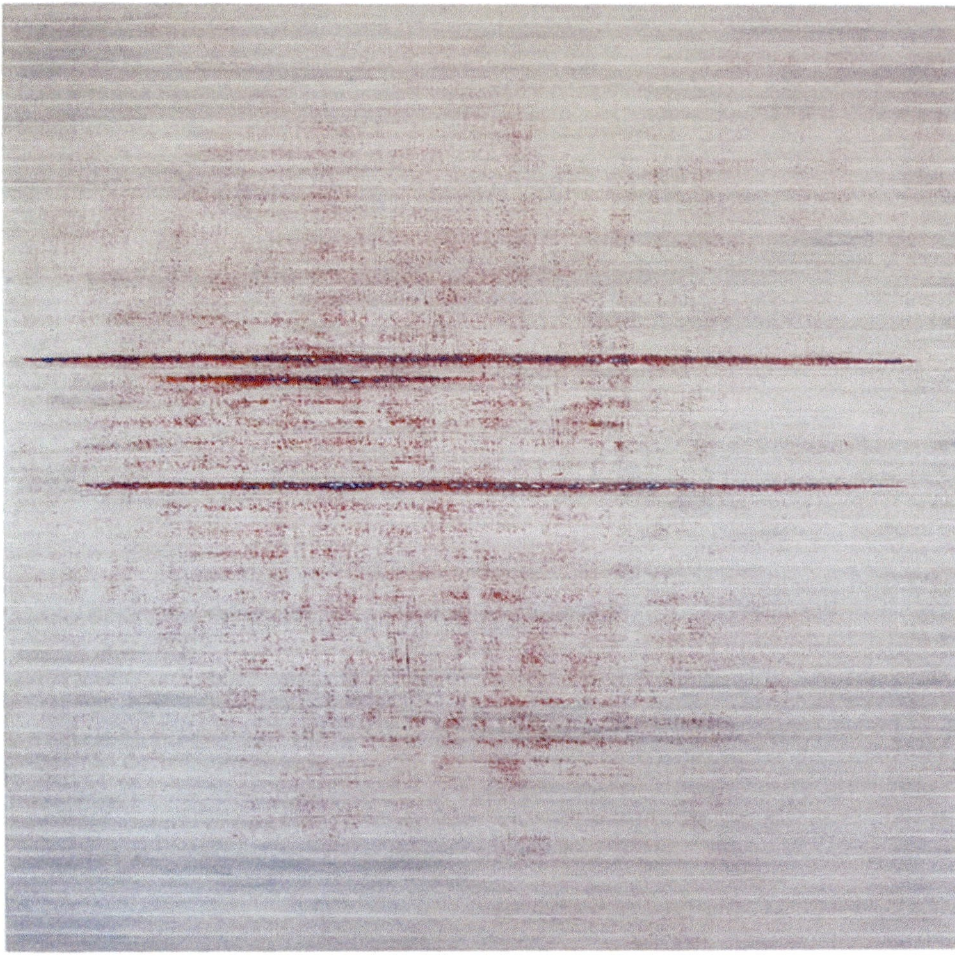

FIGURE 5.12 Susan Schwalb, *red/white/blue VII*, 2002, silverpoint, acrylic on paper on panel, 30 × 30 × 2 inches (76.2 × 76.2 × 5.1 cm), courtesy of the artist

which she combined layers of acrylic paint with metalpoint on top, applied mostly with flat pieces of metal (Figure 5.12). She writes,

> I used 3 or 4 layers of different colored Liquitex acrylic paint. I sanded each layer after it was dry. When all of the layers dried I lightly sanded the top layer enough to bring up some of the color of the layers beneath. Then I drew with flat pieces of metal to make bands of tone and then using a piece of folded sandpaper, I sanded inside the bands to reveal more of the colors underneath. This gave the illusion of gashes on the surface.[6]

Acrylics can be applied with bristle brushes, watercolor brushes, or with an airbrush; when using acrylic under metalpoint, layers of thin paint are usually applied with a soft brush. Even acrylic washes have enough tooth to act as a ground, especially when used over gesso, opening possibilities of layers of marks and transparent color (Figure 5.13).

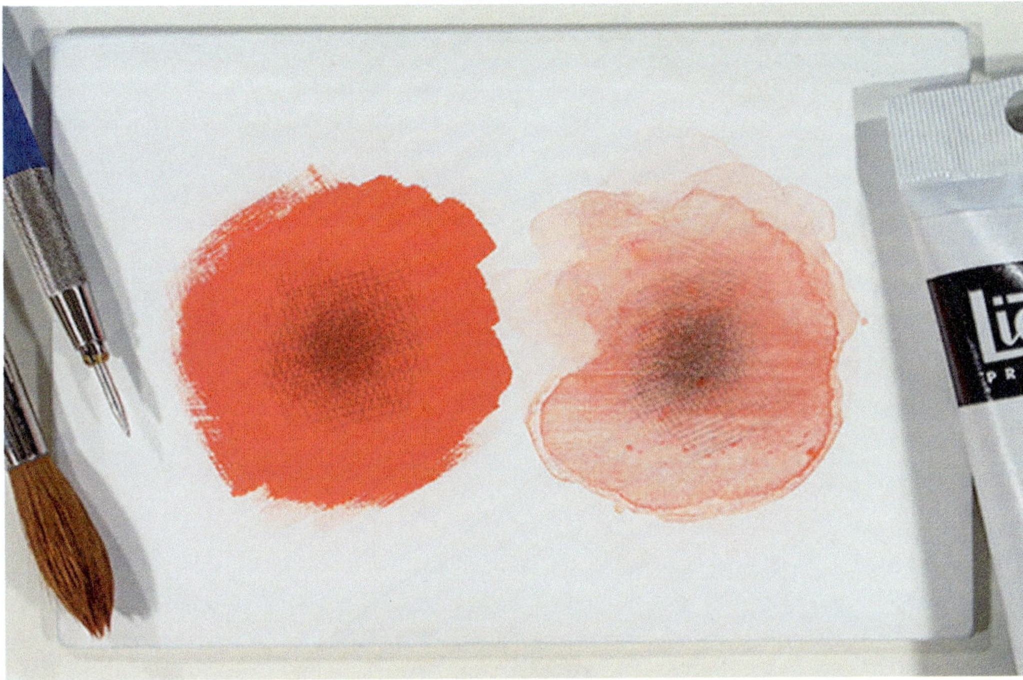

FIGURE 5.13 Silverpoint on acrylic wash and flat acrylic paint, both applied to gessoed panel

While metalpoint can work on top of acrylic paints, oil paint in general creates too smooth and tough a surface for the metal to adhere reliably. Oil paints have been around for more than half a millennium and use slow-drying linseed oil as their vehicle; their increased drying time allows the creation of minute detail and finely blended gradations of color. Widely available in many different grades and hues as a thick paste, oil paint can be thinned with linseed oil and mineral solvents, and it dries to a very smooth, permanent emulsion.

Care must be taken when preparing surfaces for work in oils; often oil paint will degrade papers, canvases, and boards unless those surfaces are first sealed, typically with acrylic gesso. To preserve paper color, clear acrylic gesso makes a good sealer. Oil paint also bonds well with Golden Absorbent Ground. Oil paint is most often used in combination with metalpoint on canvas and wood panel, where the surface has been sealed first, then prepared with a ground that works well for both oil paint and metalpoint. It should be noted that oil paint has poor adhesion on Golden Silverpoint Ground.

Sometimes artists draw in metalpoint to produce an under-drawing for oil glazes. Kate Kretz (American, b. 1963), known for intense oil glaze paintings as well as meticulous silverpoint drawings, says,

> I recently experimented with putting a transparent oil glaze down over the silverpoint drawing, to add the lightest tint of color. The silver acts as a type of resistance, and the subtle, quiet effect is quite similar to a hand-colored black and white photograph.[7]

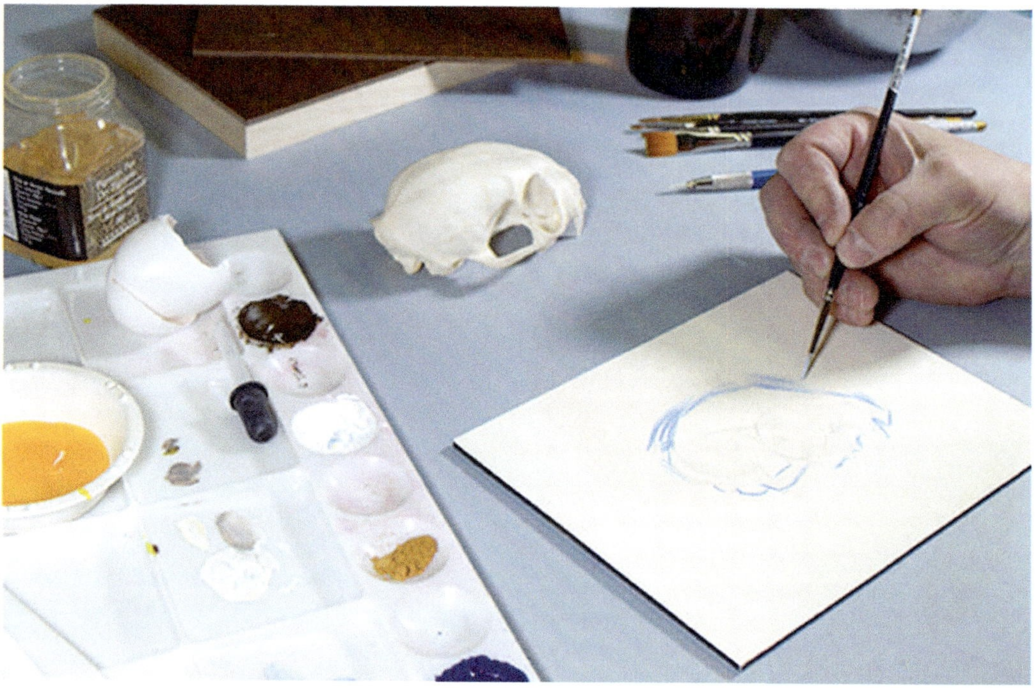

FIGURE 5.14 Materials for egg tempera and using egg tempera over a silverpoint underdrawing

Egg Tempera

Egg tempera is one of the oldest painting mediums, consisting of finely-ground pigment mixed with egg yolk, which dries to a permanent emulsion. It has been in use for thousands of years, and the technique was only superseded by oil painting in the fifteenth century. Egg tempera and metalpoint historically used the same ground: traditional gesso made of rabbit-skin glue, marble dust, and white pigment, chalk, or bone ash. Grounds for egg tempera painting are generally prepared in several layers and sanded smooth to provide a slightly chalky, porous, paper-like surface. Tempera dries quickly, so that a line of color will often be dry before the brush leaves the surface. Egg medium is notoriously inflexible and should be applied to a rigid support; the ground needs to be porous enough to hold the paint so it does not crawl when applied or crack off when dry. Natural Pigments Rublev Tempera Ground is manufactured specifically to be porous enough to hold egg tempera, and there are pre-made supports with usable smooth grounds, such as Ampersand Clayboard. Since egg tempera underpainting can be layered with oil paint, a drawing in metal is sometimes done first, with egg tempera used in areas on top of it and oil glaze used at the end (Figure 5.14). Egg tempera crawls on acrylic paint and Golden Silverpoint Ground, but it layered well on Liquitex clear gesso, Daniel Smith transparent watercolor ground, and Golden Absorbent Ground.

Artist Koo Schadler (American, b. 1962), known primarily as an egg tempera painter, also works in metalpoint, often combining the two. She uses Rublev Tempera Ground and emphasizes optical color blending through layered strokes of color (Figure 5.15). Schadler says,

> I begin by building up lines and layers using a variety of metal tips and metal wool pads until the drawing is more or less established. Next, I cover the entire surface with a fresh layer of whatever ground I initially used, often lightly tinted with pigment. I re-apply the ground so thinly . . . that the drawing underneath shows through. On top of this I once again develop the image using various metalpoints. The new layer of ground creates fresh "tooth," allowing for deeper darks to be developed. . . . Near the end I'll intensify darks, pull out highlights, and/or add a bit of color using egg tempera mostly, although I sometimes work with gouache, ink, or graphite as well.[8]

Gouache

Gouache is a water-based paint akin to watercolor, sharing a gum arabic binder, but opaque, with the addition of chalk and less finely ground pigment to increase opacity. It adheres well to acrylic gesso and traditional gesso ground, but it has a tendency to flake and chip and should be used on rigid surfaces. Heavy watercolor paper, illustration board, and Bristol board are recommended for use with gouache. Artists will sometimes use an additive like *glair* (a medium made from egg

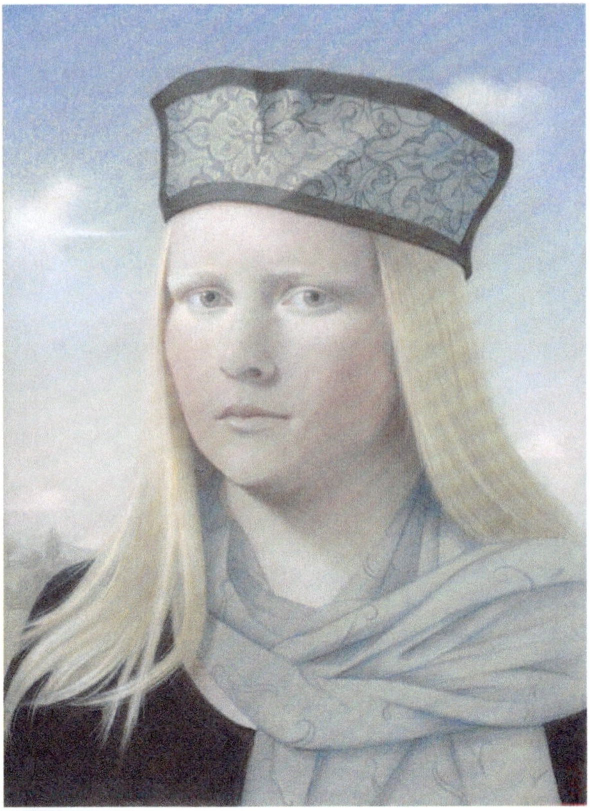

FIGURE 5.15 Koo Schadler, *Lily & Landscape*, 2018, silverpoint, aluminumpoint, and copperpoint, copper wool pad, egg tempera on blue-tinted Rublev Tempera Ground, 7 × 5 inches (17.8 × 12.7 cm), courtesy the artist

white) to increase adhesion and flexibility, but this will alter the sheen of the dry paint. Traditionally, white gouache has been used to create highlights when working in a chiaroscuro manner with metalpoint on a medium-toned paper. It can be thinned to build up areas with a fine brush or used full-strength to pack a punch of opaque color. The chalky nature of gouache makes it perfect for use under metalpoint drawing, and areas of different colors may first be *blocked in* and then detailed or worked over with metalpoint. Gouache's tendency to chip, however, means care must be taken to create both a flat surface for the metal and a thin, consistent area that the metal will not gouge.

Artist Andrea Sherrill Evans (American, b. 1982) uses gouache to add areas of dramatic color in her silverpoint drawings (Figure 5.16). She describes her process:

> Working with gouache (I use Holbein Artists' Gouache) on a metalpoint ground, as opposed to more absorbent unprepared paper, does not allow for as much fussing with the surface. I learned early on to develop the areas of color first, before the more time-consuming silverpoint drawing, in case of any errors. . . . As the gouache does not absorb very deeply into the surface, it remains rather delicate. I try to leave it as undisturbed as possible while working on the rest of the drawing.[9]

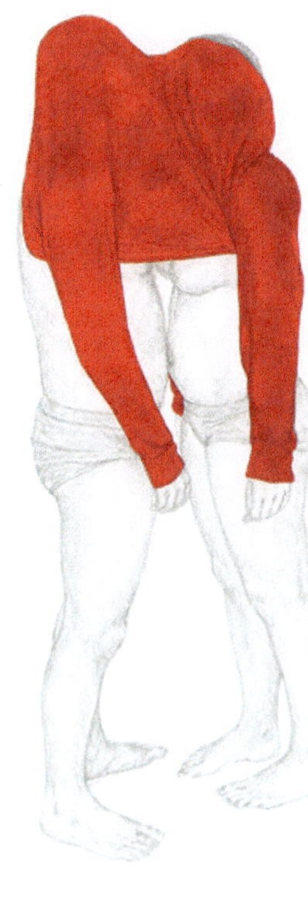

FIGURE 5.16 Andrea Sherrill Evans, *Union Suit #6*, 2007, silverpoint and gouache on prepared paper, 14 × 9 inches (35.56 × 22.86 cm), courtesy of the artist

Most fine artists have a variety of painting media available to them in the studio, and contemporary art often blurs the line between painting and drawing. Combining wet media with metalpoint is a natural idea for both traditional and contemporary artists, as long as care is taken to preserve the compatibility of both.

Additional Media

Mixed media artists are experimenters and explorers, and as new materials and technologies enter the field, they naturally invite them into their studios. One of the primary means of expression employed by contemporary artists is the use of photography, and there are even means of incorporating moving images into metalpoint work.

Digital Projection

One way of combining video with metalpoint work is to use a drawing as a background for a projected image. Using found metal objects to mark her zinc white gouache ground, Erika Winstone (British, b. 1957) combines scribbled drawings and layered writing to create metalpoint drawings with a conceptual reference to her body's gesture (to the point that her actions tear the paper in places). She documents her movement with a video, which she then projects on top of her metalpoint drawings (Figure 5.17) so that, as Winstone states,

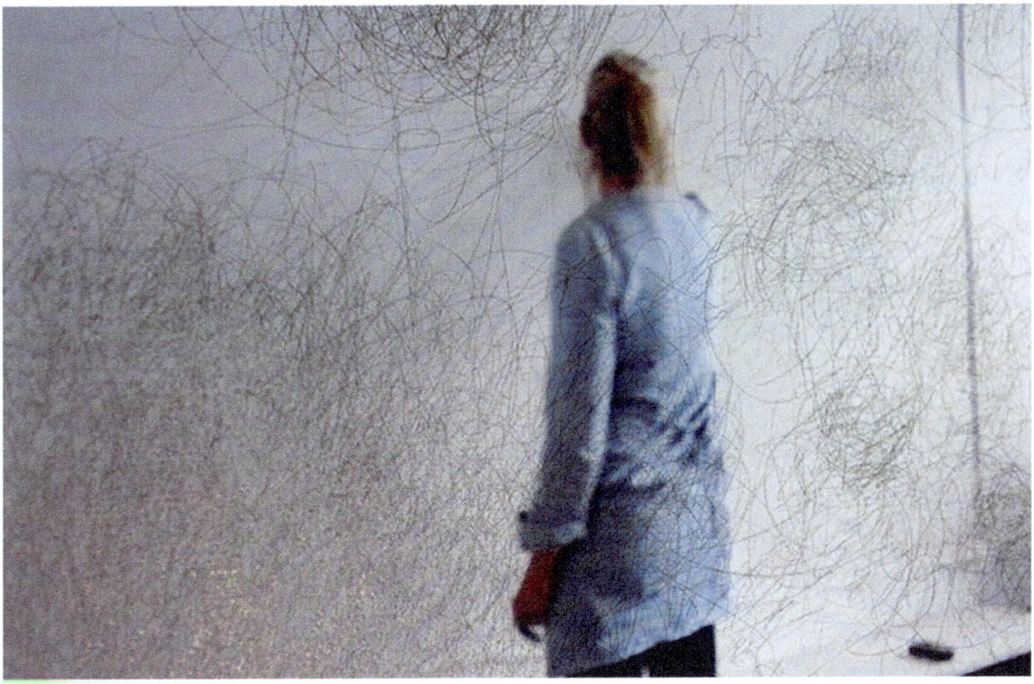

FIGURE 5.17 Erika Winstone, *The Rink and Talent Show*, 2015, HD video projection, glass panel, silverpoint, gold point, gouache, canvas, installation, 144 × 120 inches (365.75 × 304.8 cm), courtesy of the artist

> My work is the result of an ongoing dialogue between video and painting. . . . I combine both personal everyday observation and feature films including relationships between who we are, and who we would like to be. . . . The presentation creates a space . . . to contemplate a dialogue between painting and video and notice the connections and correspondences that may subsequently emerge.[10]

Inkjet Prints

Artists have used inkjet prints in their work since consumer-grade and professional computer printers became available. Over the years, the quality of ink has increased with the capabilities of graphics to allow photo-quality reproductions to be made quickly and for very little money. Adding mixed media to an inkjet print opens up a huge field for incorporating photography and computer-generated imagery with metalpoint. However, when working with metalpoint grounds on inkjet prints, it is important to consider the archival quality of the ink along with the adhesion of the inks to the ground. Prepared papers have been used with mixed success; clay-coated papers and plastic-like papers are not always suitable for water-based inkjet inks, and as the papers become thicker and lose their ink-absorbing characteristics, consumer printers work less reliably. Grounds can be applied to papers after printing. Most inkjet prints are produced with quick-drying dye-based inks which remain water soluble when dry, so sealing an inkjet print with shellac or another solvent-based varnish is recommended before applying an aqueous metalpoint ground. Several printers of this kind are on the market, and as long as there is no problem with water solubility with the ink and the ground, clear acrylic varnishes and sprays can be used with them.

Common substrates to use in printers are watercolor, printmaking, and rice papers as well as canvas and other fabrics. Less common are thin wood veneers, thin metals, and plastics. Golden Artist Colors has discontinued its digital ground for inkjet printing, but another suitable product is InkAID Clear Gloss Type II. It is an inkjet-receptive coating for paper, fabric, canvas, plastic, or practically anything you can put through your printer. It provides the same surface as many commercially produced gloss inkjet papers. InkAID is a water-based medium, and it will adhere to surfaces that work with aqueous paints. Since this medium is clear, it can be added over metalpoint drawing to create a surface receptive to inkjet printing. If additional media are to be used on top of it, it is important to know that InkAID Clear Gloss Type II is not water-resistant; care should be taken with fluid media, or else a varnish should be applied.

If metalpoint work is to be done on top of a printed image, clear gesso may be used to seal an inkjet print, and thin layers of gesso and some other grounds will serve as a suitable toothy surface for metalpoint work. Artist Elizabeth Whitely made samples of Epson Ultrachrome K3 inkjet prints on Epson Fine Art Velvet printing paper, coated with a single layer of Golden Silverpoint Drawing Ground that was toothy enough to take a metal mark (Figure 5.18).

Incorporating photographic or computer-based imagery into metalpoint work is in its infancy. But technology is moving rapidly, and this is one area of contemporary metalpoint that is fast developing.

CNC Drawing

A novel use of metalpoint has been developed by Mike Lyon (American, b. 1951), who employs a CNC (computer numerical control) machine that can hold metalpoint wire (Figure 5.19). He writes,

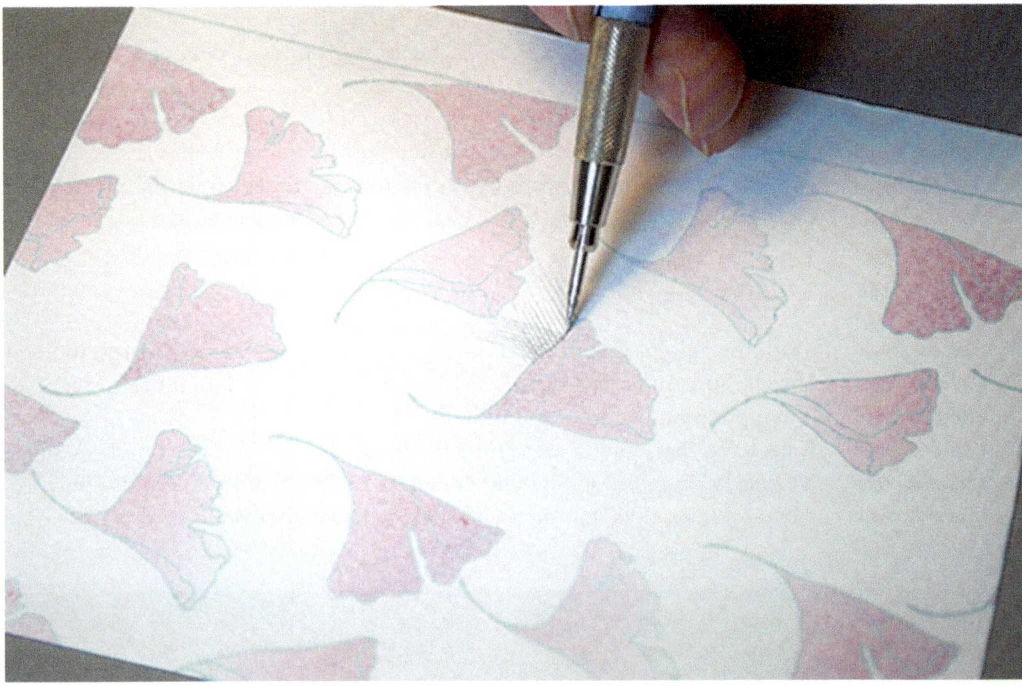

FIGURE 5.18 Metalpoint on Golden Silverpoint Drawing Ground over an inkjet print

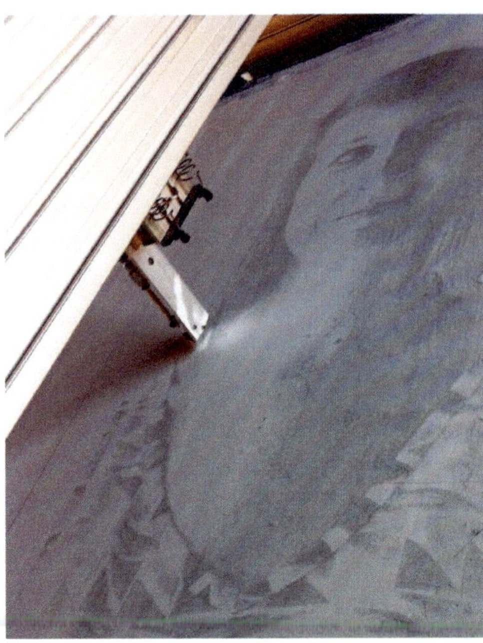

FIGURE 5.19 Mike Lyon, *Jessica*, copper point, 20 × 16 inches (50.8 × 40.64 cm), using CNC machine and specially made jig, process photograph, courtesy of the artist

> I made numerous experiments in machine drawing using silver, copper, and gold . . . on panels and papers prepared with commercial metalpoint grounds. I designed and built a number of simple jigs to hold the fine metal wires so that I could lift and drop them easily under program control using a solenoid mounted in my CNC machine. . . . In conceiving the drawings, I invented a sort of rational cross hatching by building many layers of concentric squiggles – the darkest values were over drawn many times while the palest were only drawn a few times.[11]

Unusual Supports

Sometimes the support for metalpoint is conceptually vital to the artwork. Shaped boards, molded plastic forms, found objects, and sculpted surfaces used as supports for metalpoint grounds are an emerging aspect of contemporary metalpoint multimedia work.

In one example, Kate Kretz has done a series of silverpoint drawings in the bowls of silver spoons called *Tempest/Deluge* (Figure 5.20). She was initially asked to create a silverpoint drawing for an exhibition, but five minutes after starting that drawing, Kretz discovered that

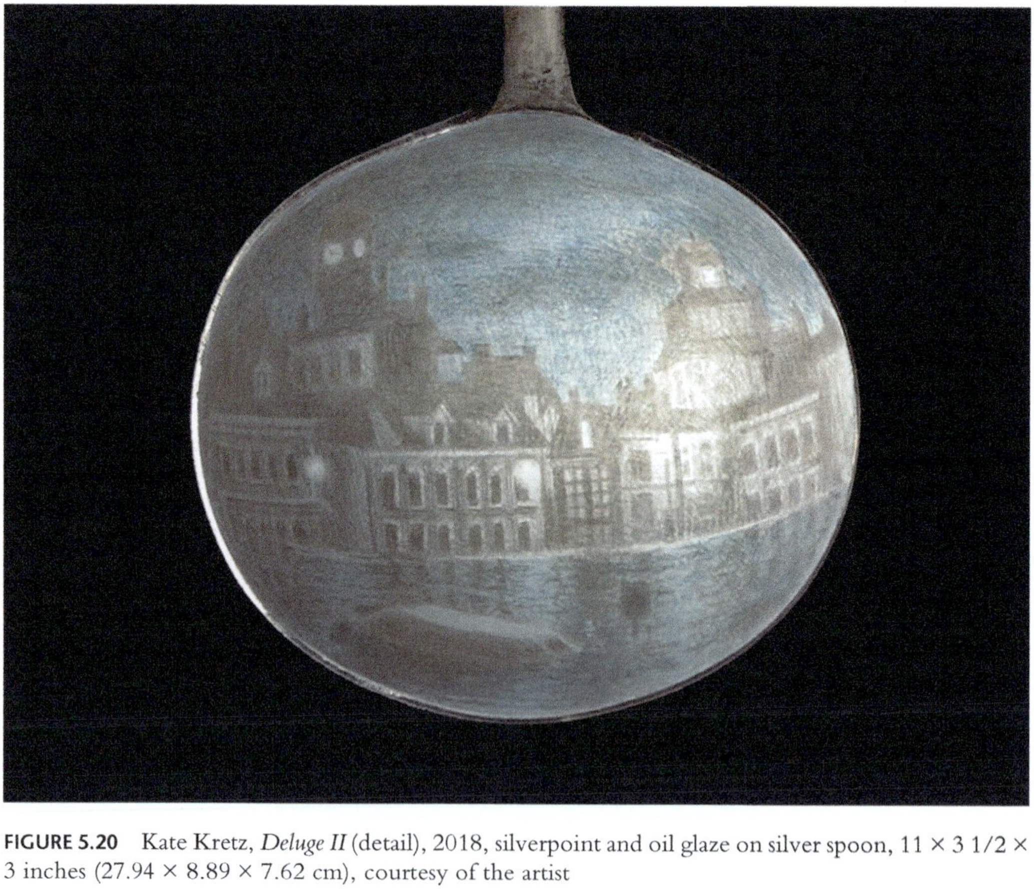

FIGURE 5.20 Kate Kretz, *Deluge II* (detail), 2018, silverpoint and oil glaze on silver spoon, 11 × 3 1/2 × 3 inches (27.94 × 8.89 × 7.62 cm), courtesy of the artist

> I knew exactly what it was going to look like when finished and lost interest. I headed to the thrift store, looking for silver objects to draw on. Spoons and ladles seemed most connected to my subject of storms and floods. I did some experiments and finally settled on a technique where I rough up the surface of the silver with sandpaper, prime it with metal primer, then use acrylic gesso. The challenge was in smoothly layering the gesso and sanding a concave surface. This was more time consuming than the actual drawing, but the challenge was motivating.[12]

Early on, Kretz drew in silverpoint over Liquitex Acrylic Gesso; recently she switched to Turner Acrylic Gouache. While she uses commercially available silverpoints, her favorite tool was made over thirty years ago by her mentor, Charles Eldred, who cut and filed her point from a piece of vintage silverware.

Carol Prusa (American, b. 1956) does metalpoint drawings over sanded and primed plexiglass spheres and domes. She hatches with silverpoint to create her drawings and deepens values with ground graphite applied with acrylic binder, then heightens with titanium white acrylic paint. Prusa often adds aluminum leaf to areas as well as fiber optic lights operated by internal programmed light emitters (Figure 5.21).

Further Examples of Metalpoint Mixed Media

Artists known for metalpoint use it as a major component of their work; however, when viewed as another drawing tool, metalpoint can accent or supplement a work without dominating it. Patricia Bellan-Gillen (American, b. 1952) is an artist known for combining painting, printmaking, and drawing methods into large scale works. She uses silverpoint to make an intimate and subtle area of drawing within her larger work, as in *Blind Spots/The Age of Discovery* (Figure 5.22). The surface for the silverpoint drawing is a mixture of high-grade, flat, interior wall paint and marble dust. Bellan-Gillen states that

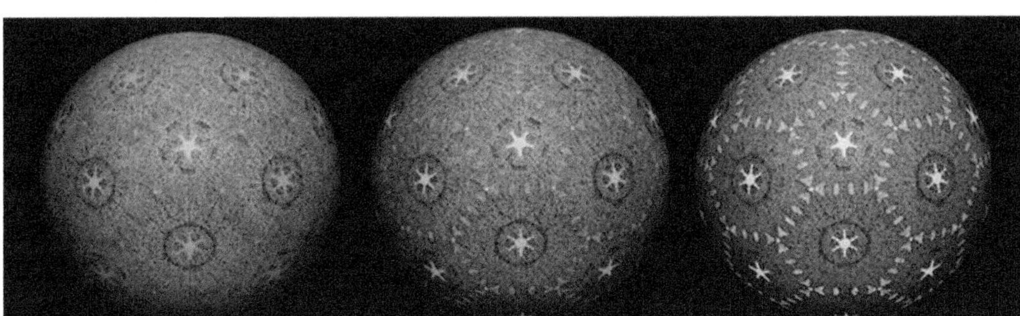

FIGURE 5.21 Carol Prusa, *Fearful Symmetry* (three views), 2013, silverpoint, ground graphite, titanium white pigment on acrylic form with programmed internal light, 36 × 36 × 36 inches (91.44 × 91.44 × 91.44 cm), courtesy of the artist

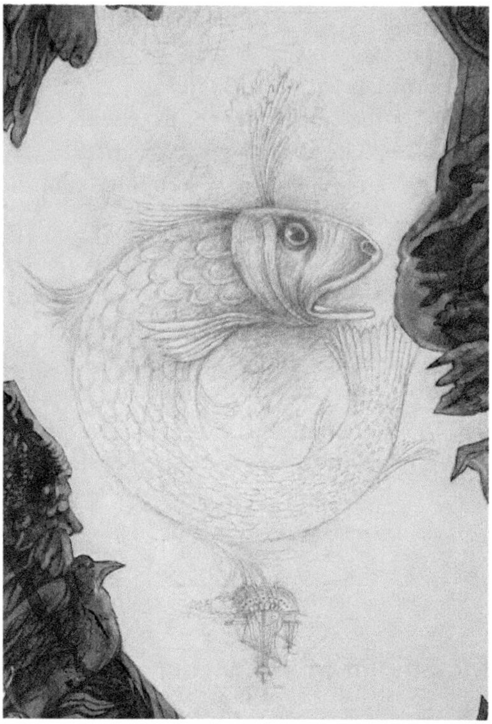

FIGURE 5.22 Patricia Bellan-Gillen, *Blind Spots/The Age of Discovery* (detail), 2017, colored pencil, acrylic, silverpoint on birch panel, 79 × 79 inches (200.66 × 200.66 cm), courtesy of the artist

> In 2015, I began a series of large-scale mixed media drawings with small bits of scrawled text on a glowing white field. . . . The physical quality of the silverpoint medium to be part of the field rather than sitting on the surface preserved the illusion of depth while making every mark of my handwriting apparent.[13]

An interesting example of multiple wet and dry media mixed with metalpoint is *Sunflower* by Gerald Hodge (American, 1920–2012), which uses carbon, conté crayon, coffee stains, and silverpoint on Video Media paper (Figure 5.23). In this work, he spilled coffee grounds and coffee onto the prepared paper to create a dynamic mottled surface, which was then controlled by his rigorous metalpoint drawing. Hodge writes, "Teaching in the scientific art field at the University of Michigan required me to be versatile in many scientific art techniques such as gouache, alkyd, acrylic, colored pencil, carbon dust, silverpoint, and pen and ink. . . ."[14]

There are many artists embracing metalpoint as more than a traditional drawing medium to be revered and practiced in the time-honored way. Since its reinvigoration in the late twentieth century, metalpoint has become one more drawing tool in the arsenal of the contemporary artist. Mixing metalpoint with other drawing media increases the value range of this otherwise pale and precious medium, and layering metalpoint with watercolor, ink, pastel, and color pencil can introduce color into what was originally only a gray drawing technique. Working on unusual substrates such as shaped forms, digital prints, and found objects is another way of continually breathing life into this traditional medium.

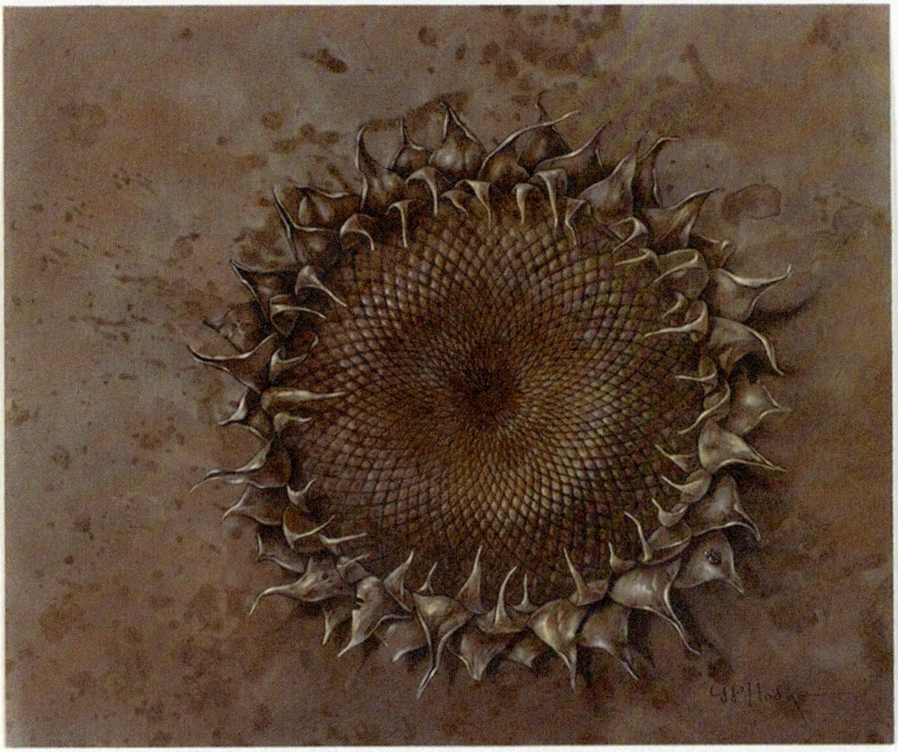

FIGURE 5.23 Gerald Hodge, *Sunflower*, 1968, carbon, conté, coffee stains, and silverpoint on video media paper, 10 7/8 × 12 3/4 inches (27.5 × 32.5 cm), Hunt Institute, Carnegie Mellon University, Accession no. 8060

Notes

1 Robyn Ellenbogen, email correspondence with the author, January 2018.
2 Susan Rubin, email correspondence with the author, January 2017.
3 Oil pastel is different from soft pastel, being an oil- and wax-based crayon that can be blended with solvents rather than with rubbing. The oil in oil pastel makes it largely unsuitable for work alongside metalpoint on prepared paper.
4 www.justpaint.org/waterproof-india-inks-and-shellac-based-primers. Accessed 3 January 2018.
5 Dale Roberts, email correspondence with the author, November 2017.
6 Susan Schwalb, email correspondence with the author, March 2017.
7 Kate Kretz, email correspondence with the author, November 2017.
8 Koo Schadler, email correspondence with the author, March 2017.
9 Andrea Sherrill Evans, email correspondence with the author, March 2017.
10 https://erikawinstone.net/site/about. Accessed 7 January 2018.
11 Mike Lyon, email correspondence with the author, November 2017.
12 Kate Kretz email correspondence with the author, November 2017.
13 Patricia Bellan-Gillen, email correspondence with the author, November 2017.
14 Ackhoff, Karen. "In Memoriam: Gerald P. Hodge," *Career Stories* (blog), Guild of Natural Science Illustrators, 20 June 2012, gnsi.org/career-stories/memoriam-gerald-p-hodge. Accessed 31 May 2018.

6

STORING, FRAMING, PHOTOGRAPHING, AND SHIPPING METALPOINT WORK

Handling and Storage

Works of art need care if they are going to last. Metalpoint drawings deserve special consideration, since they are difficult to repair or restore if they get damaged. Because these works are done on a ground, metalpoints are challenging to clean if they become stained, and works on paper are susceptible to creasing, buckling, tearing, and discoloring with age. All metalpoints share the danger of image loss should the ground separate from the underlying support. Margaret Holben Ellis discusses metalpoint conservation in a 1980 paper in the journal *Drawing*, noting that the ground may flake from the support over time, and suggests environmental causes: "A dry climate would hasten the weakening of the bond . . . with abrupt changes in humidity, the paper expands and contracts below the ground."[1] Ellis goes on to suggest that flaking, once started, only gets worse. On dealing with stains, Thea Burns notes: "Conservation treatments that involve water in its different forms and dry removal of superficial grime are not appropriate for metalpoint drawings as they may disrupt or destroy the ground, remove particles from the metal line, result in halos etc."[2] Additionally, while modern acrylic-based grounds are water-resistant, cleaning their surfaces would still abrade the thin metal image. Conservation is both a method of dealing with damage and the practice of daily care for valuable works of art. The best way to ensure longevity for metalpoint works is to use quality materials in their construction, to handle them carefully, and to store and mount them in an archival manner.[3]

Works on paper should be stored safely when not exhibited, because paper is susceptible to humidity, light, and changes in temperature. Ultraviolet (UV) radiation can cause colors to fade and paper to yellow and become brittle, which is called *light burn*. Acid-free papers are less susceptible to yellowing, but even the best quality paper suffers from the effects of light exposure. The ground applied to metalpoint paper will protect it a little, but the ground itself can fade or darken when exposed to light. Commercially prepared metalpoint papers are often made from wood pulp, and their clay coatings will not completely protect them. Works on paper can absorb moisture from the atmosphere and buckle or cockle, and uneven surfaces are especially susceptible to abrasion. The normal method of flattening works on paper by humidifying and weighting them under blotters can soften or delaminate aqueous metalpoint grounds. As with all works on paper, metalpoint drawings can be creased or torn or will fray at the edges. They are susceptible to indentation, and because of the difference in flexibility of ground and support, they should never be folded or rolled. In addition, absorbent metalpoint grounds pick up fingerprints and grease more easily than plain paper. The best way to deal with damage to a metalpoint is to prevent it in the first place by handling and storing the works as recommended by conservators.

Metalpoints should be stored flat, protected with a sheet of *interleaving* paper such as glassine, Holytex, or a sheet of acid-free drawing paper. For storing a substantial amount of work, a set of steel flat files provides the best long-term solution, but inexpensive archival storage boxes of many sizes can be bought from companies like Gaylord, University Products, or Talas. Mounting drawings on acid-free boards offers extra protection for long-term storage, and an acid-free top mat will protect the surface and neutralize acids and humidity. A folio made of hinged pieces of rigid, acid-free board is also good storage for a few loose works on paper. If possible, works on paper should be unframed between exhibitions and stored in their mounts in files or boxes to protect from long-term light exposure; the downside of this is the extra handling required (Figure 6.1).

Metalpoints done on wood panels also require special care. Works on tempered and untempered hardboard are much less susceptible to changes in humidity and are more resistant to flexing than works on paper or paperboard.[4] It is important, however to protect the surfaces from

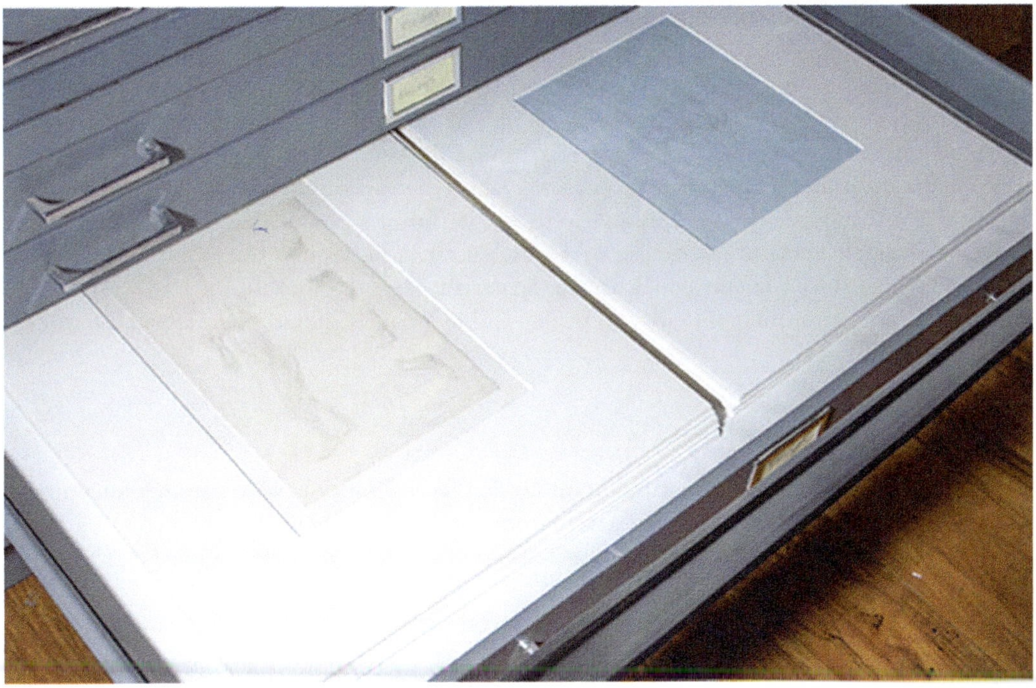

FIGURE 6.1 Metalpoint drawings, matted and stored in flat file drawers

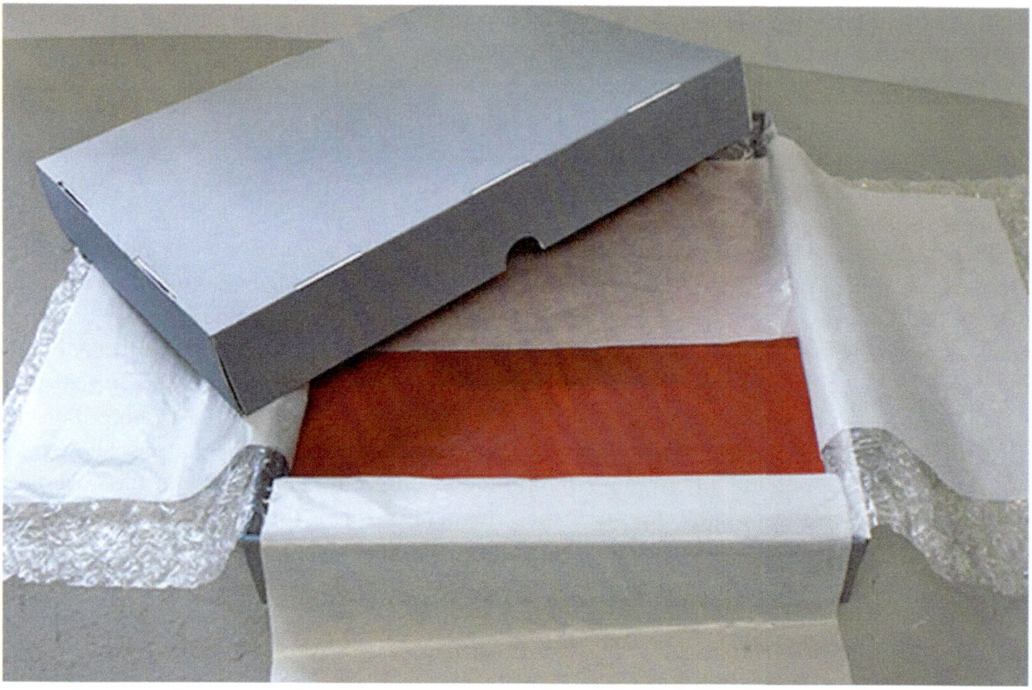

FIGURE 6.2 Talas storage box customized for a work on panel

indentations and scrapes, and finished panels and paperboards should be completely wrapped in acid-free paper. Cradled panels are generally hung, but they may also be wrapped in acid-free paper and soft foam before being stored in boxes or on shelves. Metalpoints done on wood panel are sometimes varnished, and generally an archival acrylic spray like Lascaux Fine Art Fixative is used rather than a brush-on varnish, so as to not disturb the ground and the delicate layer of marks. It is not advisable to use shellac or traditional oil varnishes like Damar on top of a metalpoint drawing, since solvents could damage materials in the ground. In the end varnish only offers protection from mild abrasion, so even varnished panels should be wrapped for storage (Figure 6.2).

Mounting and Framing

The variety of supports used in metalpoint means that the artist may have to consider uncommon ways of mounting in order to preserve, ship, store, and display them. Mounting creates a "protective housing" for artwork and serves the purpose of minimizing environmental and handling damage.[5]

For the artist who produces a large amount of work, mounts can be made in standard sizes for framing, such as 11 × 14 or 16 × 20 inches.[6] These sizes are useful for storing artworks in archival boxes and for quickly finding frames that fit the artwork. Mounts for works on paper should always be made of 100% rag, acid-free, buffered mat board, so that contaminants in the environment can be absorbed and neutralized. Cheap mounting materials made of wood pulp can leech acids into the artwork and should never be used. Four-ply mat board is the most common thickness and is rigid enough to keep the artwork flat and well-protected. Some framers mount works directly to acid-free *foam core*, which is a lightweight, rigid board made from layers of acid-free paper and polystyrene foam. Custom frame shops frequently use colored or textured mat board to enhance the decorative quality of the framed artwork, but museums and galleries will almost always require plain white or ivory mat board.

When mounting works on paper, there are many approaches used.[7] Small works on paper can be secured with photo corners, which are hidden under a top mat. One simple way to mount a work on paper is to use hinges made of acid-free tape, attached to the back of the artwork at the top corners, then secured to an archival backing board (Figure 6.3). Metalpoint drawings can become very heavy if done on thick paper coated with multiple layers of ground, and they may need larger or an increased number of hinges. Artworks are very infrequently secured with hinges at the sides or bottom; these extra hinges may cause the artwork to buckle in its mount rather than shrink and grow with changes in humidity.

A contemporary type of mount is a *float* mount, in which the artwork is hinged to a smaller mounting board, which is then secured to a larger backing board; the artwork is raised off the surface and seems to "float" (Figure 6.4). Mounts can be made for artwork on thick boards or panels as well. A *build-up* is created around the edges of the backing board, with a tight-fitting center space into which the artwork is inserted. The artwork is held in place by friction or by stiff corners hidden under a window mat.

A *top mat* or *window mat* is used to protect the surface of the artwork when in storage and to separate the artwork from the glazing when framed. A sheet of acid-free paper is usually placed

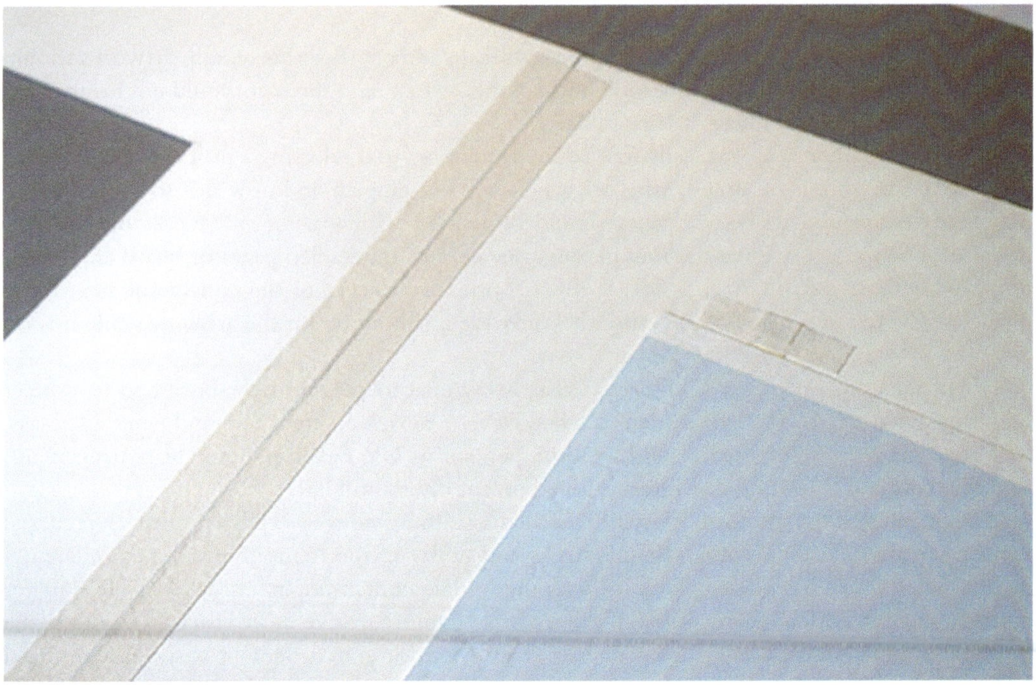

FIGURE 6.3 T-hinged artwork attached to the backer of a hinged window mat

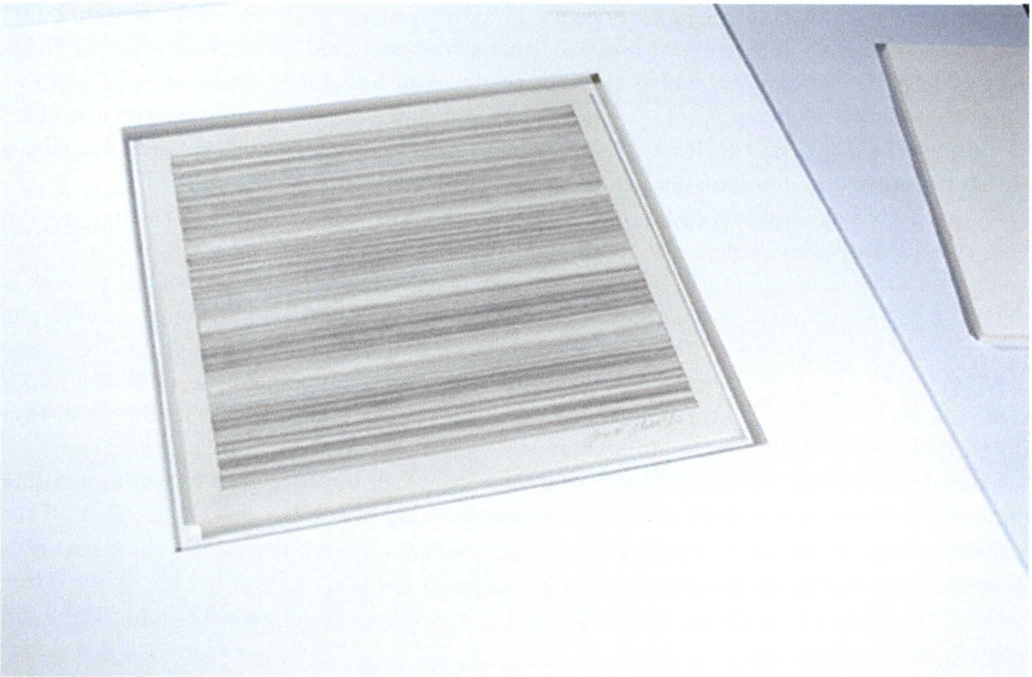

FIGURE 6.4 A float-mounted metalpoint (one of Susan Schwalb's *Strata* series, collection of Tom Mazzullo)

under the mat to protect the surface of the artwork in storage. For this reason, artworks should never be taped or glued to the underside of the window mat, and the mat should not be attached to the backing board on more than one edge.

Metalpoint drawings are typically framed for exhibition, and selecting a proper frame depends on how the artwork is mounted, whether it needs to be shipped, and how it is to be exhibited. Mounted and matted works on paper should be framed with glazing and works on panel or board may be framed with or without glazing; metalpoints on cradled panel or board are usually displayed without a frame or in a float frame. Of primary concern to the metalpoint artist is the quality of the framing materials, because they provide a safe home for the artwork while it is on display.

For metalpoints on paper, UV-filtered glass is essential to prevent light-burn and to protect colors from fading. Acrylic glazing, often called *plexi* or *plexiglass*, after the brand name Plexiglas, is also sold as Acrylite or Lucite and blocks 65 percent of UV radiation.[8] Acrylic glazing is also available with a UV coating that filters out 98 percent of harmful light.

The frame itself can be plain or ornate, finished or unfinished wood, plastic, or metal sectional frames. For the metalpoint artist, the aesthetics and utility of the frame should be considered; a natural wood frame has a classic look for drawings, while contemporary art galleries often prefer white mouldings with a square profile. Deeper profile frames can give more visual "weight" to the artwork. Simple gold-leaf and silver-gilt frames are common for metalpoint works, as are metal section frames. Works on cradled panel are often exhibited unframed but are also shown in simple black, white, and natural wood float frames (Figure 6.5). If a framed artwork is to be shipped, a

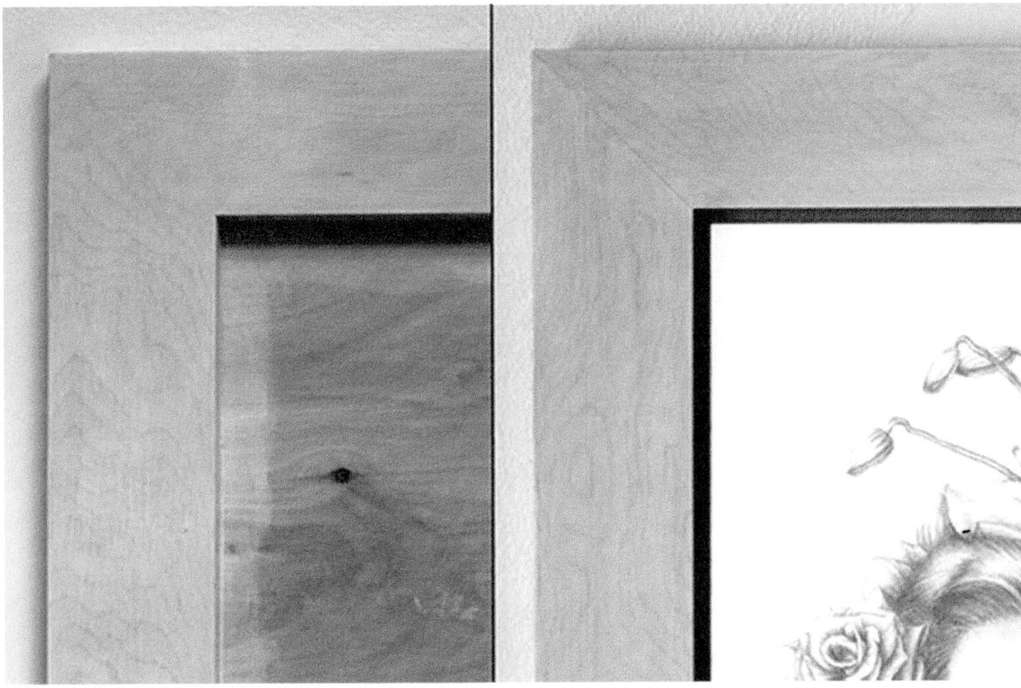

FIGURE 6.5 A float frame (empty, left) and with an artwork installed (right). Illustration from photos courtesy of Lauren Amalia Redding

sturdy, simple hardwood or metal frame is best; ornate frames can be easily chipped or scratched during transit and require extra cushioning to arrive undamaged. Framed artwork can be stored on a painting screen or wrapped and stored on shelves. Avoid laying framed artworks face-down to keep works on paper from sagging against the glass and to keep unglazed works from being damaged by contact with other surfaces.

Photography and Processing Images

Photography of metalpoint drawings is tricky. The marks are reflective, the lusters of different metals are subtle, and paper texture is hard to capture. With digital photography, it is possible to make images that represent the artwork as closely as possible.

When photographing artwork, a high-resolution DSLR (digital-single-lens-reflex) camera is recommended for control of all the exposure parameters for best picture quality. *Resolution*, in digital photography, generally refers to the total number of pixels that the camera's image sensor can record. Five megapixels represents the resolution of an 8 × 10-inch photographic print or a laptop screen. Current DSLR cameras have 24-megapixel resolution,[9] enough to zoom a screen image with excellent detail or print an 11 × 14-inch image at perfect quality.[10] Most artists need a camera that will shoot artwork at screen resolution, with the occasional need for a printed post-card, magazine ad, or book illustration. For this, a 16-megapixel digital DSLR is adequate.

A typical setup for flat artwork photography shoots the artwork on the wall using one lamp on each side of the artwork and a camera on a tripod (Figure 6.6). Reflector umbrellas are used with

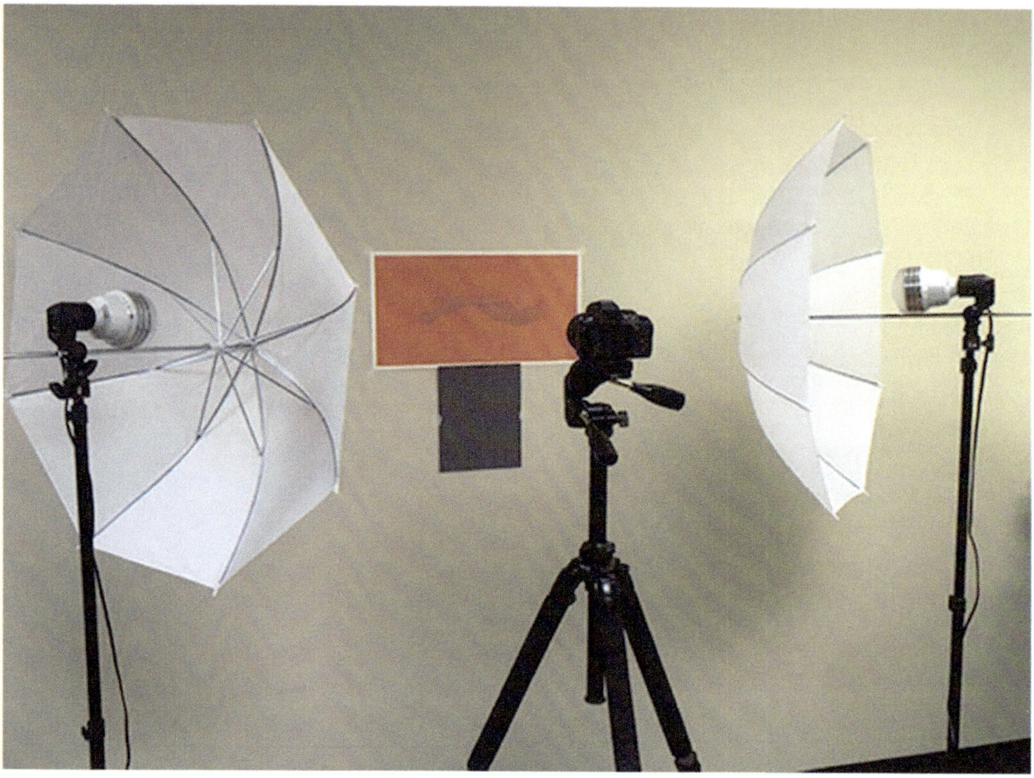

FIGURE 6.6 A typical setup for wall photography, including LED lamps and stands with diffusers, tripod and camera, artwork, and gray reference card

the lamps to diffuse the light. For large artworks, four lamps – two placed high and two placed low – should be used. The lamps should be very bright, natural-colored light, and 500-watt LED lamps are becoming less expensive and better with each passing year.[11] Place the lamps halfway between the art and the camera and take time to equalize the light across the entire artwork; even small variations in light intensity can be seen in the recorded image. Metalpoints and works under glass are especially susceptible to reflection, so place the lamps at a 45-degree angle to the artwork and look through the viewfinder to search for glare in heavily-drawn areas. Be sure to block out extraneous light sources. Moving the lamps further to the side also reduces glare but will increase exposure time. Make sure the back of the camera is parallel to the artwork and neither angled up nor down so that the image will be square, although tilting works under glass can eliminate reflections and a skewed image can be squared later, in post-processing.

For small artworks, a 50mm focal-length lens shoots the "flattest" image; a short focal-length lens can shoot large artworks, but the image will distort, creating a "fish eye" appearance. In addition, the evenness of light is affected by wide-angle lenses, creating *lens vignetting*, or a dimming of the image at the corners. A 28–55mm zoom lens allows the tripod to remain stationary while the photographer uses the zoom ring to compose the image in the viewfinder.

Select settings in the camera menu that are good for photographing artwork. Shoot RAW images, which are uncompressed files that will have the maximum resolution for post-processing work. JPG files are compressed to make a smaller file size and to fit more images on the memory card. Change the sensor ISO to the lowest setting possible, usually 100; a higher ISO is used to shoot in low-light situations, which is not the case in artwork photography. If it is an option, select settings for the type of lamps being used. Use the camera on manual exposure, stop down the aperture to increase sharpness and to decrease lens distortion, then adjust the shutter speed. Bracket the exposures; shoot one image underexposed, one at recommended exposure, and one overexposed, to give a range of images to adjust.

In addition to wall photography, small works can be photographed using a copy stand or a scanner (Figure 6.7). Scanners are ideal for imaging small metalpoint works; they reduce the reflections common to photography setups and are able to capture subtle textures. One advantage of scanning is that the artwork image can be previewed in scanning software, and adjustments can be made before the "scan" button is pressed. Images of larger artworks can be "stitched together" in image-editing software; Adobe Photoshop offers a "Photomerge" process that automatically combines images selected from scanned files.

Once the artwork is photographed, some digital processing is essential for optimizing metalpoint images. Adobe Photoshop is the standard of photo processing, but there are similar editing tools in all image software. Image processing for metalpoint artwork involves adjusting contrast and rotating and cropping the image. Advanced image processing can involve adjusting white balance, straightening distorted images, and removing lens vignetting. The intention is to match the digital image to the artwork, and to make it reproduce accurately.

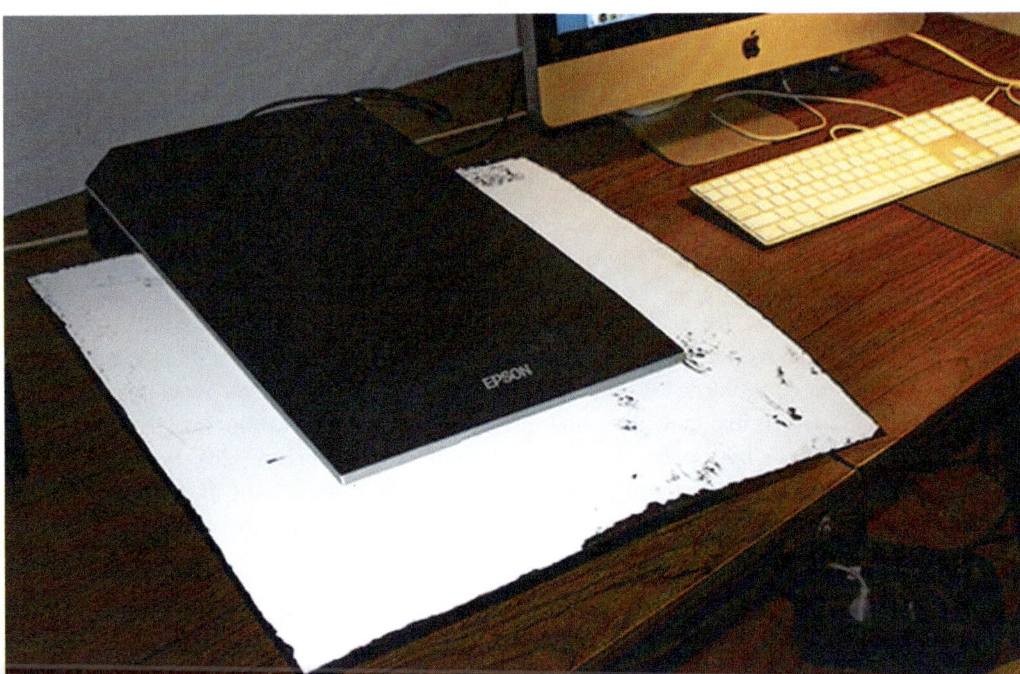

FIGURE 6.7 A large work on paper being imaged on a flatbed scanner. Multiple scans will be merged together electronically

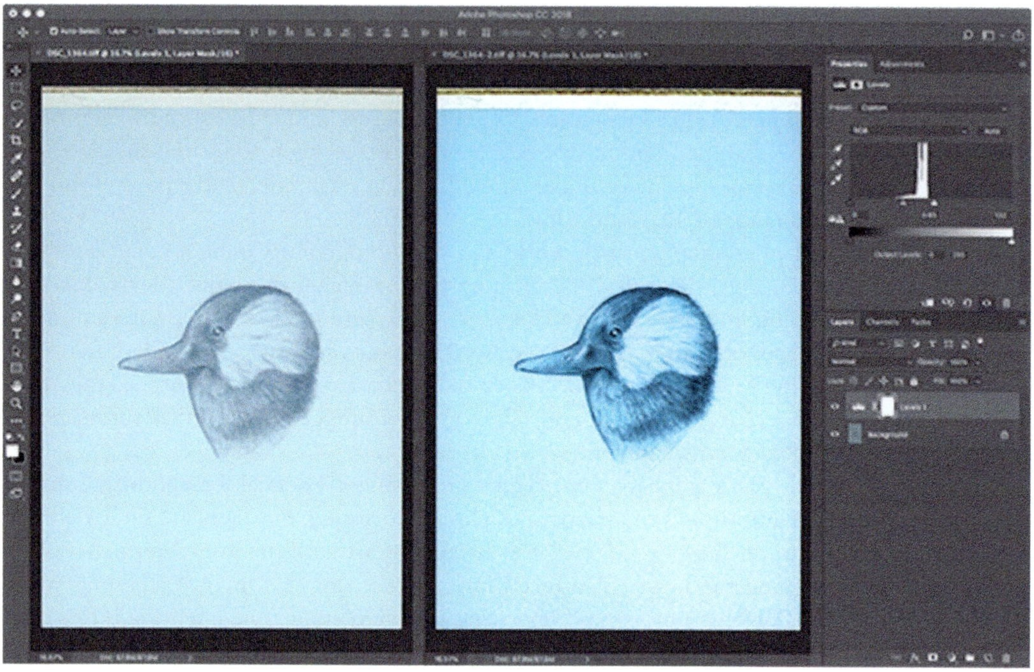

FIGURE 6.8 Two edits of the same image of a metalpoint, one with just enough image processing to reproduce the artwork (left) vs. one with too much contrast and color saturation (right). Note the histogram window showing the value range for the image on the left

A *levels* tool allows for very fine adjustments in contrast. It will present you with a *histogram*, or map, of the lights and darks in your image, and will have sliders for highlights, midtones, and shadows along the bottom. Bring the highlights (right) slider toward the center to brighten the image. Move the midtones slider to the center to improve contrast. The shadows slider at the left controls the density of darks and rarely needs adjusting for metalpoint images on light-colored grounds. Occasionally, heavily-worked areas of metal will reflect light rather than appear dark when photographed; some software applications have "shadows" and "highlights" sliders that can adjust these areas to match the rest of the image. Work in a dim, but not dark, room, and, if possible, use a calibrated monitor for accurate results.[12] Always compare the image on the screen to the artwork and try to maintain the tonal quality of metal marks as much as possible, while still achieving the proper brightness, contrast, and color balance (Figure 6.8). For multi-media metalpoints or drawings on color grounds, make minute adjustments until all the colors look as they do in real life. There are many online tutorials for different software applications that can explain these tools in detail.

Packing and Shipping

Metalpoints are more fragile than many other works of art, and there are ways of packing and shipping them to arrive at their destination in the best possible condition. In most cases, it is an artwork framed for exhibition or a "loose" drawing that needs to be shipped to a buyer or a gallery.

Shipping a loose work on paper or a drawing in a mat is the simplest way to send artwork. For a loose work, use a folio of sturdy board that is larger than the drawing. Metalpoint drawings are prone to abrasion damage as they shift inside the folio, so it is a good idea to place the drawing in a folded sheet of acid-free paper, secured to the inside of the folio with protective paper corners (Figure 6.9). Multiple sheets can be included in one folio if the drawings are on thin paper, but each should have its own interleaving. Single mounted works, single works on paperboard, and single panels can all be contained within a folio as well. When packing two or more mounted works, bundle the mounts and use extra boards to protect the top of each mount if they are not matted, and one sturdy board on the top and on the bottom of the entire bundle.

Wrap the entire folio or bundle of mounts in plastic sheeting and seal it carefully with packing tape. This is done to ensure that moisture, humidity, odors, insects, and other environmental concerns do not affect the artwork during transit. To prevent bending of larger packages, a sheet of corrugated plastic can be inserted under the plastic sheeting to provide extra rigidity. As the package becomes heavier, it is a good idea to reinforce the corners with extra cardboard triangles to protect the package if it were to be dropped. Folios and bundles of matted works can also be shipped in a box.

If you are sending framed artworks, they should be shipped in a sturdy box or crate (Figure 6.10). Many shipping companies will make boxes to order, quickly and cheaply; wooden crates are more expensive and need to be built by art-shipping specialists. When taking a framed artwork to a shipper, protect the front with a sheet of cardboard and wrap the frame in plastic sheeting

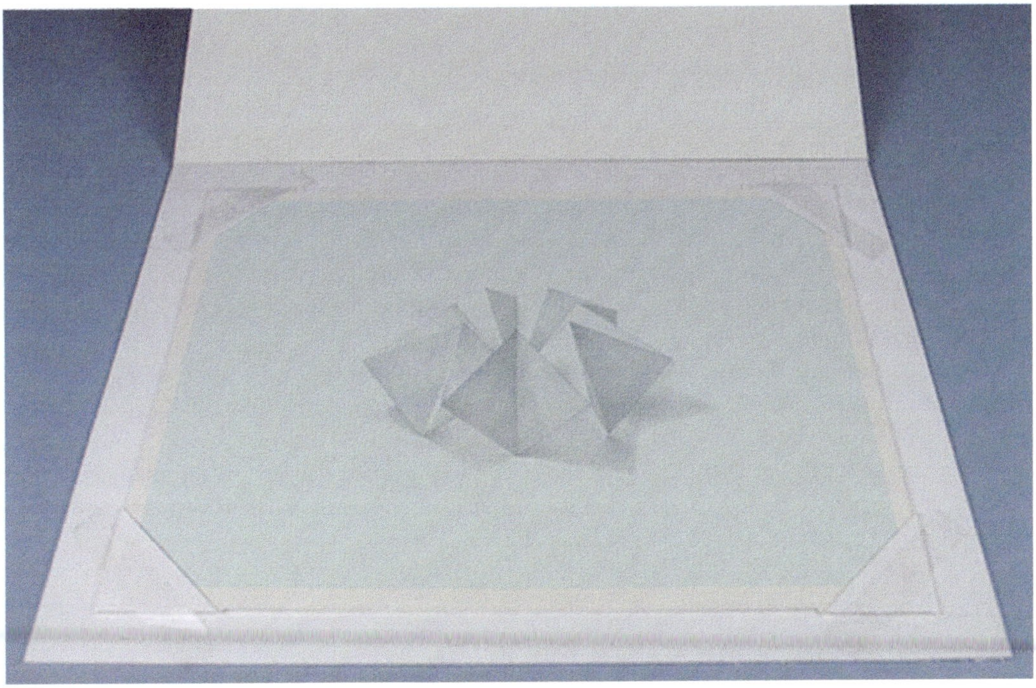

FIGURE 6.9 Several drawings in a folio secured for transport

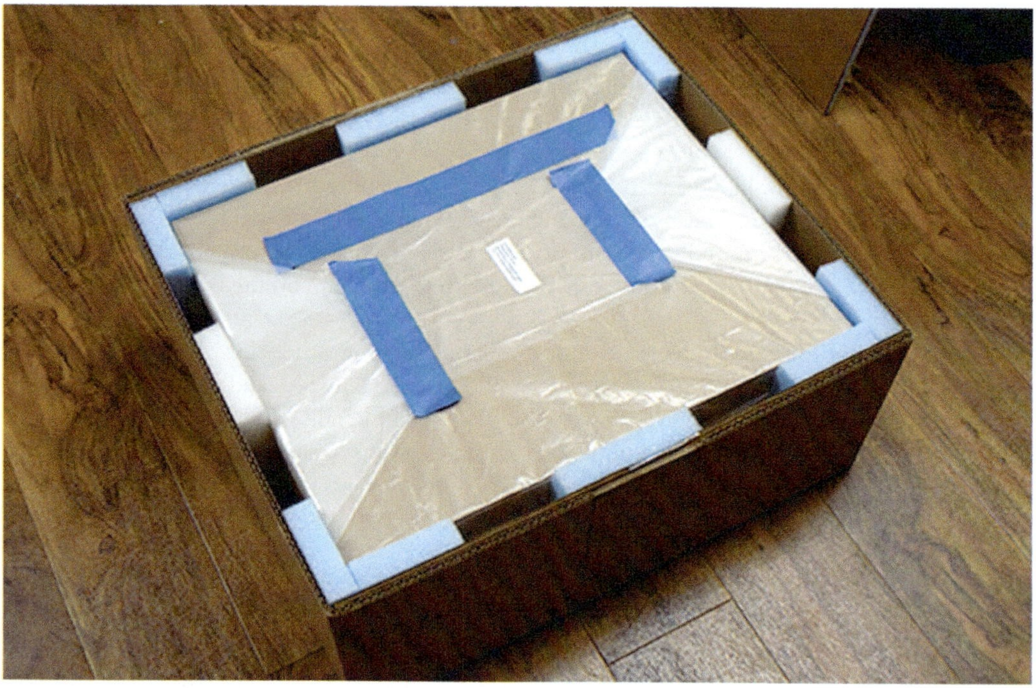

FIGURE 6.10 Framed artwork wrapped in plastic, in a shipping box with medium-density foam cushioning and double-thick cardboard construction. The lid is off in this image

sealed with packing tape to protect against moisture. The corners of the frame may need extra cushioning. Glass rarely survives shipping; taping glass does not prevent it from breaking and is only intended to grab small chips that could scratch the artwork. Shipping a framed, glazed artwork requires using plexiglass. When shipping an unglazed metalpoint, wrap it in a sheet of soft, thin paper to protect the delicate surface, then cover the front with cardboard before wrapping it in plastic sheeting. It is also a good idea to cover the hanging hardware on the back of each frame with a small square of foam to prevent it from tearing through the wrap. Ship one framed work per box for maximum safety, or for economy, wrap two or three frames together with layers of cardboard and foam in between to hold them firmly together.

It is hard to imagine the trouble a package could encounter in transit, so use packing and shipping suitable for the value of the artwork inside. It is best to ship art using a dedicated art shipper, one who understands the needs of handling fragile items. A national package shipper such as FedEx can be used, but there are restrictions, such as insurance limits on shipping artwork.[13] Packing and shipping artwork is very expensive, but like all other aspects of caring for artwork, cost should not be spared if the works are valuable.

Notes

1 Ellis, Margaret Holben. "Metalpoint Drawings: Special Conservation Problems for Collectors." *Drawing* 2, no. 4 (1980): 59–61.

2 Burns, Thea. *The Luminous Trace: Drawing and Writing in Metalpoint* (London: Archetype, 2012), 203.

3 Prestowitz, Brook. Assistant Paper Conservator, Williamstown Art Conservation Center, email correspondence with the author, March 2018.
4 https://ampersandart.com/the-story-of-hardbord.php. Accessed 7 February 2018.
5 Kosek, Joanna M. *Conservation Mounting for Prints and Drawings: A Manual Based on Current Practice at the British Museum* (London: Archetype Publications, 2014), xiii.
6 These measurements are American standard picture frame sizes. The British Museum has been using slightly different standard sizes for over a century.
7 For many examples of proper mounts for display and storage, Kosek, *Conservation Mounting* is an excellent and standard reference. Another excellent reference for archival mounting is Vivian Carli Kistler. *The Library of Professional Picture Framing*, vol. 4, 7 vols., *Conservation Framing* (Akron, OH: Columbia, 2004). A more accessible source for general mounting information can be found in a one-volume handbook by the same author: Kistler, Vivian Carli. *The Complete Photo Guide to Framing and Displaying Artwork* (Minneapolis, MN: Creative Pub. International, 2009).
8 www.eplastics.com/Plastic/plastics_library/UV-Ultra-Violet-Filtering-Plexiglass. Accessed 8 February 2018.
9 Or more. As of this writing, the Nikon D850 offers massive 45.4-megapixel resolution. www.techradar.com/reviews/nikon-d850-review. Accessed 13 March 2018.
10 http://improvephotography.com/34880/how-big-print-with-megapixel-camera. Accessed 12 March 2018.
11 For a lot of artists, a kit such as the "Savage 500W LED Studio Light Kit" is affordable and provides an adequate lighting setup.
12 Apple MacOS, for example, has a built-in display calibration app. For more information, see ISO/TC 42 3664:2009: "Graphic Technology and Photography: Viewing Conditions." www.iso.org/obp/ui/#iso:std:iso:3664:ed-3:v1:en. Accessed 21 August 2018.
13 Policy as of March 2018. Please check with the shipper for any policy changes or further details. FedEx Custom Critical is a special service tailored just for art museums and galleries. It is best for shipping a lot of valuable artwork. http://customcritical.fedex.com/us/services/market-industry/art.shtml. Accessed 13 March 2018.

7

CONTEMPORARY METALPOINT DRAWING

Introduction

In 1985 *The Fine Line: Drawing with Silver in America* opened at the Norton Museum of Art in West Palm Beach, Florida. It inspired numerous metalpoint exhibitions, and many artists began to work in metalpoint. For most of the first part of the twentieth century silverpoint drawing was dominated by figuration. Many of these artists were influenced by Renaissance masters, but gradually work began to emerge in a more contemporary style. One can divide the practice of contemporary silverpoint into several directions. There are those who have continued in the long tradition of figurative work and those who have made image-based works but have expanded the technique to create very unique drawings. Then there are artists who have pushed metalpoint into abstraction and combined it with other media (see Chapter 5) and lastly, there are those who have moved silverpoint into conceptual art, wall works, and performance-based artworks, so that they have expanded the technique beyond anything artists of the past could have ever imagined.

Figuration

One of the earliest American artists to develop a body of metalpoint work was Joseph Stella (American, 1877–1946), who focused on portraits, plants, and flowers. Often he combined silverpoint with colored pencils or pastels, and he was very free in applying his grounds so that one could see the brush strokes. In some of his self-portraits the force of his line tore the surface of the paper, whereas in other portraits the line is refined. In Stella's drawings of flowers and plants, such as *Untitled (Yellow Orchid)* (Figure 7.1), the drawing has a very elegant line, and it is easy to see how Stella integrated the colored pencil into the drawing.

Other artists who worked in metalpoint include Marsden Hartley (American, 1877–1943), who primarily drew landscapes, John D. Graham (American, 1881–1961), August Mosca (American, 1909–2002), who explored portraiture, and John Storrs (American, 1885–1956), who made abstract drawings, besides portraits, as sketches for his sculptures.

Paul Cadmus (American, 1904–1999) also used very free brush strokes to make his grounds, which were often in color (light pinks, greys, yellows, and blues), inspired by some of the

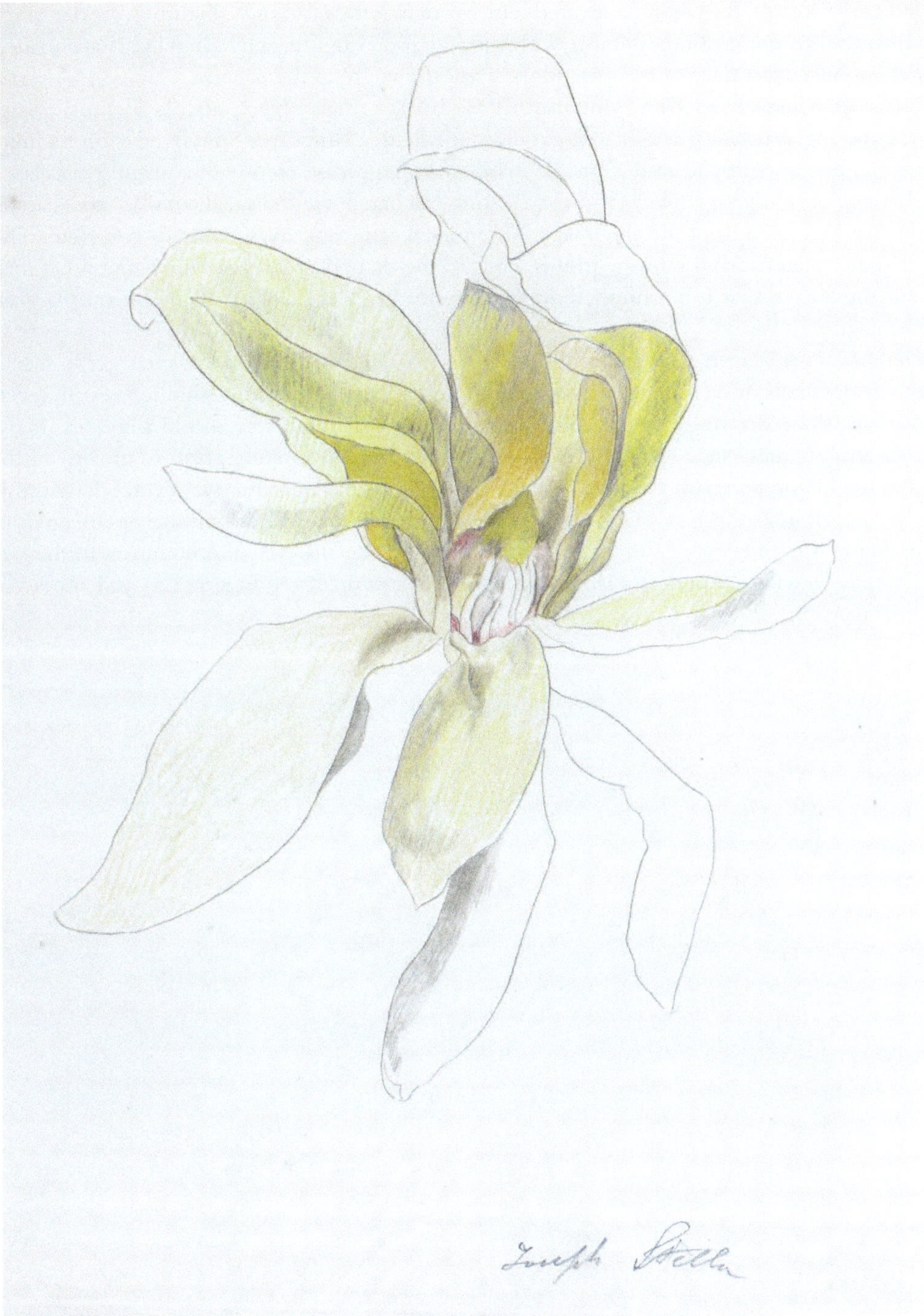

FIGURE 7.1 Joseph Stella (1877–1946), *Untitled (Yellow Orchid)*, c.1920, silverpoint, graphite and colored pencil on paper, 12 7/8 × 9 1/2 inches / 32.7 × 24.1 cm, 12 1/2 × 8 3/4 inches / 31.8 × 22.2 cm, sight size, signed lower right: *Joseph Stella*, courtesy of Michael Rosenfeld Gallery LLC, New York, NY

traditional colors of Renaissance grounds. In his drawing *Male Nude* (Figure 7.2), the vertical brush strokes of the ground contrasts with the horizontal figure, while highlights are made by scratching into the surface of the ground to reveal the white of the paper.

In the drawings of Leo Dee (American, 1931–2004) a single object, such as a lemon or a part of an envelope, is transformed into an exquisite meditative landscape. So refined is his technique that it can be very difficult to discern the mark-making process even with a magnifying glass. In his drawing *Small Drapery Study* (Figure 7.3), one can barely see the small circular cross hatching marks that Dee used to create the image. Often his works took over a year to complete. There is a definite reference and homage in this work to the drapery studies of Dürer, but what makes it contemporary is that it is a finished drawing (instead of a sketch) and its dominant placement on the page.

Dennis James Martin (American, 1956–2001) managed to give his 24-karat goldpoint and platinum drawings of reclining nudes a voluptuous and almost pornographic softness. Executed on vellum, these drawings have a soft, blurry quality that resembles an old film still. Harvey Dinnerstein's (American, b. 1928) work ranges from powerful-looking plants to unconventional models (including pregnant women), usually drawn from his community. Several drawings pay special attention to the hair of his models (either facial or head), an unusual focus obviously suggested by the fineness of the silverpoint line, something that was also common in the work of Thomas Dewing (American, 1851–1938) (for an example, see Figure 1.4) and other early American artists.

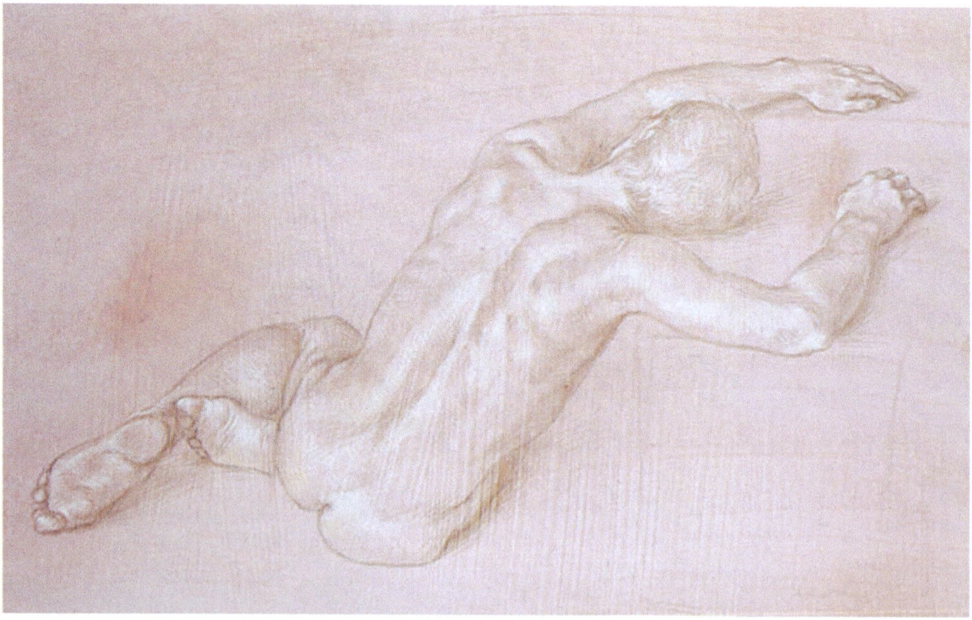

FIGURE 7.2 Paul Cadmus (1904–1999), *Male Nude (NM #62)*, 1968, silverpoint and egg tempera on gessoed board, 12" × 20" / 30.5 × 50.8 cm sheet size, 11" × 17 1/2" / 27.9 × 44.5 cm sight size, signed and dated, Courtesy of Michael Rosenfeld Gallery LLC, New York, NY, © Jon F. Anderson, Estate of Paul Cadmus/Licensed by VAGA, New York, NY

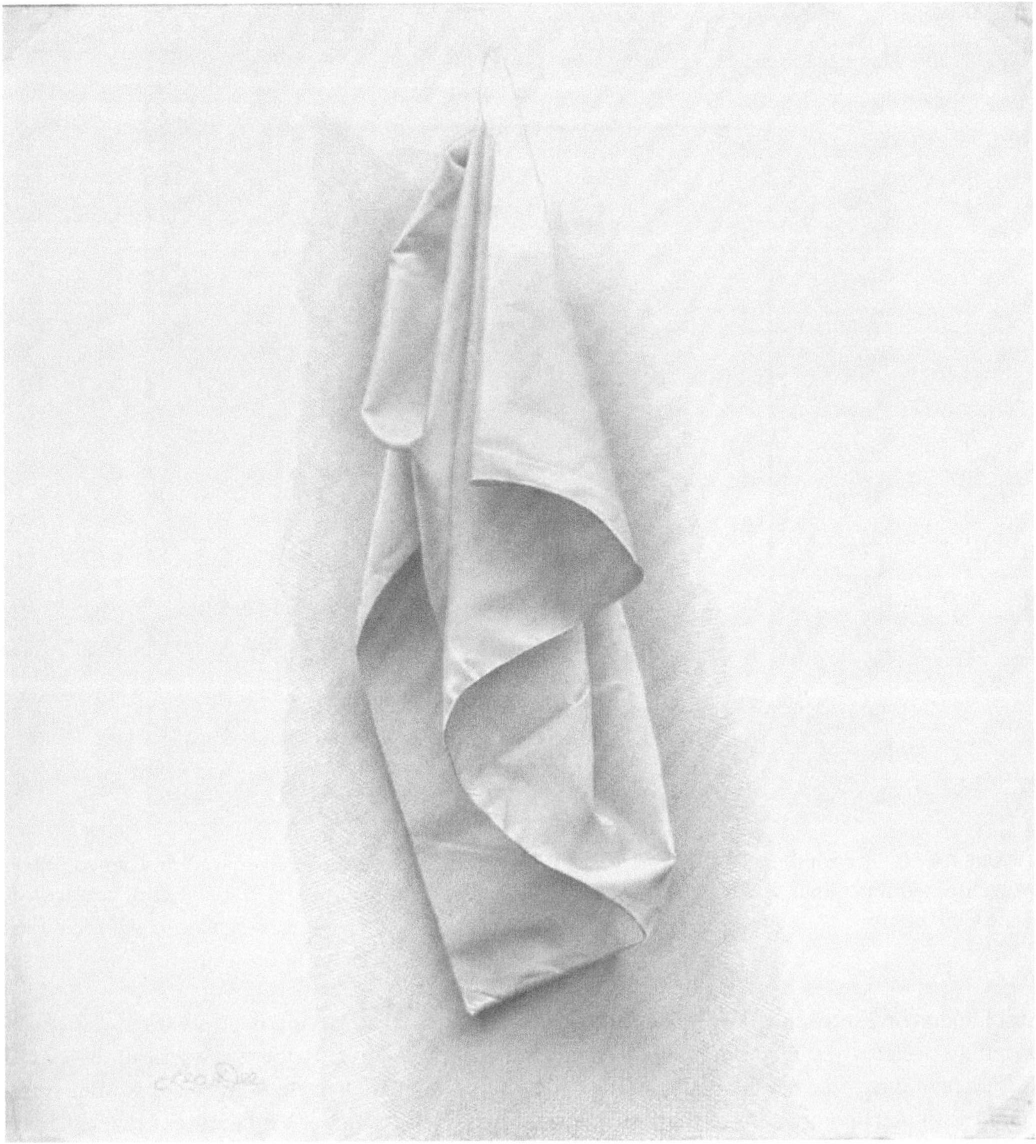

FIGURE 7.3 Leo J. Dee (1931–2004), *Small Drapery Study*, 1983, silverpoint on prepared rag board, 9 3/4 × 8 3/4 inches (24.8 × 22.2 cm), Portland Museum of Art, Maine, Gift of Mrs. Charles Barker King, 2001.16

Roger Anliker (American, 1924–2013) taught drawing at both Carnegie Mellon University (CMU) and Tyler School of Art; when he taught silverpoint, he would require his CMU students to spend at least a month preparing a perfect ground before he allowed them to begin to draw. This obsessiveness carried over into his own work, where he often spent as many as ten years working on a drawing. In *Pods with Patterned Paper, Pleated* (Figure 7.4), he carefully builds up an exquisite

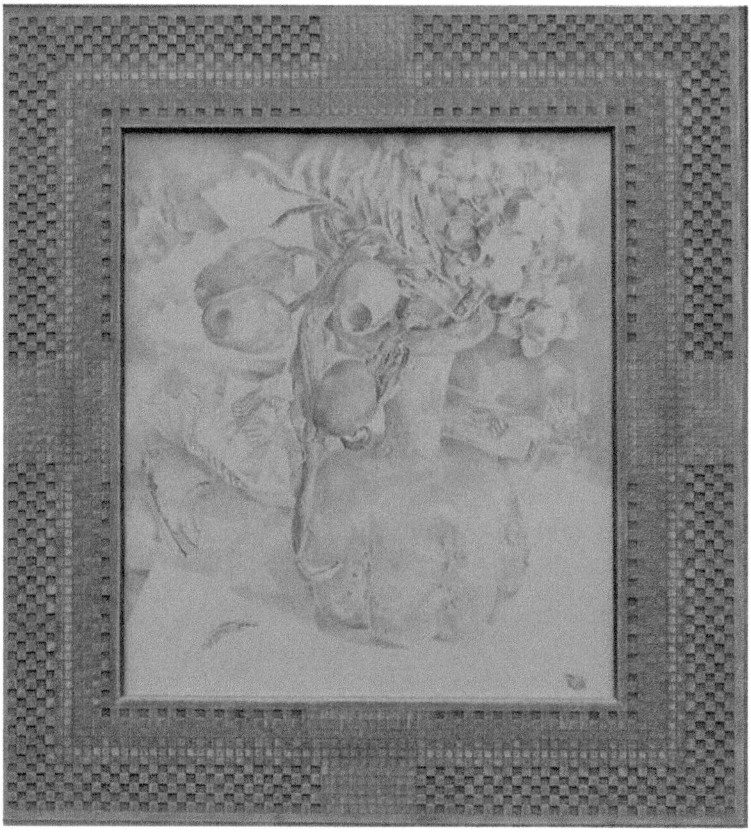

FIGURE 7.4 Roger Anliker, *Pods with Patterned Paper, Pleated*, 1972–1987, silverpoint on Cameo paper, polychromed relief liner and mat by the artist, 7 1/2 × 6 1/2 inches (19.05 × 16.51 cm), courtesy of Dale O. Roberts

still life drawing surrounded by a detailed, pleated mat, scored at varying depths with a scalpel and carefully peeled away to produce the desired step effect.[1] Dale O. Roberts (American, b. 1959), a student and friend of Anliker's who currently handles the Anliker estate, uses ink washes combined with metalpoint to make his beautiful still lifes (for an example, see Figure 5.11).

Jasper Johns (American, b. 1930), whose career has covered numerous mediums and directions, turned to silverpoint briefly in 1984, after being given some tools and paper. He made three detailed drawings based on a group of paintings from the early 1980s, including his *Ventriloquist* (1983, Museum of Fine Arts, Houston), which features a compositional design with overlapping grids and interweaving straight, curved, and hatched lines.[2] In *Untitled* (Figure 7.5), Johns draws with a delicate and elegant line using crosshatching.

Marjorie Williams-Smith (American, b. 1953) focuses her practice on images of flowers, particularly roses. She often draws the flower alone, placed on a pure white ground that has been carefully polished. Usually she concentrates on a part of a flower that encourages the viewer to marvel at a detail while seemingly caught up in an interior world. Recently she

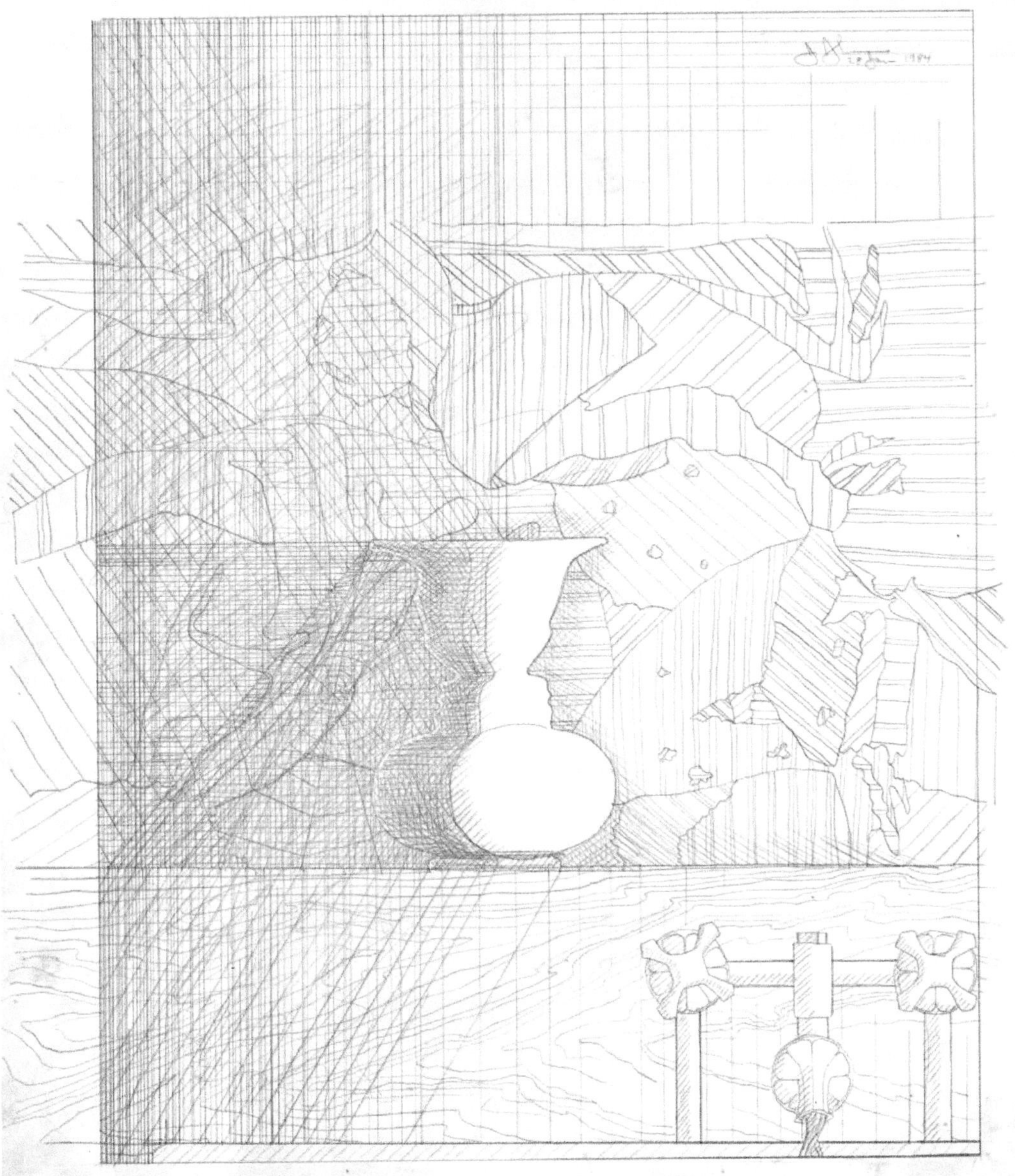

FIGURE 7.5 Jasper Johns, *Untitled*, 1984, silverpoint on white prepared paper, 17 1/4 × 13 5/8 inches (43.82 × 34.61 cm), collection of the artist, Art © Jasper Johns/Licensed by VAGA, New York, NY

began working with black grounds and has created luminous images, such as *Lines* (Figure 7.6), using aluminumpoint.

Smith's husband, AJ Smith (American, b. 1952), known for his pencil and graphite drawings, has also taken up metalpoint to create poignant portraits for his *Faces of the Delta* series. About *Delta Blues* (Figure 7.7), Smith writes,

> Silverpoint and a variety of other metals allow me to capture subtle personality traits in the faces of my subjects – this I feel is due to the very fine 'pin-point' sharpness one can get when using metals on several different surface preparations. . . .[3]

Another husband-and-wife team of silverpoint artists are Laura Shechter (American, 1944–2018) and Ben Shechter (American, 1940–2016), who was born in Israel. Both have made small-scale works often using silverpoint on light yellow Cameo paper. In *The Yellow Spurges* (Figure 7.8) two very similar drawings are matted side-by-side, one drawn on white clay-coated paper and the other on light yellow Cameo paper. Both artists use very sharp points in their styluses, and Laura uses a single-hatching technique that almost eliminates the white of the paper in her piece *Still Life on a Red Cloth* (Figure 7.9).

Some of the most interesting image-based works are by artists dealing with surrealist or symbolist themes. One of the masters was John Wilde (American, 1919–2005), who favored a style drenched in imagination and fantasy sometimes described as *magic realism*. Wilde was fascinated by the process of transformation and his human figures frequently morph into birds and other forms, as in the work *Lady-Bird Series #9* (Figure 7.10).

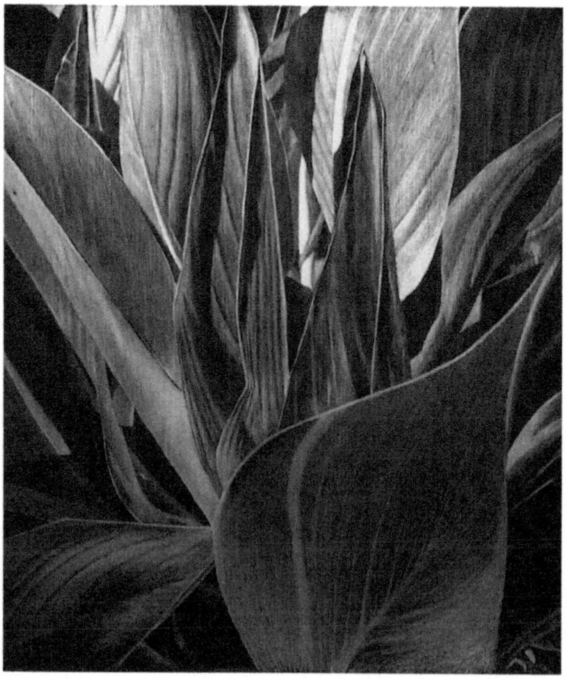

FIGURE 7.6 Marjorie Williams-Smith, *Lines*, 2017, aluminumpoint on black acrylic gesso, 9 3/4 × 6 1/4 inches (25 × 16 cm), private collection

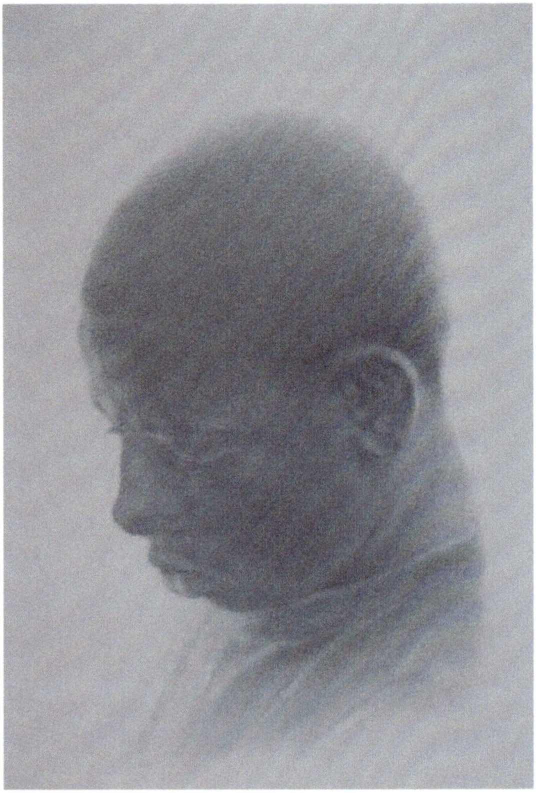

FIGURE 7.7 AJ Smith, *Delta Blues: Faces of the Delta Series*, 2012, silverpoint on paper, 16 × 14 inches (40.64 × 10.16 cm), collection Delta Cultural Center, A Museum of the Arkansas Department of Heritage, Helena, AR

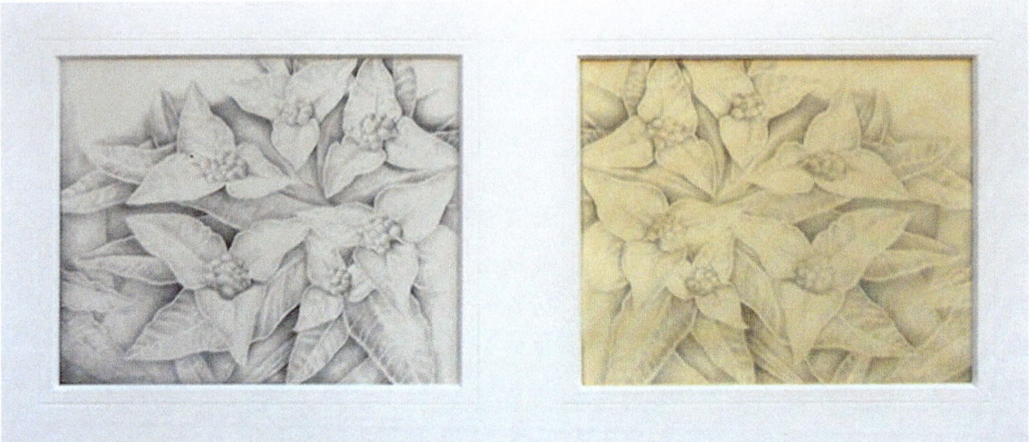

FIGURE 7.8 Ben Shechter, *The Yellow Spurges* (detail), 1981, clay coated paper and cameo paper, each panel 4 3/4 × 4 3/4 inches (12.07 × 12.07 cm), courtesy of the estate of Ben Shechter, Brooklyn, NY

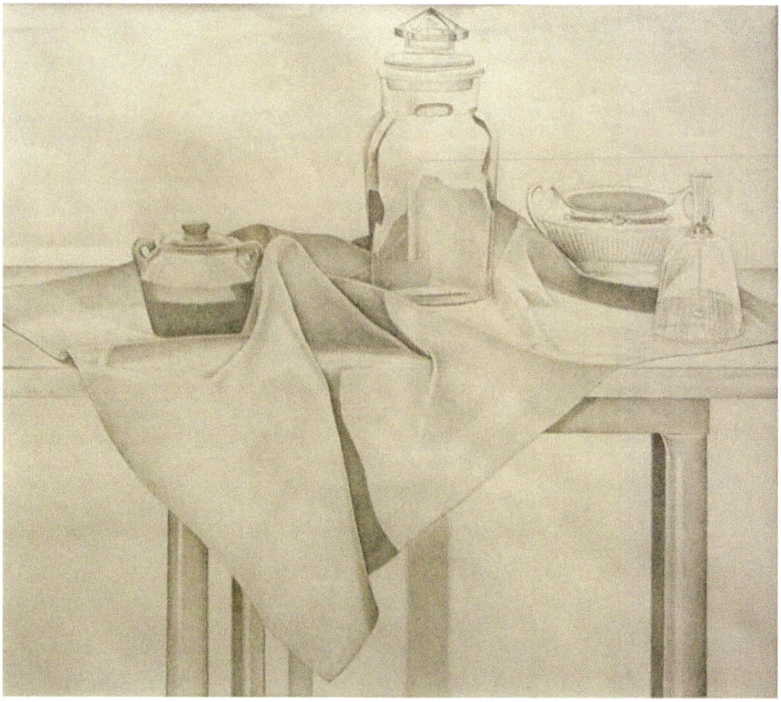

FIGURE 7.9 Laura Shechter, *Still Life on a Red Cloth*, 1976, silverpoint on cameo paper, 7 1/2 × 8 inches (19.05 × 20.32 cm), private collection

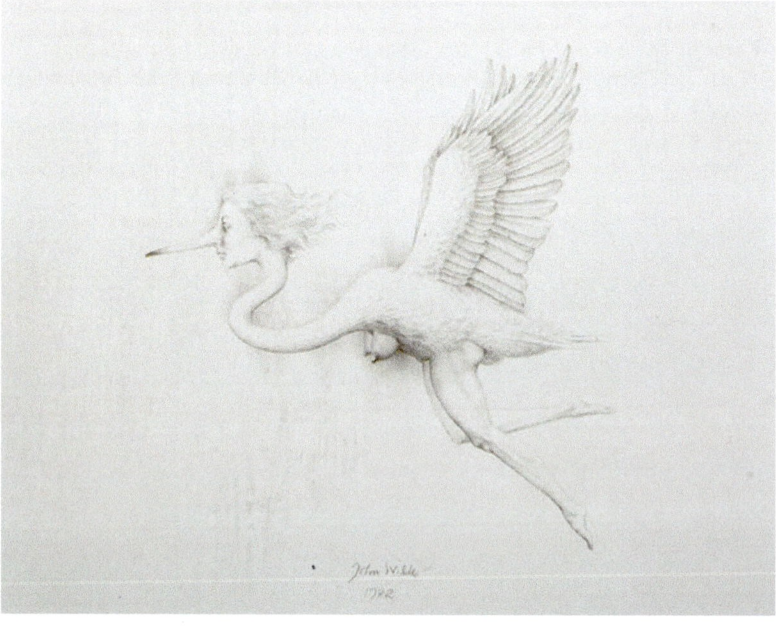

FIGURE 7.10 John Wilde (American, Milwaukee, Wisconsin, 1919–2006, Milwaukee, Wisconsin), *Lady-Bird Series #9 (Emily Egret)*, 1982, silverpoint on paper, 8 × 10 1/4 inches (20.3 × 26.0 cm), Arkansas Arts Center Foundation Collection: Purchase, Tabriz Fund. 1983.024.002. Courtesy of the Shirley Wilde Trust

Lori Field (American, b. 1955) is another artist who explores personal myths and fantasies. Drawing on a freely painted ground, she is partial to doll-like figures that often seem to float in a parallel universe with animal heads or masks instead of faces; viewing Field's work is like falling down the rabbit hole in *Alice in Wonderland*. About *Freckles* (Figure 7.11) she writes, "I especially love using imagery from nature combined with figures in suits of armor; I love the contrast between the depiction of a soft, natural form with the hard, metal surface of the armor."[4]

Like many contemporary artists, George Sorrels (American, b. 1944) is self-taught and has made images that combine nature with glimpses of parts of a figure. About *The Garden Time, Times and Time Again* (Figure 7.12), Sorrels writes,

> I am a purist at heart. There is no heightening with white nor darkening with ink, charcoal or graphite. My shading is a matter of touch. As I draw, I have to concentrate intensely on the fact that I cannot press down, as I would with a graphite pencil; my darks come about through a gentle layering process . . . it takes several months or even years for me to complete a silverpoint drawing. . . .[5]

Numerous artists have focused on portraiture in metalpoint, including Lauren Amalia Redding (American, b. 1987), Aaron Board (American, b. 1971), Koo Schadler (American, b. 1962), Roy Eastland (British, b. 1964), Charles Schmidt (American, b. 1939), and Nancy Lawton (American, 1950–2007). Redding's work often contrasts silverpoint drawing with gold or silver leaf. About *San Soldado/St. Soldier* (Figure 7.13) she writes, "I was playing with subverting the scale typically

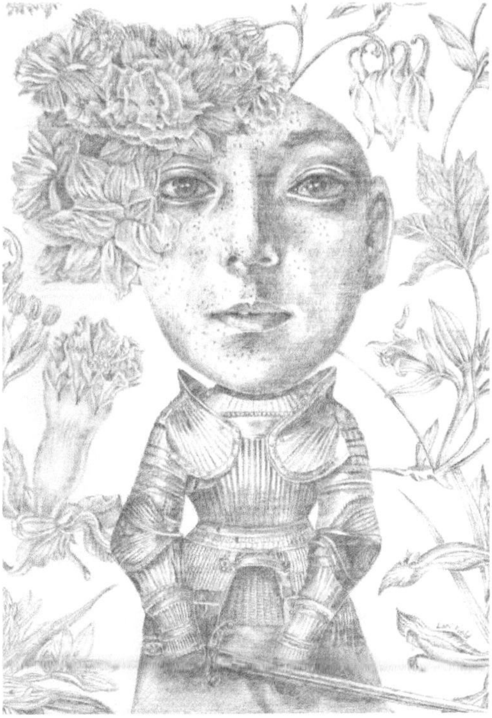

FIGURE 7.11 Lori Field, *Freckles*, 2012, silverpoint and gesso on paper, 9 × 4 inches (22.86 × 10.16 cm), courtesy of the artist

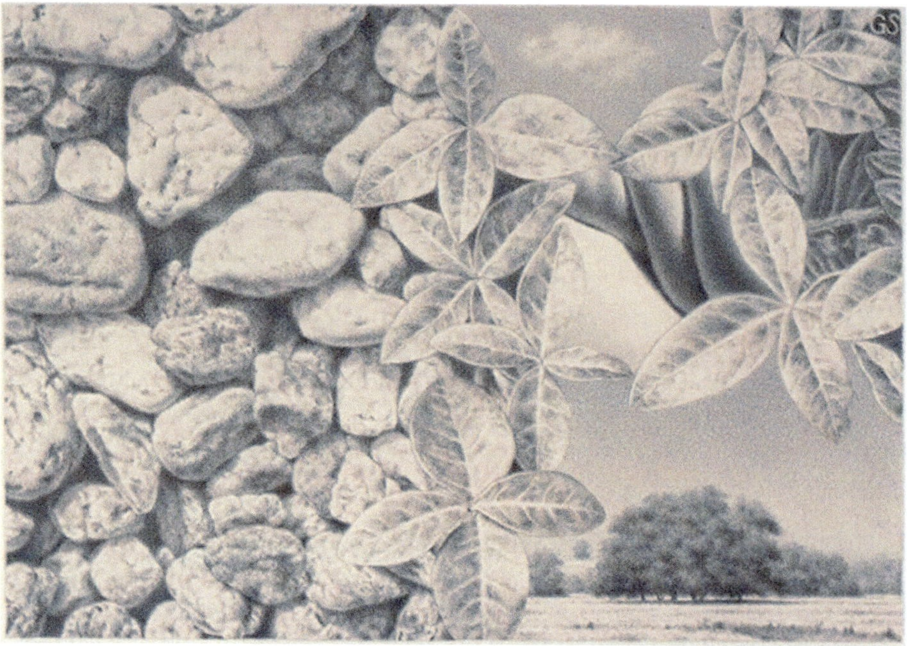

FIGURE 7.12 George Sorrels, *The Garden Time, Times and Time Again*, 1986, silverpoint, light-colored ground on paper, 4 1/2 × 6 inches, (11.43 × 15.24 cm), private collection

associated with representational silverpoint drawings . . . my drawing is larger in scale but is comprised of a blown-up, much-larger-than-life size snippet of a face."[6] Aaron Board's work (Figure 7.14) often combines metalpoint drawing with three-dimensional wood forms making a kind of mandala or religious icon in which he portrays his family. Koo Schadler paints and draws numerous portraits of people (for an example, see Figure 5.15), but her animal works, which combine silverpoint with tempera and gold leaf, are especially appealing. Roy Eastland's photo booth series (Figure 7.15) is loosely based on old images of his parents, exploring ideas involving presence and memory. Using very fine wire, along with needles and a scalpel blade, he repeatedly draws and redraws the image. The hand-written text beneath the portrait is based on lines of remembered speech and family stories.[7] Charles Schmidt has done numerous works in metalpoint and was an influential teacher of numerous artists, including Tom Mazzullo and Dale O. Roberts, while he was at Tyler School of Art. In *Portrait of Larry* (Figure 7.16) Schmidt emphasizes the structural aspect of the head by using horizontal and diagonal lines to accentuate the planes of the head; the drawing is deliberately left unfinished.[8] Nancy Lawton, known for her drawings of flowers and for her portraits, was inspired to start metalpoint after seeing the catalogue for the exhibition *The Fine Line*. She often contrasted her abstract treatment of space with hyper-realistic, subtly toned drawing. In Lawton's portrait of her son, *Forrest Holding Oriental Lilies* (Figure 7.17), she has contrasted the fine line of silverpoint with the bold use of acrylic paint.

In another take on portraiture, Michael Nichols (American, b. 1973) has used a lineless approach to silverpoint by creating faint veils of tone that create a sort of fuzzy haze over his subject (for an example, see Figure 4.9). Often, he has created a much more abstract image by placing a geometric form (square or circle) to cover the face. Katherine Vetne (American, b. 1987), in her drawing *Self Portrait in a Curved Mirror* (Figure 7.18), has set up a challenge of sorts to the great

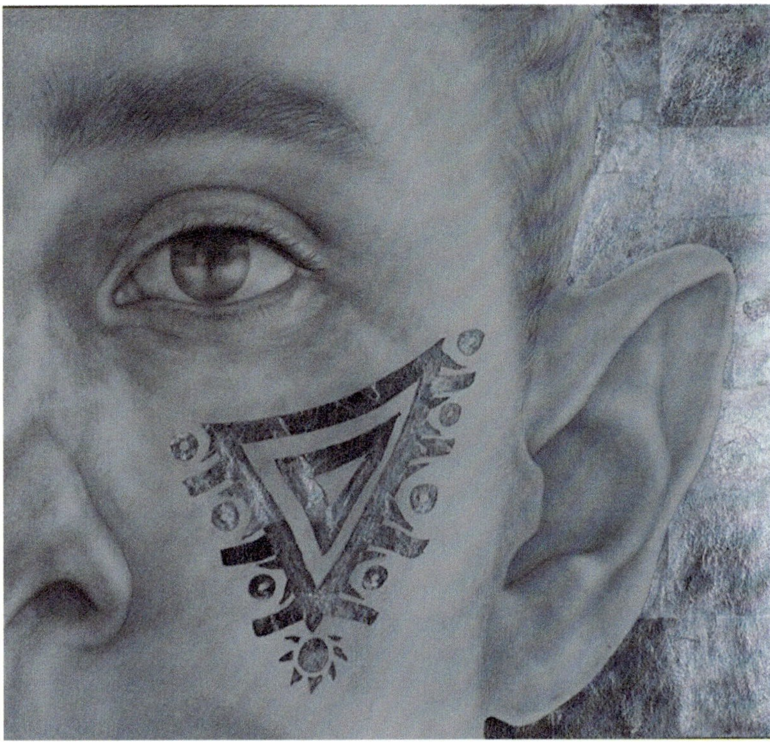

FIGURE 7.13 Lauren Amalia Redding, *San Soldado/St. Soldier*, 2016–2017, silverpoint and silverleaf on panel, 21 × 20 inches (53.34 × 50.8 cm), courtesy of the artist

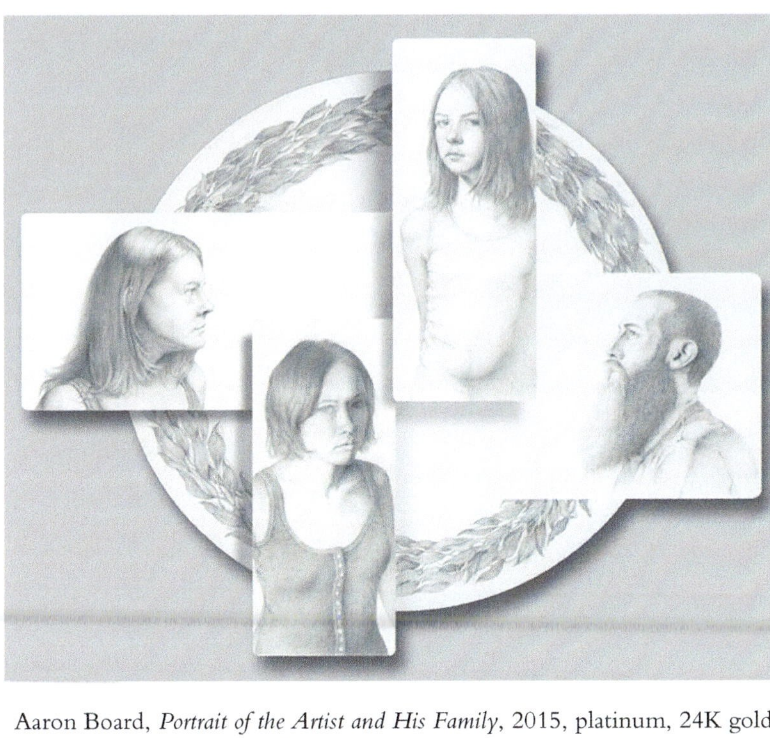

FIGURE 7.14 Aaron Board, *Portrait of the Artist and His Family*, 2015, platinum, 24K gold and silver on MDF, 21 × 26 × 2 inches (53.34 × 66.04 × 5.08 cm), courtesy of the artist

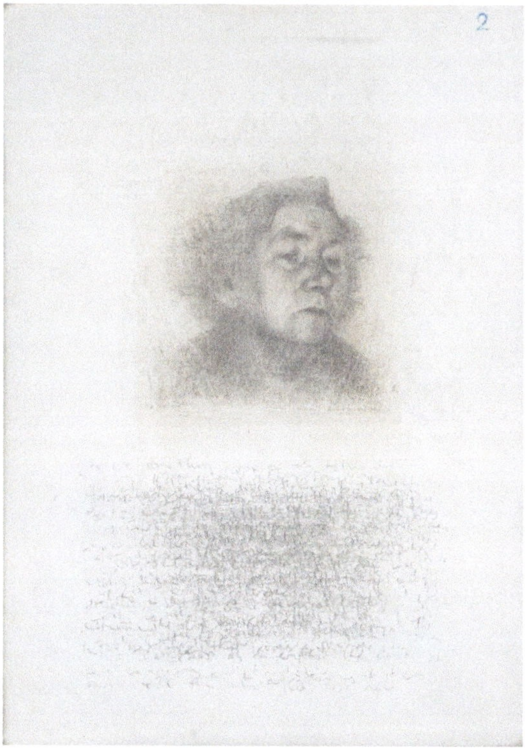

FIGURE 7.15 Roy Eastland, *Photo Booth Portrait Drawing 2*, 2014–2016, silverpoint on gesso on board, 8 1/4 × 6 3/4 inches, (21 × 14.5 cm), courtesy of the artist

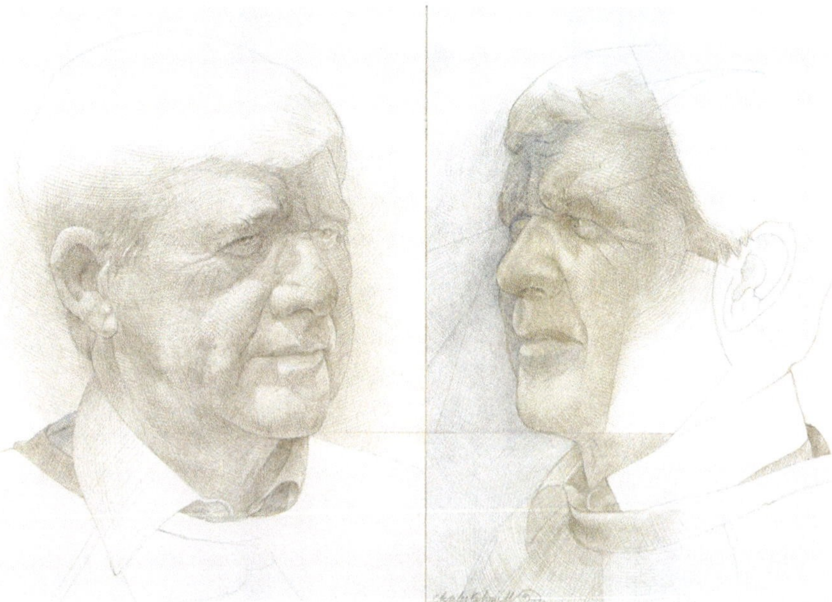

FIGURE 7.16 Charles Schmidt, *Portrait of Larry*, 1989, silverpoint on paper, 9 × 15 inches (22.85 × 38.1 cm), private collection

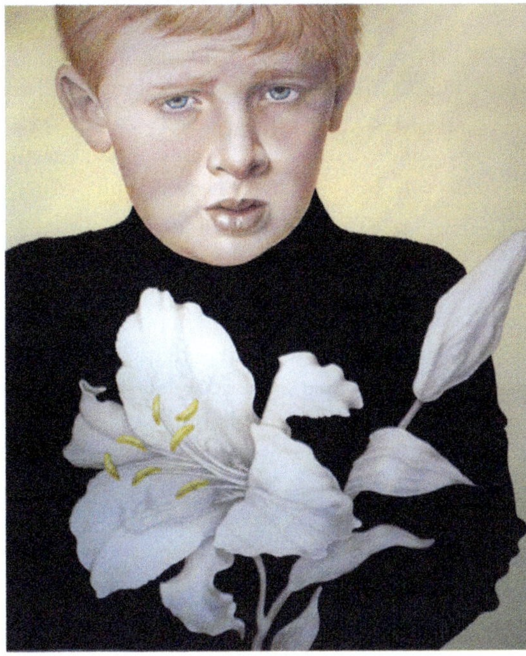

FIGURE 7.17 Nancy Lawton, *Forrest Holding Oriental Lilies*, 2005, silverpoint, acrylic on prepared paper 17 7/8 × 15 3/16 inches (45.40 × 38.57 cm), courtesy of the Nancy Lawton Estate

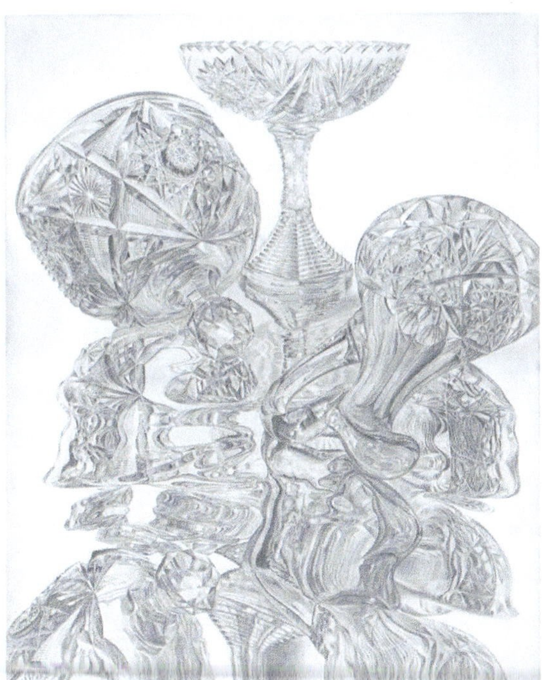

FIGURE 7.18 Katherine Vetne (American, b. 1987), *Self Portrait in a Curved Mirror*, 2017, goldpoint, graphite, and egg tempera on toned chalk ground on panel, 26 × 20 inches, (66.04 × 50.8 cm), courtesy of the artist. Photo credit: John Janca

masters of the Renaissance by paraphrasing her title from Parmigianino's *Self Portrait in a Convex Mirror*. About the drawing, which is composed of numerous crystal glasses, jars, and objects that seem to melt into each other, the artist states, "I see the crystal as a kind of self-portrait, perhaps for another version of myself had I come from a different class background."[9]

Jeannine Cook (British-American, b. 1944) and Sherry Camhy (American, b. 1940) are artists who have not only made numerous works in metalpoint but have also done a great deal to advance the medium by curating exhibitions, giving workshops, and writing on metalpoint. While living in Palma de Mallorca, Spain, Cook did a series of drawings of tree bark on black grounds entitled *Apovos IV* (Figure 7.19) as a memorial to her mother. Camhy, who has taught metalpoint at the Art Students League, has explored classic themes such as figures and plaster casts, but it is her large series of drawings of the sky (Figure 7.20) that are among her best works in the medium.

Dennis Angel (American, b. 1955) has also made drawings of cloudscapes. On the drawing *Taos, New Mexico #3* (Figure 7.21), which is quite subtle and delicate, he writes,

> Ironically, the very atmosphere that I am representing will gradually alter the metal surfaces of the drawings through the oxidation process. As the tones of the finished drawing subtly shift over time, the work will assume a life independent of my choices, echoing the transient nature of the clouds. . . .[10]

Joanne Hopper (American, b. 1962), has been making drawing tools since elementary school and for the past ten years has been making thick silverpoint tools that she sells online. Her delicate

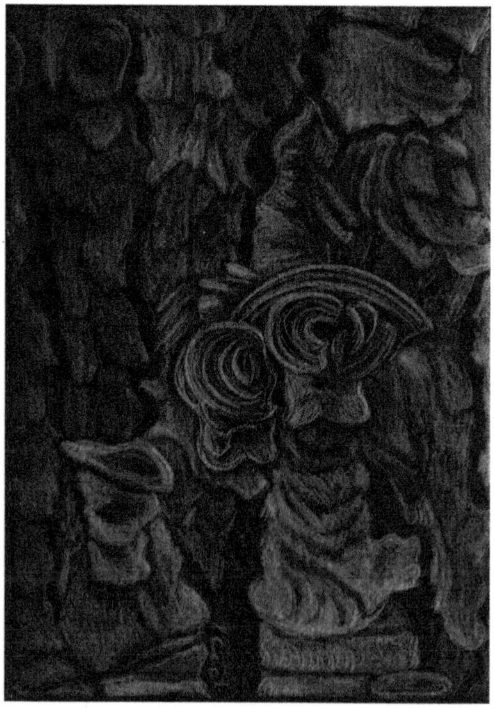

FIGURE 7.19 Jeannine Cook, *Apoyos IV: Pine Tree Bark*, 2011, silverpoint on black ground on paper, 5 × 3 1/2 inches (12.7 × 8.89 cm), courtesy of the artist

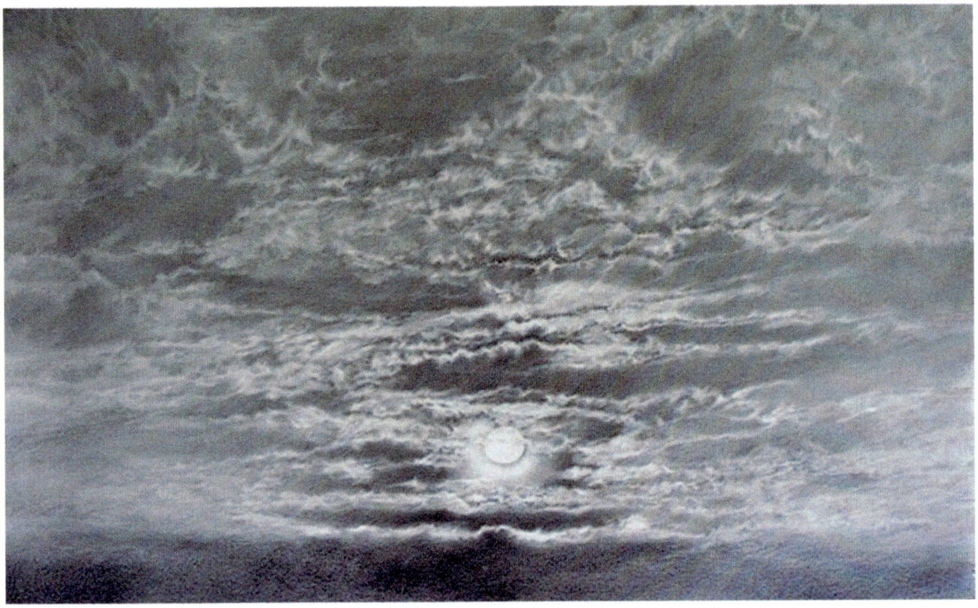

FIGURE 7.20 Sherry Camhy, *Silver Sky*, 2006, sterling silver on clay coated paper, 30 × 40 inches (76.2 × 101.6 cm), collection Evansville Museum of Arts, History and Science, Evansville, IN

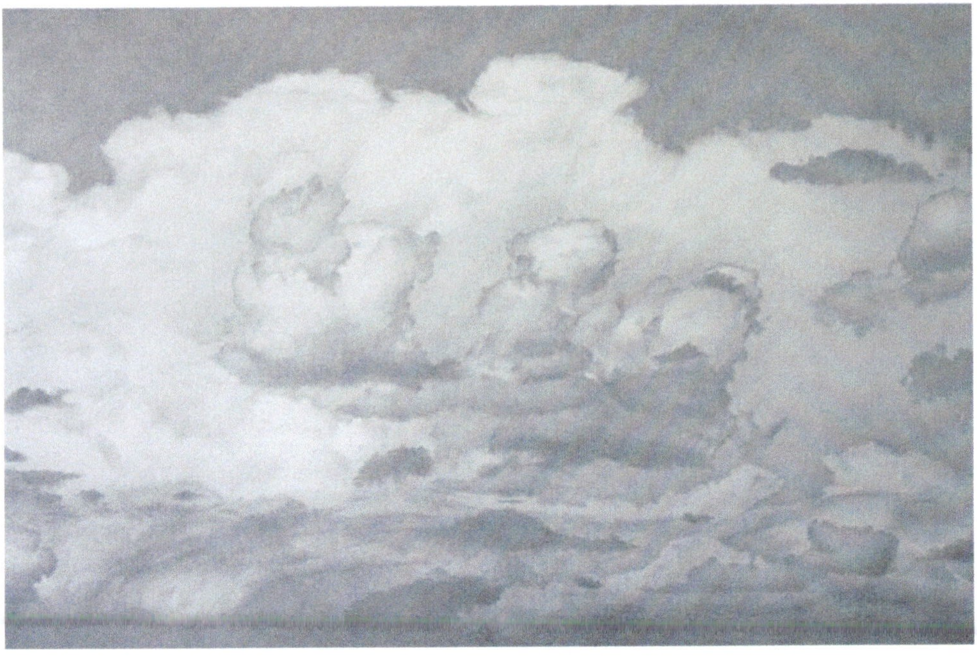

FIGURE 7.21 Dennis Angel, Taos, New Mexico #3, 2017, soft silver, sterling silver and 24K gold on primed paper, 22 × 30 inches (55.88 × 76.2 cm), courtesy of the artist

drawing *Summer Silversword* (Figure 7.22) depicts dried flowers from the Haleakala Mountains in Maui, hanging in front of an abstract watercolor background.

One of the masters of silverpoint and watercolor is Victor Koulbak (Russian, b. 1946), who currently divides his time between Paris and Malta. He began working in metalpoint quite by accident when, during an artist's block in Paris, he happened into an art supply store and reached for a book on a high shelf; it fell open on his head to a page with a silverpoint drawing. Intrigued, he began reading and going to museums to see original art. This experience changed his life, and now his precise drawings combined with watercolor of portraits and animals are prized by collectors worldwide (Figure 7.23).

Other artists who have made numerous drawings of animals and birds include Tom Otterness (American, b. 1952) and Kandy Vermeer Phillips (American, b. 1954). Otterness, who is known for his cartoonish metal sculptures of animals and children, turned to metalpoint in 2014 to create a series of drawings using a ground of clay, ash, and pigments. Many of the drawings, like *Rabbit* (Figure 4.3), were done on lightly tinted sandpaper-like grounds and are some of the most amusing images ever done in metalpoint. Phillips has focused her metalpoint practice on small-scale drawings of birds. *Marsh Wren Nest* (Figure 7.24), drawn from a museum specimen and a photo, is made of numerous built-up lines that create an intricate and almost abstract image.

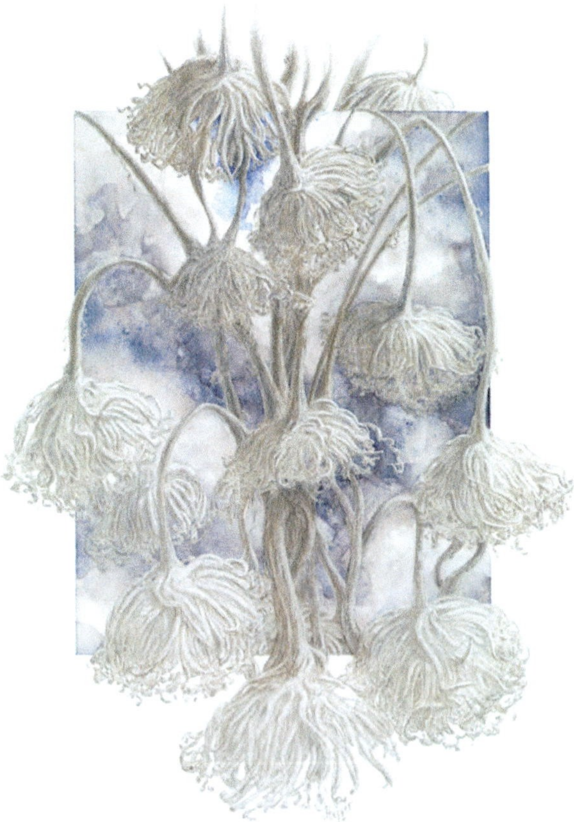

FIGURE 7.22 Joanne Hopper, *Summer Silversword*, 2017, silver, copper, platinum, goldpoint, silverpoint ground over watercolor on paper, 20 × 15 inches (50.8 × 38.1 cm), courtesy of the artist

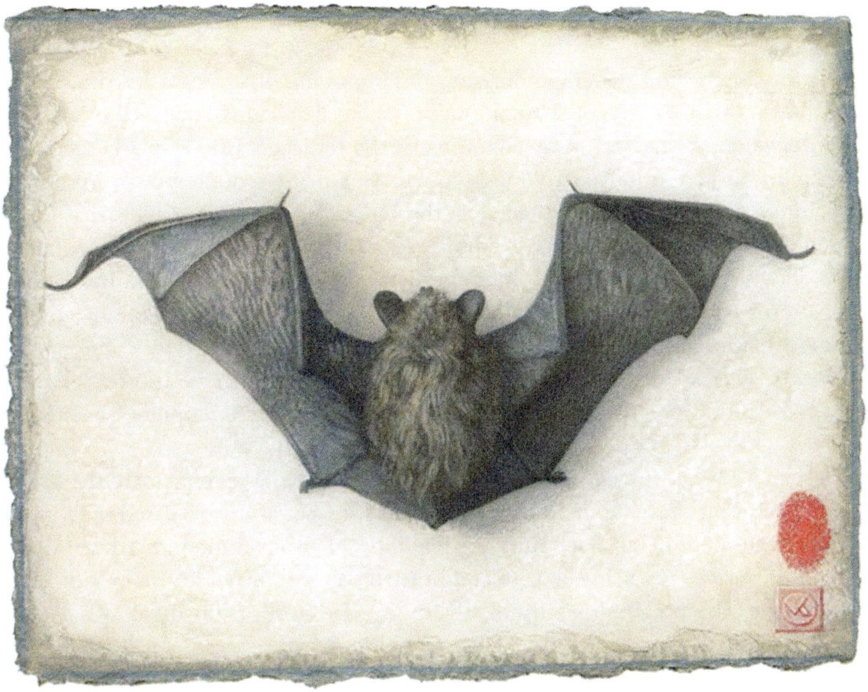

FIGURE 7.23 Victor Koulbak, *Bat*, 2009, silverpoint, watercolor on handmade paper, 10 × 12 1/2 inches (25.4 × 31.8 cm), courtesy Didier Aaron, Inc., New York

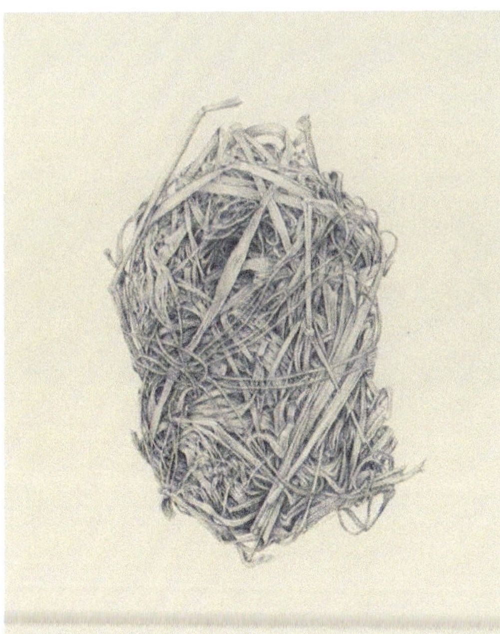

FIGURE 7.24 Kandy Vermeer Phillips, *Marsh Wren Nest*, silverpoint and goldpoint on Colourfix paper, 8 × 6 inches (20.32 × 15.24 cm), courtesy of the artist

Abstraction

One of the most interesting developments in contemporary silverpoint drawing has been the emergence of artists who are devoted to abstraction as well as conceptual and minimal art. One of the first to develop abstraction in metalpoint was the Chicago artist Paula Gerard (American, 1907–1991), who studied in Italy as a young woman. She first encountered silverpoint while living in Paris, but it wasn't until she returned to the United States in the 1940s that she began to devote herself almost exclusively to the medium. At first her work was figurative, but gradually she began to draw silver- and goldpoint lines over her watercolor abstractions. In *Currents* Gerard uses linear patterns and tone to build up a biomorphic world where one might glimpse waves or sea creatures that inhabit the bottom of the ocean. She is one of the few contemporary artists who also worked with metalpoint on parchment, and in one of her best known works, *Vortex* (Figure 7.25), swirls of tone create a sensual vision not unlike how one might imagine riptides or whirlpools.

For more than 40 years Susan Schwalb (American, b. 1944) has been part of the revival of the technique of silverpoint drawing in America. Her work began as image-based drawings of flowers, which gradually became abstract, and her handling of the technique has been quite varied. In works from the late 1970s Schwalb tore and burned paper to provide an emotionally-free and dramatic contrast to the precise linearity of silverpoint. In works from the 1980s she combined silverpoint with flat expanses of acrylic paint or gold leaf (for an example, see Figure 5.12). In 1996 she began her signature work when she abandoned the stylus altogether in favor of wide metal bands that achieved a shimmering atmosphere reminiscent of the luminous transparency of watercolor, as in *Strata #295* (Figure 4.10). This drawing was featured in the seminal historical metalpoint exhibition *Drawing in Silver and Gold: Leonardo to Jasper Johns* at the National Gallery of Art, Washington, DC in 2015.

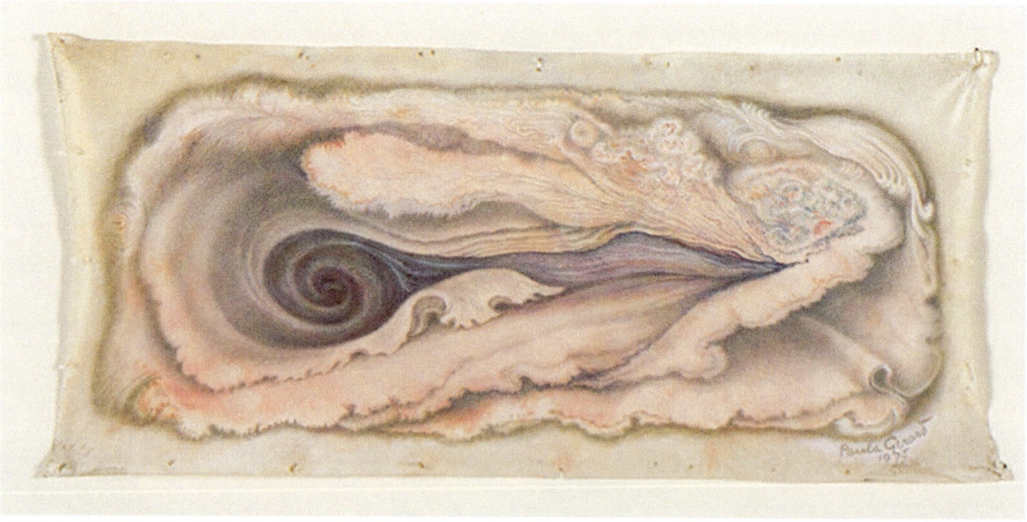

FIGURE 7.25 Paula Gerard, American (Brighton, England, 1907–1991, Chicago, Illinois), *Vortex*, 1975, silverpoint, goldpoint, watercolor on casein-coated parchment, 4 × 8 inches (10.2 × 31.8 cm), Arkansas Arts Center Foundation Collection: Purchase. 1985.065

In 2010 Schwalb returned to the stylus to create numerous works on panel and coated papers (Figure 7.26). At this point she added metallic bronze, brass, copper, and aluminum wool pads, as well as metal brushes, to her arsenal of tools. As Bruce Weber writes in his essay for her exhibition *A Luminous Line: Forty Years of Metalpoint Drawings by Susan Schwalb* at the Arkansas Art Center in Little Rock in 2018,

> In the *Polyphony* pieces, she layers squares on top of squares to create the illusion of depth, and she varies the type of lines (thick versus thin) to create a sensation of movement. . . . For the *Harmonizations* series. . . . She focuses her attention on the arrangement and layering of squares, and draws them in patterns of vertical, horizontal, or diagonally oriented lines [for an example, see Figure 2.4].[11]

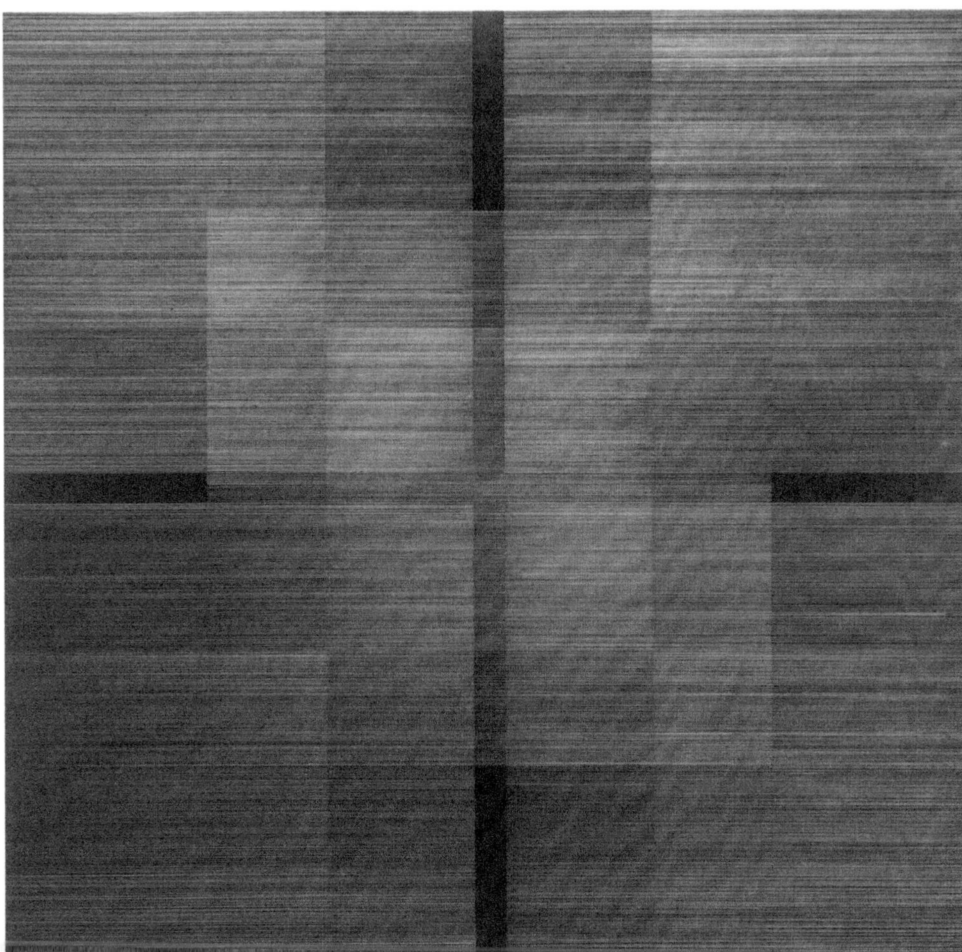

FIGURE 7.26 Susan Schwalb, *Polyphony XIII*, 2016, silverpoint, goldpoint, and copperpoint on black gesso on paper on panel, 24 × 24 × 2 inches (60.96 × 60.96 × 5.08 cm), courtesy of the artist

Sal Hunter (British, b. 1966), who is also a neuroscientist, works with silverpoint combined with gouache, which she treats like watercolor. In her circular-shaped drawings, such as *Specimen 19* (Figure 7.27), she builds up layers of silver over free-form, painterly shapes related to biological patterns.

Shona Macdonald (American, b. 1969) and Fran Siegel (American, b. 1960) are two artists working with landscape but in a distinctly abstract manner. MacDonald's work *Ground Covering Large #1* (Figure 7.28), "uses silverpoint for conceptual reasons. The faint, diaphanous delivery of the metal to the paper is the best material I have found to represent and depict the ghost-like imagery I have been interested in over the past few years."[12] Siegel, on the other hand, has made Los Angeles her subject since moving there, using aerial photographs taken during flights into LAX airport (Figure 7.29). Robyn Ellenbogen (American, b. 1953) is another artist whose metalpoint drawings on black and brightly colored grounds evoke images that suggest swirling seas, mountains and oceans (for an example, see Figure 5.3).

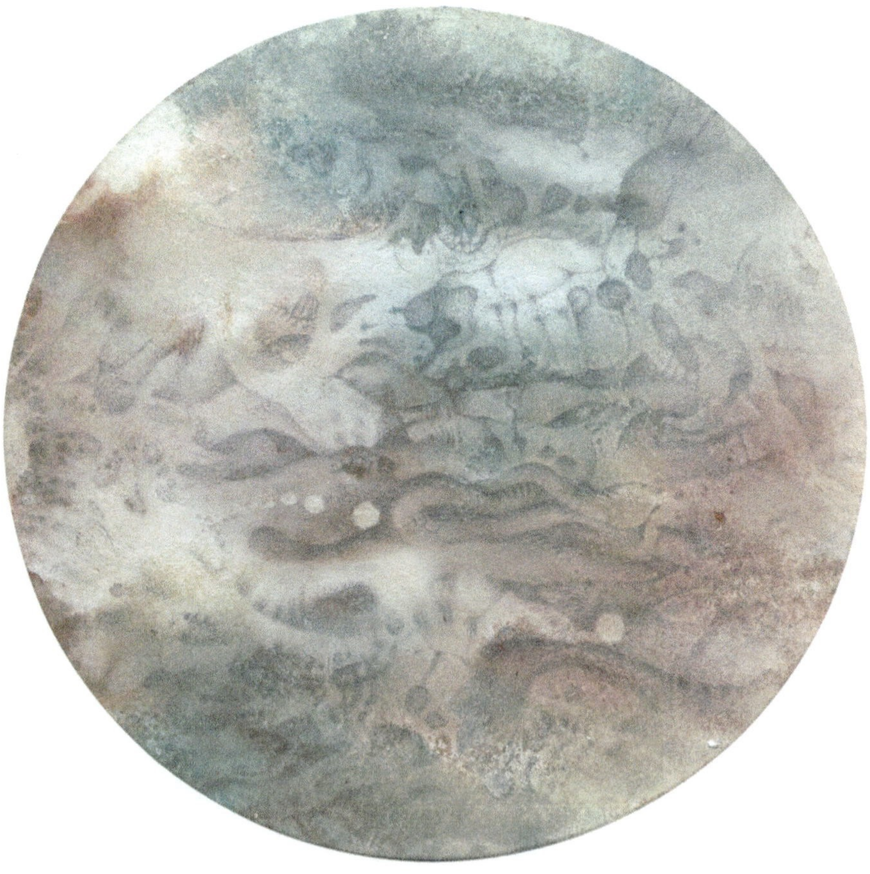

FIGURE 7.27 Sal Hunter, *Biofilter Series Number 19 – Specimen 19*, 2013, silverpoint and gouache on qualitative grade cellulose laboratory filter paper, 5 inches (12.5cm) diameter, courtesy of the artist

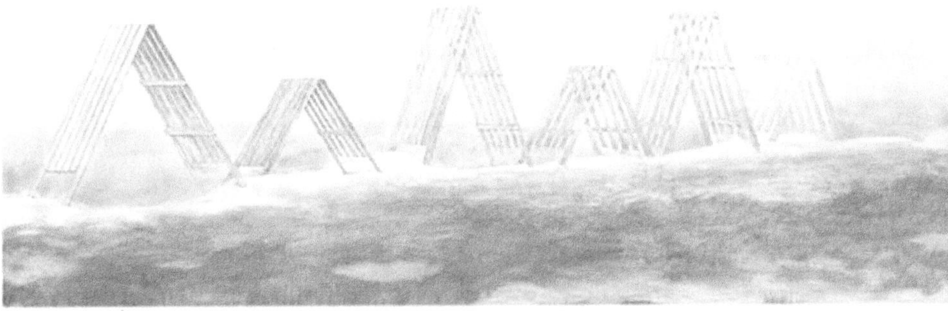

FIGURE 7.28 Shona Macdonald, *Ground Covering Large #1*, 2017, silverpoint and graphite on TerraSkin paper, 30 × 48 inches, (76.2 × 121.92 cm), courtesy of the artist

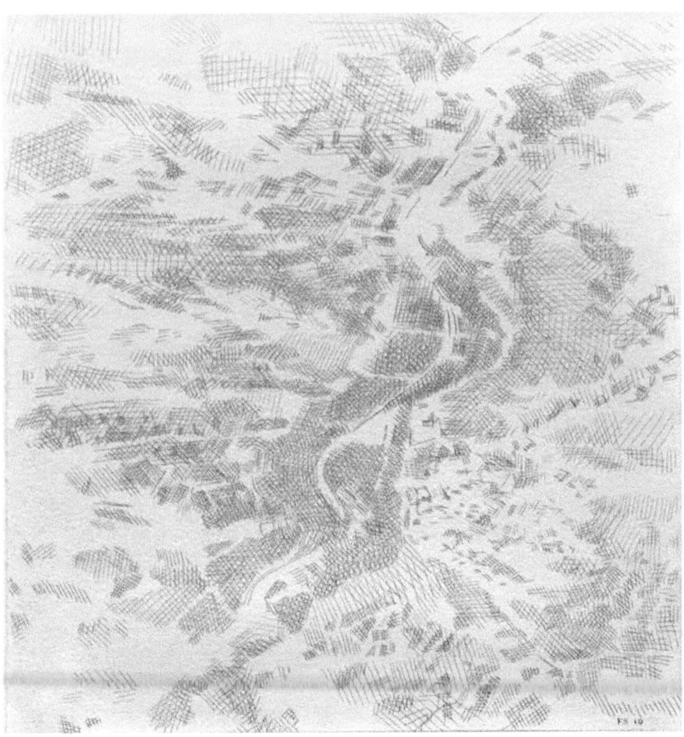

FIGURE 7.29 Fran Siegel, *Tracks for Overland 1.1*, 2010, silverpoint on hand-coated clay paper, 19 × 18 inches (48.26 × 45.72 cm), courtesy of the artist

Denver-based artist Tom Mazzullo (American, b. 1968) has spent over 30 years devoted to silverpoint drawing. For Mazzullo, silverpoint offers a connection with those artists who first turned to the natural world to inform their work. He has studied the work of the Old Masters, with particular attention to Leonardo, Albrecht Dürer, Hendrick Goltzius, and Jaques de Gheyn II. Although he draws many different subjects, the more abstract drawings of twisted, coiled, and torn paper are some of his best known works (Figure 7.30). He writes,

> My process has remained simple: I prepare a sheet of hot-press watercolor paper with two thin coats of tinted casein, sketch an object from life, sight-size, working up the drawing in meticulous 16th-century-style crosshatching in sterling silver. The goal is always to show form and to produce a realistic expression of the object. If a mistake is made, the drawing is restarted or abandoned. The subject floats in the center of the paper demanding exclusive attention. The drawing itself is a journal of time spent with the subject, every line agonized over, deliberated; nothing is arbitrary. Silverpoint demands exact, patient work to make a successful drawing.[13]

Shirazeh Houshiary (Iranian, b. 1955), who lives in London, turned to silverpoint around 2000. She made a series of large, 6-foot-square works on canvas using silverpoint. *Shroud* consists

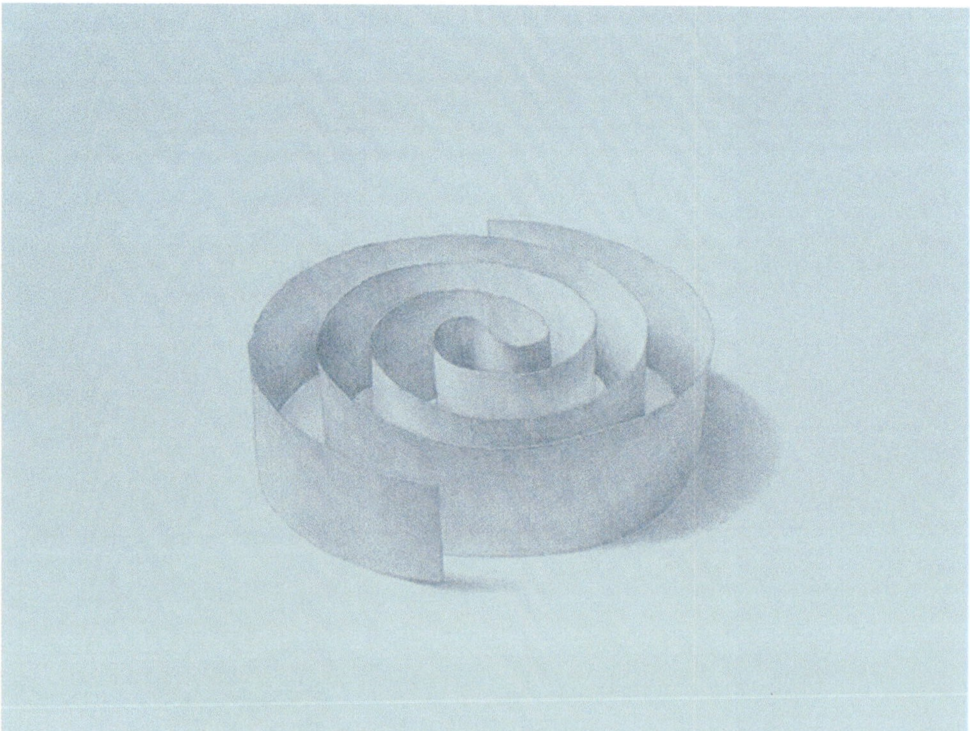

FIGURE 7.30 Tom Mazzullo, *Fermat*, 2016, silverpoint on prepared paper, 10 × 12 inches (25.4 × 30.48 cm), courtesy of the artist

of a pristine white acrylic ground over which the artist has delicately "etched" minute Arabic words and phrases expressing Sufi thoughts. She used pencil and silverpoint with varying degrees of pressure, but it is almost impossible to see the images with the naked eye. The work is the most minimal and subtle silverpoint drawing one might encounter.[14]

Cynthia Lin (American, b. 1964) has created small drawings that seem abstract but are actually (according to the artist) *trompe l'oeil* portraits of dust and hair (Figure 7.31). Frequently placed on a shelf, they play with the confusion between reality and imagination. Marietta Hoferer (German, 1962) and her husband, Michael Kukla (Czech, b. 1963), who divide their time between New York and France, have both been working in silverpoint for around ten years. Hoferer is known for her minimalist, process-oriented, tape-and-pencil drawings. As if in a meditative state, she draws grids of fine lines on black Plike paper. In *Feb 20, 2015* (Figure 7.32), although each line was drawn against a straight edge, the hand of the artist is still evident, and slight deviations and accidents are an essential part of the process. Kukla continues his use of the hexagon as his basic structural element. In *sp mx 1* (Figure 7.33) he starts in the center, and as he draws outward he creates a visual field shifting across the page.[15]

Jonathan Higgins (American, b. 1962), who runs Manneken Press, a fine art print publisher in Illinois, was inspired to take up metalpoint drawing after seeing the exhibition *Drawing in Silver and Gold: Leonardo to Jasper Johns* at The British Museum in 2015. In *Untitled III* (Figure 7.34) marks were made with wide brass and silver wire twisted and pressed into the black ground of the paper, giving the illusion of raised or embossed marks. Ron Janowich (American, b. 1948) first created a geometric abstract form over which he drew a grid of small squares made up of diagonal

FIGURE 7.31 Cynthia Lin, *Itch #10* (detail), 2001, silver on gesso on paper, 7 × 9 inches of 11 × 14 total (27.94 × 35.56 cm), courtesy of the artist

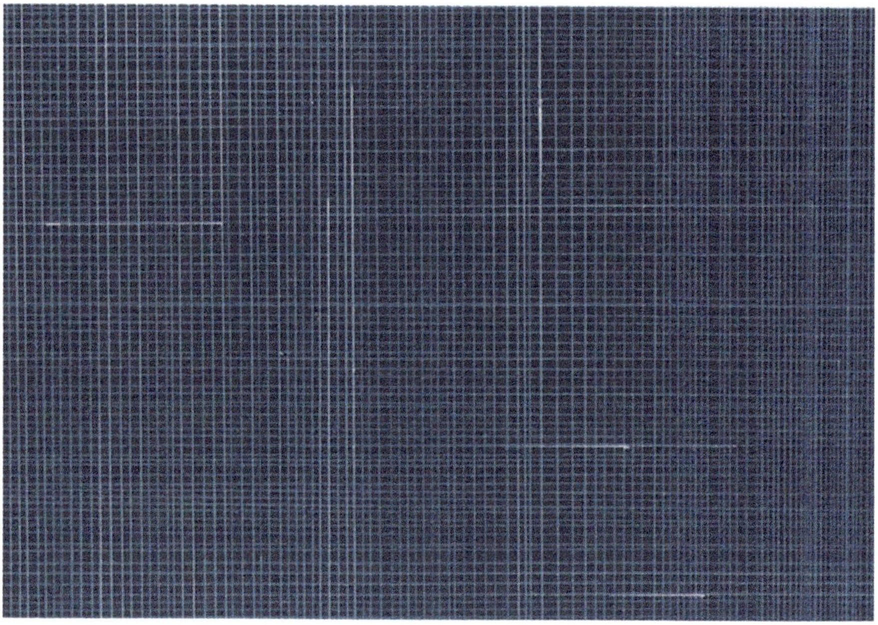

FIGURE 7.32 Marietta Hoferer, *Feb 20, 2015* (detail), 2015, silverpoint and graphite on black Plike paper, 12 × 12 inches (30.48 × 30.48 cm), courtesy of the artist

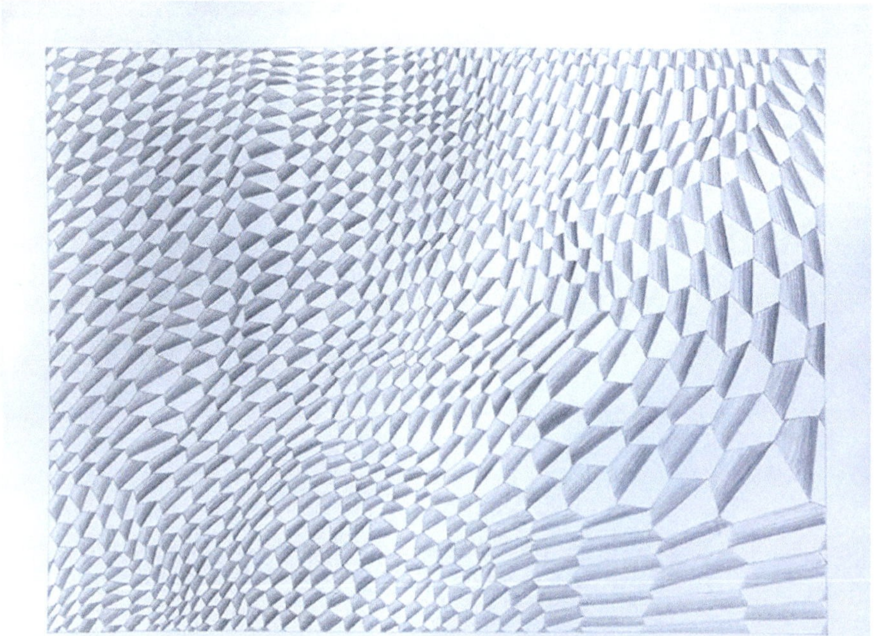

FIGURE 7.33 Michael Kukla, *sp mx 1*, 2018, silverpoint on clay coated paper, 14 × 18 inches (35.56 × 45.72 cm), courtesy of the artist

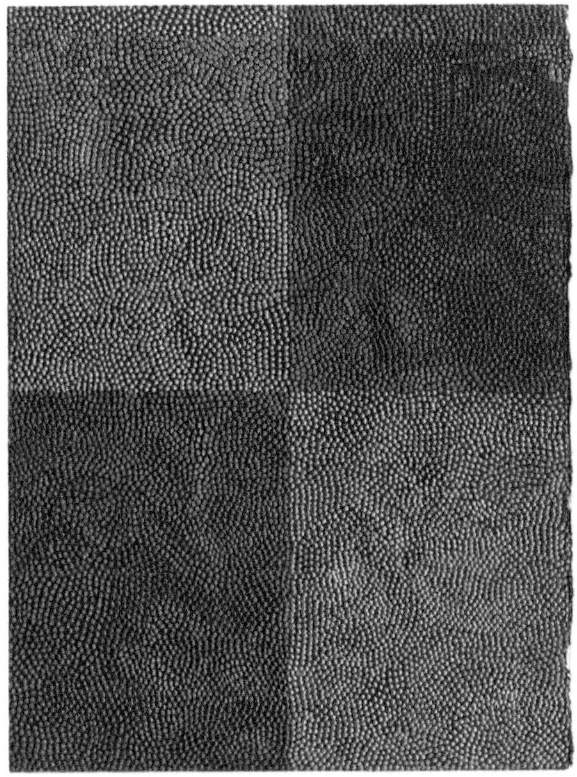

FIGURE 7.34 Jonathan Higgins, *Untitled III*, 2017, silver and brass on black gesso on Fabriano Rosaspina paper, 12 × 8 3/4 inches (30.48 × 22.22 cm), courtesy of the artist

lines. Once this pattern was complete, an act of complete bravery impelled him to fling colored encaustic onto the paper in the manner of Jackson Pollock or Franz Kline (Figure 7.35).

Lucie Beppler (German, b. 1961) has done a body of elegant line drawings combining the medium with etching and engraving needles. She scratches into the surface building up relief-like abstract compositions[16] (Figure 7.36). Also using very fine lines, Sam Messenger (British, b. 1980) constructs web-like designs to form an intricate and geometric pattern that conveys an illusion of depth. He often makes enormous wall-sized drawings which can only be appreciated on very close inspection (Figure 7.37).

Conceptual Work

Several artists have pushed metalpoint off the surface of paper onto walls. Linda Hutchins (American, b. 1957), has used her grandmother's silver spoon to make large, 9 x 12-foot wall drawings. In *Lineal Silver (pool)* she drew with her spoon to create a network of lines that swirl and undulate across the wall. In recent works she incorporated sterling silver thimbles (for an example, see Figure 4.11) into her practice. In *Clapping Music Notation Study 5* (Figure 7.38) the pattern of marks was made by striking the drawing according to the rhythms of Steve Reich's *Clapping Music* (1972).

Natalie Loveless (Canadian, b. 1971) uses the medium in context-based performances. In an early work entitled CoOperation, 2004, she moved in to the gallery space for five days and

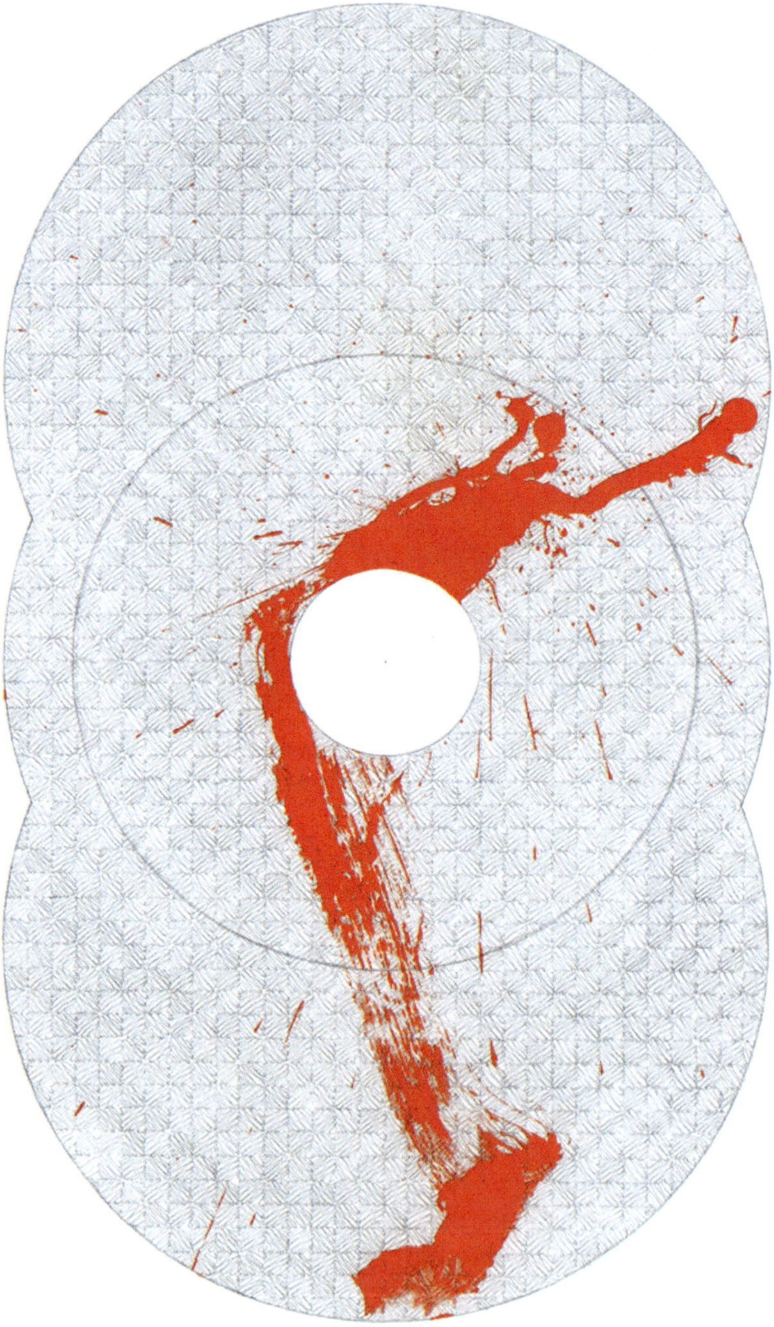

FIGURE 7.35 Ron Janowich, *Untitled*, 2011, silverpoint and encaustic on clay-coated paper, 18 × 14 inches (45.72 × 35.56 cm), courtesy of the artist

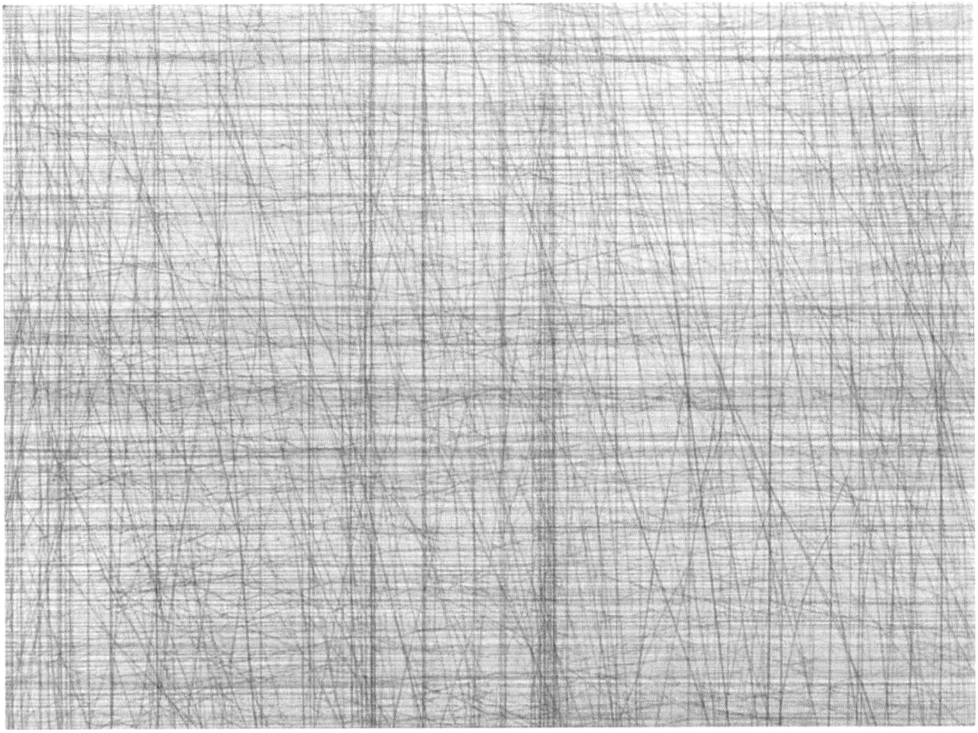

FIGURE 7.36 Lucie Beppler, *Untitled*, 2014–2015, pencil, silverpoint, etching needle, gesso on paper, 29 1/2 × 39 1/4 inches (75 × 100 cm), private collection

communicated with friends and strangers through email. She invited her participants to tell her stories of mourning and memory, from which she drew a complex map on the wall, marking their location around the world. For an installation at the Kentler International Drawing Space in 2009, she invited friends to determine how she should behave with the wall, whether to throw things at it, kiss it, etc. After performing these actions, Loveless then used a stylus to draw lines around each image.

Ram Samocha (Israeli, b. 1966), who lives in England, has developed a 3-D technique using the stone paper TerraSkin. He explains about *Silver Sun* (Figure 7.39), "As my work is very physical and repetitive I tried to see how much this paper can take and started to understand that it became distorted only by putting force on it as I drew."[17] His work is very performance-oriented, and when there are breakthroughs or accidents he usually embraces them; a recent drawing entitled *Sea of Lead* took three months to make and measured 400 × 100 cm (approximately 13 × 3 feet).

Several artists combine video with metalpoint. Erika Winstone (British, b. 1957), in *The Rink and Talent Show* (Figure 5.17), combines video projections with fine silverpoint line. One of the most unusual artists currently working in metalpoint is Carol Prusa (American, b. 1956), based in the Miami area. Prusa became interested in silverpoint after a trip to the Uffizi Gallery in Florence in 2002. She works on three-dimensional plastic domes, some as large as 60 inches in diameter,

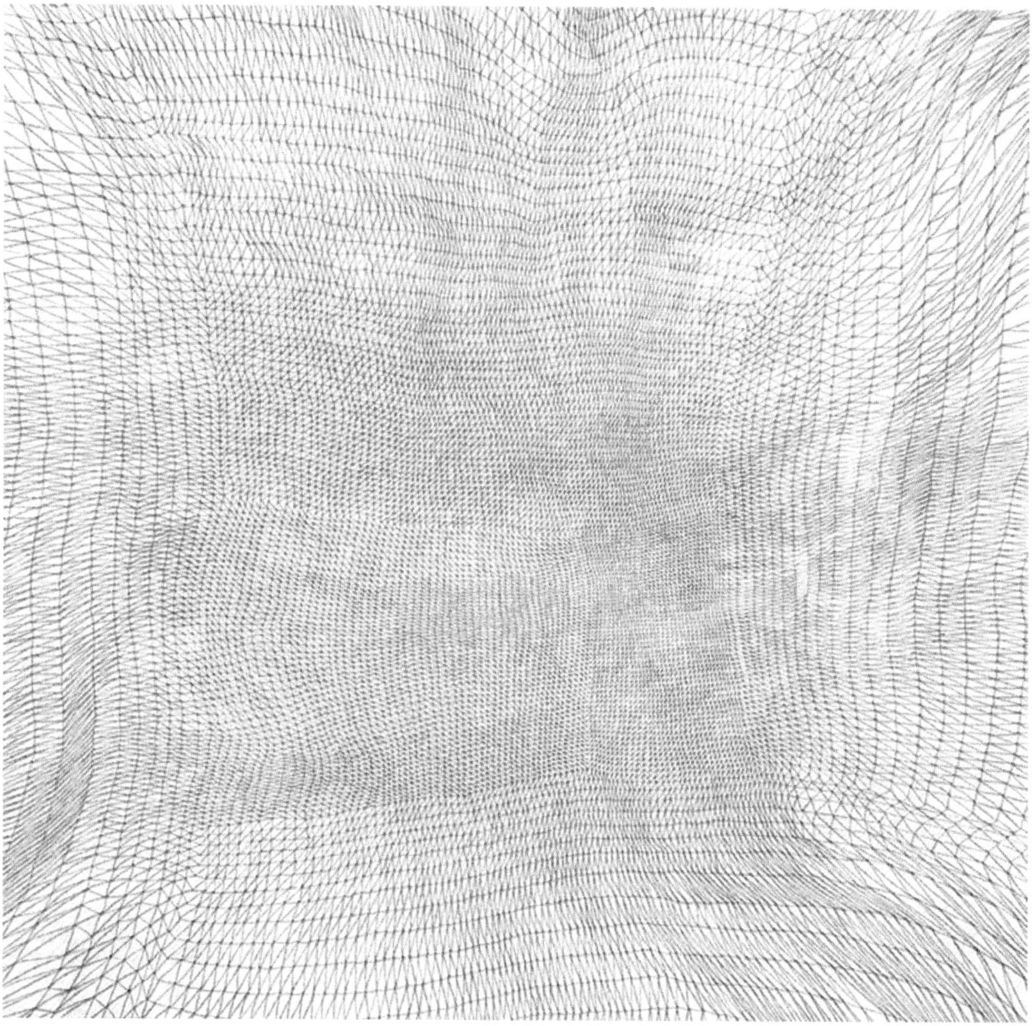

FIGURE 7.37 Sam Messenger, *Veil from Rhea*, 2013, silverpoint, graphite and gesso on paper, 18 × 18 inches (45.72 × 45.72 cm), courtesy of Davidson Contemporary, New York, NY

which generally hang on the wall. Using silverpoint, silver leaf, acrylic, fiber optics, and video, she covers her domes with intricate drawings of cosmic shapes, plant-like forms, and designs. About a recent work entitled *Thirst (insatiable)* (Figure 7.40) she writes,

> I was thinking about our insatiable consuming thirst so made a dome forming a "Tower of Babel" and in the center is a lens to view a video of water poured incessantly into my mouth so that it overspills and can't be swallowed. . . . The sound is of trickling, spilling water. Each tongue-like form ends in a tiny flickering light from a fiber optic cable that runs to a programmed light emitter housed with the video player inside the work[18]

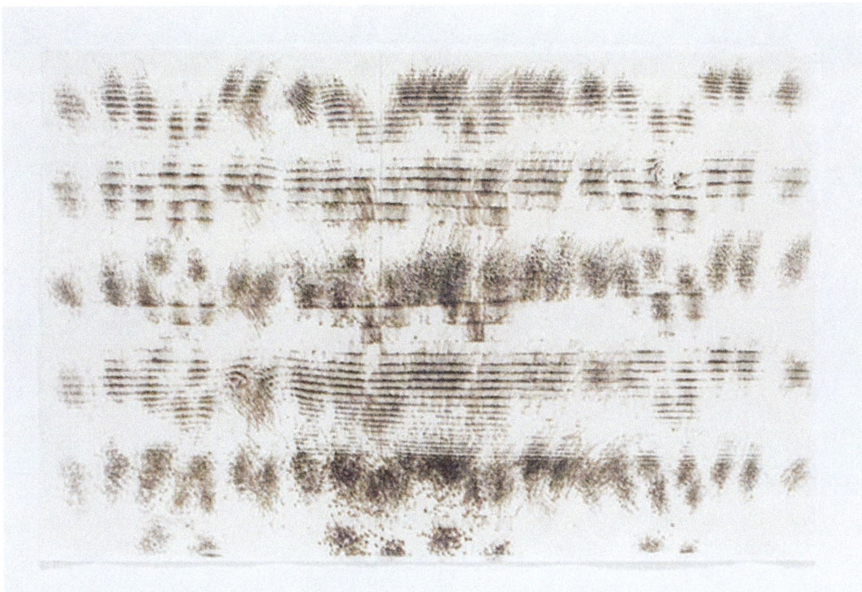

FIGURE 7.38 Linda Hutchins, *Clapping Music Notation Study 5*, 2016, silver on prepared paper, 12 × 18 inches (30.48 × 45.72 cm). Photograph by Dan Kvitka, courtesy of the artist

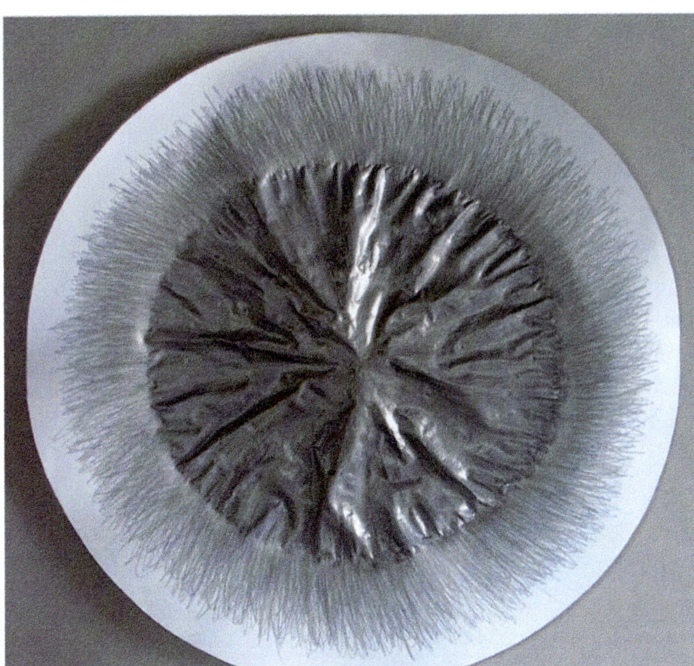

FIGURE 7.39 Ram Samocha, *Silver Sun*, 2012, silverpoint on stone paper, 24 inches (60.96cm) diameter, courtesy of the artist

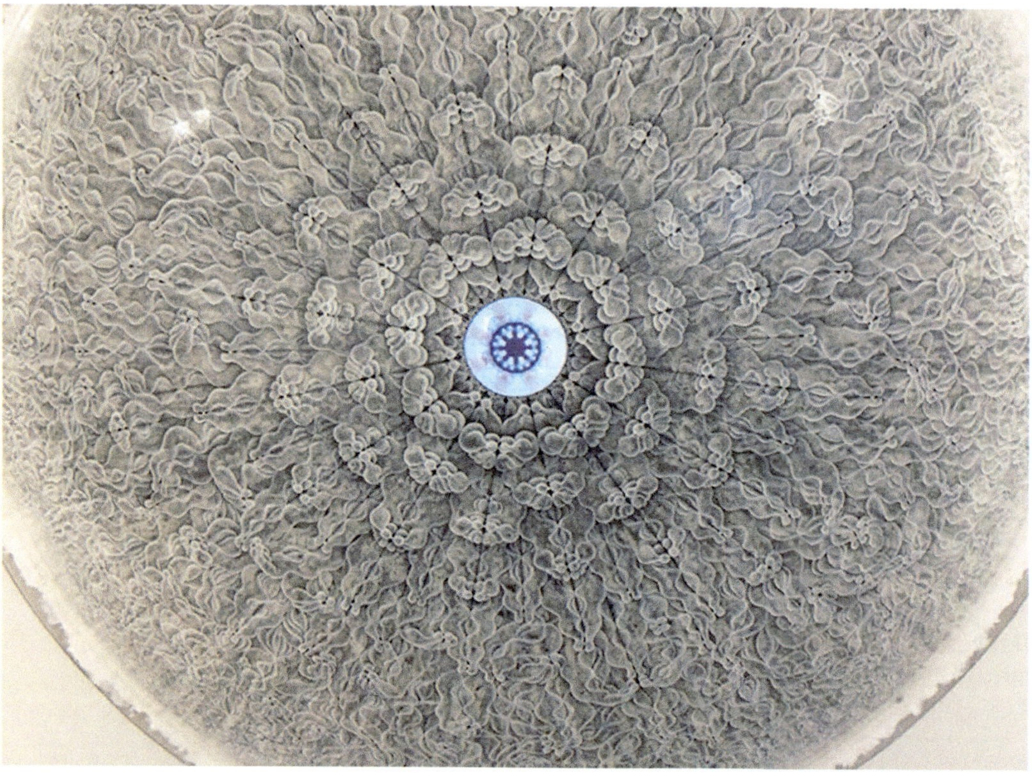

FIGURE 7.40 Carol Prusa, *Thirst (insatiable)* (detail), 2017, silverpoint, graphite, titanium white pigment with acrylic binder on acrylic dome with lens, fiber optics, light emitter and video with video player, 50 × 50 × 10 inches (127 × 127 × 25.4 cm), courtesy of the artist

Conclusion

Metalpoint drawing continues to be a medium for quiet, refined, and meditative work, but contemporary artists have been radically pushing the boundaries of this time-honored technique. Whether it is combined with other media, used for marking a wall, or for creating large, oversized works, silverpoint can no longer be primarily regarded as an ancient technique tied to a conservative sensibility. It is hoped that, as more artists explore metalpoint drawing, they will find many unusual and unique ways of using it.

Notes

1 Dale Roberts, email correspondence with the author, November 2017.
2 Weber, Bruce. "Modern and Contemporary Drawing in Metalpoint." In *Drawing in Silver and Gold: Leonardo to Jasper Johns*, Stacey Sell and Hugo Chapman (Washington, DC: National Gallery of Art, 2015), 234.
3 AJ Smith, email correspondence with the author, 8 February 2018.
4 Lori Field, email correspondence with the author, 24 April 2018.
5 George Sorrels, email correspondence with the author, 19 September 2017.
6 Lauren Amalia Redding, email correspondence with the author, 26 April 2018.

7 Roy Eastland, email correspondence with the author, 27 April 2018.
8 Charles Schmidt, telephone conversation with the author, 28 April 2018.
9 Katherine Vetne, email correspondence with the author, 26 April 2018.
10 Dennis Angel, email correspondence with the author, 26 April 2018.
11 Weber, Bruce. "A Luminous Line: Forty Years of Metalpoint Drawings by Susan Schwalb." In *A Luminous Line: Forty Years of Metalpoint Drawings by Susan Schwalb*, Susan Schwalb (Little Rock: Arkansas Art Center, 2018), 16.
12 Shona Macdonald, statement from the artist dated 19 February 2018.
13 Tom Mazzullo, statement from the artist dated 16 June, 2018.
14 Information taken from www.tate.org.uk/art/artworks/houshiary-shroud-t07777. Accessed 30 April 2018.
15 Information taken from the website of the artist http://mkukla.com. Accessed 30 April 2018.
16 Heide, Patrick, and Verena Platzgummer. *Patrick Heide Contemporary Art Ten Years*. (London: Patrick Heide Contemporary Art, 2017), 238.
17 Ram Samocha, email correspondence with the author, 11 November 2017.
18 Carol Prusa, email correspondence with the author, 28 April 2018.

Appendix

LIST OF SOURCES FOR MATERIALS

Art Boards Archival Artist Panels – Online source for cradled and uncradled hardwood panels as well as paper-mounted panels, gesso panels, and Art Board Superior Quality Panel Gesso. Online at www.art-boards.com

Cheap Joe's Art Stuff – Online retailer of general art supplies and a full line of Holbein colored gessoes. Online at www.cheapjoes.com

Couleurs du Quai Voltaire – Magasin Sennelier – Art supplies since 1887 in Paris, France. Famous for creating materials for Picasso, Serra, and others. Retailer of Sennelier Papier Pointe d'Argent Furioso clay-coated silverpoint paper in sheets and pads. Located at 3 quai Voltaire, 75007 Paris, Phone: +33 01 42 60 72 15, and online at www.magasinsennelier.com

Dick Blick – Large supplier of artist materials, including paper, boards, and grounds. Over 50 stores across the United States and online at www.dickblick.com

Gaylord Archival – Full range of archival storage boxes and supplies. Online at www.gaylord.com

Golden Artist Colors, Inc. – Information about Golden products, including a wide variety of artist resources. Online at www.goldenpaints.com

Heartstone Paper Company – Makes TerraSkin paper, made of stone. Online at http://heartstonepaper.com/products

Jerry's Artarama – Discount art supplies at 17 locations in the United States. Jerry's NY Central is located at 111 Fourth Avenue, New York, NY 10003 and online at www.jerrysartarama.com

Jackson's Art Supplies – London art supply retailer that carries Roberson metalpoint tools and wires, Zecchi styluses, Sinopia and Golden grounds, and Art Spectrum Colourfix papers. Located at 1 Farleigh Place, London, N16 7SX, Phone +44 0 20 7254 0077, and online at www.jacksonsart.com

Joanne Hopper Artist Website – Custom-made metalpoint tools, including thick silver and copper points, also platinum points. Online at https://joannehopper.com

Kremer Pigments – Supplier of traditional fine art materials, including papers, linen, pigments, tools and brushes, rabbit-skin glue, bone ash, and calcium carbonate, as well as silverpoint tools and silver brushes. Stores in New York and Germany. Located at 247 West 29th Street New York, NY 10001, Phone (212) 219–2394 or 1-(800)-995–5501, and online at https://shop.kremerpigments.com/en/

L. Cornelissen & Son – London art supply retailer located near the British Museum and that carries Roberson metalpoint grounds, wire, tools, and metalpoint paper. Located at 105 Great Russell Street, London WC1B 3RY, Phone: +44 0 20 7636 1045, and online at www.cornelissen.com

Legion Paper Company – Makes Legion paper, suitable for silverpoint. Must be ordered in quantities of 300 sheets. Online at https://legionpaper.com/legion-art-cover/

Lustersheen Products – An online store for metal wool pads, including brass, bronze, aluminum, and copper in several grades and sizes. Online at www.lustersheen-online.com

Myron Toback Inc. – Jewelry supplier selling fine metals and wire, with a catalog that can be viewed online. Local address for New Yorkers: 545 Fifth Avenue, Suite 1000, New York, NY 10017. Phone (212) 398–8300, info@myrontoback.com, and online at www.myrontoback.com

NaturalPigments.com – Rare artist colors and materials, metalpoint grounds, kits, wire, and tools. Online at www.naturalpigments.com

Rio Grande.com – Online retailer of silver, gold, and platinum, including fine round wire and sheets. Located at 7500 Bluewater Rd NW Albuquerque, NM 87121, (800) 545–6566. Online at http://riogrande.com

Ross Metals Corp. – Supplier of metals in wire, sheets, and findings. Local address for New Yorkers: 54 W 47th St, New York, NY 10036. Phone (212) 869–1407 and online at https://rossmetals.com

SilverpointWeb.com – Comprehensive site with history, links, and products. Online at www.silverpointweb.com

Talas Bookbinding, Archival and Conservation Supplies – Full line archival boxes, glassine, and papers. Located at 330 Morgan Avenue, Brooklyn, NY 11211, (212) 219–0770 and online at: www.talasonline.com

University Products – Full line of archival materials and boxes. Online at www.universityproducts.com

Wet Paint Art – Online art supply store. Golden silverpoint ground, Aurum metal points, and Art Spectrum Colourfix papers are available. Online at www.wetpaintart.com

Zecchi – Based in Florence, Italy. Sells colored and white commercial silverpoint paper and different points, as well as many art supplies. The site can be viewed in English or Italian. Online at www.zecchi.it

INDEX

References to figures are indicated in *italics*. References to endnotes consist of the page number followed by the letter 'n' followed by the number of the note. When the author or subject mentioned in the endnote is not directly identified in the main text, the text page is added in brackets, e.g. 19n75 (12) refers to endnote 75 on page 19, and the note number is to be found in the main text on p. 12.